T0332721

STRING SEARCHING
ALGORITHMS

LECTURE NOTES SERIES ON COMPUTING
Editor-in-Chief: D T Lee (*Northwestern Univ., USA*)

Lectures Notes Series on Computing – Vol. 3

STRING SEARCHING ALGORITHMS

Graham A Stephen

School of Electronic Engineering and Computer Systems
University of Wales
Bangor, Gwynedd, UK

 **World Scientific**
Singapore • New Jersey • London • Hong Kong

Published by

World Scientific Publishing Co. Pte. Ltd.

P O Box 128, Farrer Road, Singapore 9128

USA office: Suite 1B, 1060 Main Street, River Edge, NJ 07661

UK office: 73 Lynton Mead, Totteridge, London N20 8DH

ISBN: 981-02-1829-X

Printed in Singapore by Utopia Press.

Preface

A number of important string-searching algorithms have been collected together and presented in this volume in a uniform format and notation. The topics covered include exact and approximate string-matching, edit-distance related problems, and problems involving repeated patterns.

The text is intended for computer scientists, software developers, computational biologists, and others with an interest in string-processing techniques. A fairly high level of familiarity with programming concepts has been assumed. The material is therefore suitable for readers at an advanced-undergraduate or postgraduate level.

This book started life as a technical report that surveyed a number of string algorithms. It has since evolved, though, having been subject to much revision, correction, and augmentation. The aim has been to provide comprehensive coverage of the selected topics. But inevitably, as with any project of this nature, there are certain to be omissions. Nonetheless, the text should prove to be useful. For those interested in learning about the methods described here, the level of detail should make this a self-contained reference. And for those involved in wider research, this book can also act as an initial guide for further forays into the literature.

The reader is invited to browse through the overview section of each chapter before delving into the nuts and bolts of specific algorithms. These overviews are intended to pave the way by providing a gentle introduction to the concepts involved in the principal algorithms. They also offer a historical perspective to the development of the major techniques in each area.

Acknowledgments

I am indebted to Mike Engber, Duncan Buell, and an anonymous referee for making helpful comments concerning this text. Many other individuals provided me with various items of useful information. In particular, I should like to thank Bill Chang, Kiem-Phong Vo, Esko Ukkonen, Gene Myers, Vaughan Pratt, Jorma Tarhio, Tao Jiang, Ming Li, Laurent Thomas, Timo Raita, C. Pandu Rangan, Xiaoqiu Huang, Brenda Baker, Peter Sibbald, Shiping Zhang, Thomas Dowling, and Dawn Chambers.

Thanks are also due to Der-Tsai Lee and the staff at World Scientific Publishing for their encouragement and support. The subvention of the United Kingdom's Science and Engineering Research Council under Grant GR/G51565 is gratefully acknowledged. I also offer my thanks to the School of Electronic Engineering and Computer Systems, here at the University of Wales, Bangor, for providing an environment in which this book could be written.

And finally, I should like to thank my wife, Heather, for her patience and under-standing.

Bangor, Wales   **Graham A. Stephen**
21 February 1994.

Contents

List of Figures

1

Introduction

It could be said of me that in this book I have only made a bunch of other men's flowers, providing of my own only the string that ties them together.
— Michel de Montaigne (1533–1592), *Essais*.

What could be more natural than grouping together various collections of symbols in sequences? This creation of strings — a fundamental aspect of communication — is such an everyday occurrence that it is easy to take them for granted. The sequence of the symbols in a string can endow it with some special significance that an unsequenced grouping of the same symbols could never convey. But such semantic considerations of what is that strings, or indeed their component symbols, actually symbolise need not really concern us. For it is only methods of performing useful operations on strings by exploiting the sequence, or syntactic ordering, of their symbols that are considered here. And, as implied by the title, the emphasis is placed on those operations that in some sense involve a search, such as seeking: strings within strings; common parts between strings; and sections that are repeated within strings. Judging by the wealth of published literature in this area, the pursuit of efficient techniques for performing such tasks runs through an oft-trodden field, but one whose soil nonetheless remains fertile.

Although the methods reviewed in this book are presented largely from a theoretical standpoint, there is certainly no scarcity of relevant, practical application areas. String-searching techniques are, for example, of import in milieux such as data processing, information retrieval, text-editing and word-processing, linguistic analysis, and also areas of molecular biology such as genetic sequence analysis.

Some Definitions

Before going any further, it might be useful to prepare the ground by giving some basic definitions. Note that the string notation described below is summarised in Appendix B, and that the terms introduced here are also detailed in the glossary given in Appendix C.

First of all, *symbols*, or characters, are taken to be our elemental building-blocks. It is true that certain encodings of symbols, such as ASCII characters, may be further decomposed, but the symbols of any particular level of description may be regarded as indivisible at that level. A specific set of symbols is termed an *alphabet*. A *string* over an alphabet is a sequence of instances of symbols belonging to the alphabet. To give an example, both aeb and ecddab are strings over alphabet {a, b, c, d, e}.

The *length* of a string x, say, is the number of instances of symbols comprising the string, and is denoted by $|x|$. If x is of length m, then it may be written as $x_1 x_2 \ldots x_m$, where x_i represents the ith component symbol. The *empty string*, ϵ, is the special string having a length of zero.

Two strings may be *concatenated* by appending one to the other. The concatenation of strings x and y is written as the 'product' xy, and is equal to the string $x_1 x_2 \ldots x_{|x|} y_1 y_2 \ldots y_{|y|}$. In a similar vein, string *exponentiation* may be defined such that $x^i = x^{i-1} x$, for integer exponents i greater than zero, with the special case $x^0 = \epsilon$. For example, if $x = $ abcde, then the *square* x^2 is equal to abcdeabcde.

A *language* is a set of strings over a particular alphabet. C^* (the Kleene closure of C) is, for instance, the language comprising all the strings, including ϵ, over alphabet C.

Next we come to consider various subgroupings of the symbols within a string. A *substring* of x is a string given by a contiguous group of symbols within x. It may thus be obtained by deleting zero or more symbols from the beginning and end of x. The substring of x, $x_i x_{i+1} \ldots x_j$, where $i, j \leqslant |x|$ and $j \geqslant i$, shall be denoted by $x(i, j)$. For cases where $j < i$, the reversed substring $x_i x_{i-1} \ldots x_j$ shall be denoted explicitly by $x_R(i, j)$. Taking $x = $ trismegistus, for example, the substrings $x(7, 10)$ and $x_R(7, 4)$ are equal to gist and gems, respectively. A *prefix* of x is a substring of x comprising zero or more symbols from the extreme left-hand end of the string. Similarly, a *suffix* of x is a substring of x comprising zero or more symbols from the extreme right-hand end of the string. Returning to the previous example, tris is a prefix and istus a suffix of trismegistus.

Similar to a substring, but more general, is a *subsequence*. This comprises a sequence of symbols in the same order that they occur in the string. Note that their appearances in the string need not be consecutive. A subsequence may thus be obtained by deleting zero or more symbols from anywhere within the string. As an example, the string rieiu is a subsequence of trismegistus.

Finally, it should be noted that a string x itself and the empty string are both prefixes, suffixes, substrings and subsequences of x. The qualifier *proper* may therefore be used with these subgroupings to exclude such cases explicitly, e.g. a proper prefix of a string is any prefix of that string other than ϵ and the string itself.

Algorithm Presentation

The prime concern when presenting the algorithms described in the forthcoming chapters has been one of clarity. It is to be hoped that the simple, concise pseudocode employed for this purpose adequately conveys the basic mechanism of each algorithm. Non-essential detail has been minimised, but the level of description given should, nevertheless, permit any of the algorithms presented to be implemented in an actual programming language without too much difficulty.

All the algorithms given are based on a single-processor, *random access machine* (RAM) model of computation (Aho, Hopcroft and Ullman, 1974), in which instructions are executed strictly sequentially.

The pseudocode is intended to be fairly self-explanatory. A couple of points worth bearing in mind, however, are as follows. Block structure, for example delineating the bodies of loops and conditional constructs, is indicated by the relative indentation of the code. Variables are *italicised*, reserved words **emboldened**, and — comments prefixed with a dash.

Chapter Preview

To round off this chapter, a brief preview of the contents of those still to come is now given. Each one deals with a particular problem area and is relatively self-contained. Any significant dependencies between chapters are, however, highlighted below in the summaries.

The structure of each chapter generally conforms to a uniform format. First of all, an introductory *overview* section surveys the main approaches that have been proposed to tackle the particular problems in question. The aim of this section is to describe briefly the underlying ideas of the techniques and to give a historical perspective to their development. This is then followed by an *algorithms in detail* section, which strives to give a more in-depth presentation and discussion of selected algorithms identified in the overview. Finally, relevant surveys and other sources of reference are mentioned in the *further reading* section.

Chapter 2 is concerned with *string-matching* methods for locating patterns occurring as substrings of a particular string. Such keyword searches are a common requirement in, for example, word-processing and information-retrieval applications. Also considered in this chapter is the problem of simultaneously searching for occurrences of any of a set of different keywords.

Chapter 3 introduces the concept of the *distance* between strings: a measure used to assess degrees of similarity. The distance between two strings may be evaluated in order to find the most economical way of transforming one into the other. String distance measures are also important in certain applications in molecular biology involving, for example, the study of the similarities between genetic sequences.

Closely linked to the computation of the distance between two strings is the problem of finding a *longest common subsequence* of the strings, i.e. a subsequence of maximal length common to both strings. In addition to this, various related problems, involving, for example, *shortest common supersequences*, *shortest common superstrings*, and *heaviest common subsequences* are also discussed in this chapter.

Chapter 4 looks at a very useful data structure known as the *suffix tree*. This is a tree which embodies a compact index to all the distinct, non-empty substrings of the input string. Use is made of this data structure in some of the algorithms discussed in Chapters 5 and 6. Suffix trees also find application in other areas, such as problems involving data-compression and the search for longest common substrings, for instance.

Chapter 5 deals with *approximate string matching* — a generalisation of the string matching covered in Chapter 2. Here, occurrences within a text string of substrings approximately equal to a given pattern string are sought. The acceptable degree of approximation is normally quantified using one of the string distance measures discussed in Chapter 3. A related problem involves strings containing wild-card symbols which are permitted to match any other symbol. Also, briefly mentioned in this chapter are some parallel hardware designs and algorithms suited to approximate-matching and sequence-comparison tasks.

Chapter 6 examines the detection of repeated substrings within a string. Two variations of the problem are considered, namely those involving *repetitions* and *longest repeated substrings*. In the former case, consecutive instances of repeated substrings are sought; in the latter, the restriction on substring contiguity is relaxed. Also for the latter case, both the problems of locating the single longest repeated substring of a given string and of finding all of its repeated substrings of maximal length are discussed. The principal approaches outlined in this chapter involve the construction of the suffix tree of the input string.

Finally, some additional material is to be found in the appendices, and is organised as follows. Asymptotic notation involving, for example, O, Ω, and Θ is described in **Appendix A**. This notation is commonly employed to characterise the performance of algorithms with respect to the variation in the time they take and the storage space they consume as the size of their inputs is increased. As mentioned earlier, the string symbology employed throughout this book is summarised in **Appendix B**, while **Appendix C** provides a glossary of selected string-related terms.

2

String Matching

2.1 Overview

One of the most common problems involving strings is that of searching for occurrences of a given pattern as a substring of a larger text string. This problem crops up in many diverse applications; an obvious one being the keyword search facility of text editors and word processors. This *String-Matching Problem* may be formulated as follows.

> Given pattern string x, with $|x| = m$, and text string y, with $|y| = n$, where $m, n > 0$ and $m \leqslant n$, if x occurs as a substring of y then determine the position within y of the first occurrence of x, i.e. return the least value of i such that $y(i, i + m - 1) = x(1, m)$.

The problem is sometimes extended such that the positions of all the occurrences of x within y are to be found. Algorithms satisfying the former requirement may be extended easily to satisfy the latter.

The range of approaches to tackling this problem is broad, and includes: brute-force searching; the seminal Knuth-Morris-Pratt and Boyer-Moore algorithms, together with a host of variants based thereon; and certain hashing-based schemes. These techniques are examined below — first of all in overview, and later in greater depth.

2.1.1 Brute Force

The intuitive, or *Brute Force*, approach to the problem is simply to attempt to match x with substrings from y at successive positions in the text string. This requires the input text string to be buffered since backtracking in the text is required in the event of an unsuccessful match. In the worst case, this method runs in $O(mn)$ time, but for practical applications, such as searching English text, the expected performance is $O(m+n)$.

2.1.2 Knuth-Morris-Pratt and Boyer-Moore Approaches

A theorem about deterministic, two-way pushdown automata, derived by Cook (1972), led to the result that there exists an algorithm solving the string-matching problem in $O(m+n)$ time in the worst case. In fact, Rivest (1977) demonstrated that, in the worst case, any string-matching algorithm must examine at least $n - m + 1$ symbols from the text string. This shows that no solution to the string-matching problem may have behaviour sublinear in n in the worst case.

In 1970, Knuth learned of Cook's theorem and from it derived a string-matching algorithm. This was then modified by Pratt so that its running time was independent of the size of the symbol alphabet. The resulting algorithm was also independently arrived at, without knowledge of Cook's theorem, by Morris in 1969 for application in a text editor so as to avoid having to backtrack in the text string. The operation of their algorithm (Knuth, Morris and Pratt, 1977) is described briefly below.

The basic idea behind the algorithm is to avoid backtracking in the text string in the event of a mismatch by taking advantage of known information. The text string is processed sequentially from left to right. When a substring match attempt fails at symbol x_j, say, the previous $j - 1$ text symbols will be known since they will be given by $x(1, j - 1)$. This fact can be exploited to determine how far to shift the pattern to the right for the next match attempt. An auxiliary *next* table containing this shift information is computed in $O(m)$ time from the pattern before searching the string.

The worst-case performance occurs for Fibonacci pattern strings, for which the algorithm runs in $O(m + n)$ time. Although the method performs well for highly self-repetitive patterns and text, this situation occurs only rarely in actual applications. Thus, in practice, the Knuth-Morris-Pratt algorithm is not likely to be significantly faster than the Brute Force approach. It does, however, have the advantage of never having to backtrack in the input text, obviating the need for involved buffering-schemes when reading from sequential text streams, for example.

Pirklbauer (1992) has discussed a variation of the Knuth-Morris-Pratt algorithm using right-to-left comparison of the pattern and text, as in the Boyer-Moore approach described below. An improved average-case performance was reported, but at the cost of sacrificing the strictly sequential nature of processing the input text.

A much faster string searching method was discovered in 1974 by Boyer and Moore, and also independently by Gosper. The algorithm was later presented in a revised form (Boyer and Moore, 1977) taking into account suggestions from B. Kuipers, D.E. Knuth and R.W. Floyd.

The speed of the Boyer-Moore algorithm is achieved by disregarding portions of the text string which cannot possibly participate in a successful match. For a large alphabet and small pattern, the expected number of symbol comparisons is about n/m, and is $O(m+n)$ in the worst case. In this method, the pattern is scanned across the text string from left to right, but for each trial position the symbol comparisons between pattern and text are performed from right to left. Thus, the first comparison is between x_m and y_m. If y_m does not occur anywhere in x, then there can be no match for x starting anywhere in the first m symbols of y. The next potential pattern starting position would therefore be $m+1$, and the next comparison would be between x_m and y_{2m}. The actual pattern shift is determined by taking the larger of the values from two precomputed, auxiliary tables. One of these — the *skip* table — is indexed by the offending text symbol causing the mismatch (the *occurrence* heuristic), whilst the other — the *shift* table — is based on the *next* table of the Knuth-Morris-Pratt algorithm (the *match* heuristic). In a postscript to Knuth, Morris and Pratt (1977), Knuth presented an algorithm to compute the *shift* table in time linear in m. The algorithm did not, however, do so correctly in all cases. A corrected version was developed in 1977 by Mehlhorn (Smit, 1982), and Rytter (1980) has also put forward a corrected algorithm.

The worst-case number of symbol comparisons necessary to determine *all* the occurrences of the pattern in the text has been a matter of some interest. In these circumstances, the original Boyer-Moore algorithm requires $O(n+rm)$ time, where r is the number of matches found. Knuth, Morris and Pratt (1977) presented a modified version of the Boyer-Moore algorithm requiring at most $6n$ comparisons for the case where the pattern does not occur in the text. Guibas and Odlyzko (1977) improved this figure to $4n$, and conjectured a tighter bound of $2n$. Galil (1979) also put forward a variant of the algorithm, which was improved upon by Apostolico and Giancarlo (1986). Their version requires at most $2n$ symbol comparisons, regardless of the number of occurrences of the pattern in the text. This is at the cost of only slightly increased pattern-preprocessing overheads, which are still linear in m. Also, a recent Boyer-Moore variant due to Lecroq (1992) involves at most $3n$ comparisons. These methods do not, however, provide any significant improvement in the average case. Recent work by Colussi, Galil and Giancarlo (1990) has resulted in a further reduction of the worst-case upper bound — neglecting preprocessing — to $(4n-m)/3$ symbol comparisons. Theirs is an algorithm based on both the Knuth-Morris-Pratt and Boyer-Moore approaches.

Horspool (1980) has shown that a simplified form of the Boyer-Moore algorithm, employing only a single auxiliary table—indexed by the mismatching text-symbols—results in a performance comparable to that of the original version. In fact, Baeza-Yates (1989a, 1989c) has observed, from both analytical and empirical studies, that the Boyer-Moore-Horspool method is the best of the known algorithms in terms of average-case performance for nearly all pattern lengths and alphabet sizes.

The average-case performance of the Boyer-Moore-Horspool, the Knuth-Morris-Pratt, and the Brute Force algorithms has been analysed by Baeza-Yates (1989b). His analysis was for the case of finding *all* the pattern occurrences, and was based on random strings (i.e. concatenations of symbols chosen independently from the alphabet with a uniform probability distribution) for the pattern and text. Empirically-validated tight bounds were derived for the expected number of symbol comparisons involved in the search methods. A hybrid algorithm, combining the Boyer-Moore and Knuth-Morris-Pratt approaches, was proposed. In practice, the hybrid performed slightly better than the Boyer-Moore-Horspool method for searches of English text.

For the Boyer-Moore approach, the average running time improves with larger alphabets or longer patterns. Improved performance can therefore be obtained by increasing the size of the alphabet. This technique has been considered by Knuth, Morris and Pratt (1977) and by Schaback (1988). Baeza-Yates (1989a) has proposed a simple alphabet transformation, leading to a practical implementation of a Boyer-Moore-Horspool variant. Essentially, this involves grouping k symbols of the pattern together as a *supersymbol*. This reduces the pattern size, $|x|$, to $m - k + 1$ and increases the size of the alphabet to $|C|^k$, where C is the original alphabet. This approach has been shown to be practicable for small alphabets or large patterns, and experimental increases in speed of 50% have been reported (e.g. for $k = 2$, $|C| = 8$ and random text).

Baeza-Yates (1989a) also put forward suggestions for improving the efficiency of searching non-uniformly distributed texts, such as English. He considered the optimal ordering of pattern symbol comparisons, based on their probability distribution within the text. This may be obtained either by preprocessing the text or from a priori information about the text source. Rarer symbols could, for example, be compared before more frequent ones, thereby increasing the probability of an early detection of a mismatch.

The order in which the pattern symbols are compared has also been investigated by Raita (1992) in an attempt to minimise the effects of dependencies between successive text symbols. For searches of English text, speed increases in the region of 25% have been reported for a variant of the Boyer-Moore-Horspool algorithm based on this criterion.

Sunday (1990) has suggested using the symbol in the text immediately *following* the one that caused a mismatch to address the occurrence-heuristic table of the Boyer-Moore algorithm. Using this approach, he developed three variations, each differing in the manner in which the order of the symbol comparisons between the pattern and the current text-substring is determined. In the *Quick Search* algorithm, the comparisons are performed from left to right. The *Maximal Shift* algorithm orders the comparisons such that the distance to the next pattern position in the event of a mismatch is maximised. Finally, the *Optimal Mismatch* algorithm uses the idea, discussed by Baeza-Yates, as mentioned above, of comparing statistically rarer symbols first. Smith (1991) has developed an adaptive version of Sunday's Optimal Mismatch technique with the advantage that it assumes no prior knowledge of the given text.

A family of algorithms based on the general structure of an optimised implementation of Boyer and Moore's (1977) method, involving a fast skip loop, has been investigated by Hume and Sunday (1991). Two new variants conforming to this structure were developed — the *Tuned Boyer-Moore*, and the *Least Cost* algorithms.

2.1.3 Hashing Functions

An alternative approach to the string-matching problem involves the use of hashing functions. Such a method to test for the occurrence of a pattern within a text string, but not to find its location, was proposed by Harrison (1971). This technique is based on the comparison of string *signatures* and requires the text to be preprocessed. It would therefore be applicable to the searching of large, static, text files, for example.

Karp and Rabin (1987) also put forward an algorithm involving the use of hashing, but one which does not require preprocessing of the text to be searched. Their approach is similar to that of Brute Force searching, but rather than directly comparing the m-symbol strings at successive text positions, their respective signatures are compared. This reduces the task of comparing two strings to the simpler one of comparing two integers. A carefully chosen hash function allows the text-substring signatures to be calculated easily in an incremental manner. The algorithm is not restricted to string matching and may be extended to multi-dimensional pattern matching. In the worst case, which is extremely unlikely, the algorithm takes $O(mn)$ time, but the expected performance is $O(m + n)$.

2.1.4 Comparative Performance

The comparative performance of the various algorithms described above has been studied both theoretically and empirically by many investigators (e.g. Horspool, 1980; Smit, 1982; Baeza-Yates, 1989a, 1989c; Davies and Bowsher, 1986; Pirklbauer,

1992). The overall conclusion of these studies is that, for general applications, the Boyer-Moore-Horspool is the best available algorithm. As noted earlier, this is the recommendation given for almost all pattern lengths and alphabet sizes by Baeza-Yates (1989a, 1989c). In the extreme cases of very small patterns (i.e. $m \leqslant 3$) and pattern lengths commensurate with the text length (i.e. $m \approx n$), the Brute Force approach is preferable. Horspool (1980) observed that his simplified variant gave an average performance comparable to that of the Boyer-Moore algorithm, and outperformed a Brute Force method coded using special-purpose machine instructions for symbol searching when $m \geqslant 6$.

Despite its theoretical elegance, the non-backtracking Knuth-Morris-Pratt algorithm provides no significant speed advantage over the Brute Force method in practice. It may, however, be a good choice when $|C| \approx n$ (Baeza-Yates, 1989a), or when dealing with binary strings, i.e. when $|C| = 2$ (Davies and Bowsher, 1986). Although it may inspect text symbols more than once and may backtrack in the input string, the Boyer-Moore approach provides, on the whole, a significantly faster search method.

In terms of execution time, the Karp-Rabin hashing technique fares badly in competition with the other methods, but is extendible to higher-dimensional problems. It may therefore be used for pattern matching in image-processing applications, for example.

With regards to Sunday's variations of the Boyer-Moore approach, Pirklbauer (1992) recommends the Sunday Quick Search in addition to a simplified Boyer-Moore variant. However, he advises against the use of the Maximal Shift and Optimal Mismatch algorithms, on the grounds of the resulting length of code and excessive preprocessing loads, especially significant when searching for only the first occurrence of a pattern. Hume and Sunday (1991) report a significant improvement in performance over the original Boyer-Moore algorithm for their new methods. Again, however, preprocessing loads were not taken into account in the measurements.

Space Optimality

Some attention has been given to the problem of minimising the extra space required by string-matching algorithms over and above that necessary to store the pattern and text strings themselves. Note that the extra space required by the Knuth-Morris-Pratt and Boyer-Moore algorithms is linear in m. Linear-time algorithms requiring only constant extra space have, however, been developed (Galil and Seiferas, 1983; Crochemore and Perrin, 1989; Crochemore, 1992).

Unlike the two earlier approaches, that of Crochemore (1992) does not involve any preprocessing, and performs symbol comparisons from left to right in the pattern. But, the algorithm is mainly of theoretical interest, as it cannot compete in practice with the average-case sublinearity of the Boyer-Moore approach and its derivatives.

2.1.5 Popularity

Although providing a high performance, the degree to which the Boyer-Moore approach has been put into practice may have been curbed to a certain extent by conceptual difficulties in the preprocessing, particularly with the match heuristic. Horspool (1980) observed that *"many programmers may not believe that the Boyer and Moore algorithm (if they have heard of it) is a truly practical approach."* Sedgewick (1983) also noted that *"both the Knuth-Morris-Pratt and the Boyer-Moore algorithms require some complicated preprocessing on the pattern that is difficult to understand and has limited the extent to which they are used."* In fact, Morris discovered that after a few months his initial search implementation in a text editor, being too difficult to understand by other systems programmers, had been ruined by various gratuitous 'fixes' (Knuth, Morris and Pratt, 1977).

Hume and Sunday (1991) add that *"partially because the best algorithms presented in the literature are difficult to understand and to implement, knowledge of fast and practical algorithms is not commonplace."* Arguing for a more consistent approach to algorithm development, and against *"widespread chaotic algorithm presentation,"* Woude (1989) asserts that the Knuth-Morris-Pratt preprocessing should be no more difficult to understand than the actual search procedure itself. There have also been some attempts of late to popularise the Boyer-Moore approach, particularly in its simplified form (e.g. Menico, 1989). As a step towards elucidating this field, Hume and Sunday (1991) have presented a means of classifying the various string-matching algorithms based on the Knuth-Morris-Pratt and Boyer-Moore approaches. A taxonomy of string-matching algorithms, including these two aforementioned approaches, has also been put forward by Watson and Zwaan (1992).

2.1.6 Multiple-String Searches

An extension of the string-matching problem involves searching the text string for an occurrence of any one of a set of N pattern strings, $X = \{x_1, x_2, \ldots, x_N\}$.

The repeated application of a linear-time, string-matching algorithm, such as Boyer-Moore, in this situation would lead to an $O(m + Nn)$ running time, where m is the sum of the lengths of the pattern strings, i.e. $m = \sum_{x \in X} |x|$. The search process can, however, be accomplished more efficiently in $O(m + n)$ time by employing a pattern-matching machine, or automaton, to search for the pattern strings simultaneously (Aho and Corasick, 1975). This technique is a generalisation of the Knuth-Morris-Pratt approach to string matching. The automaton may be constructed from the set of keyword strings in $O(m)$ time, and may then be used to search the text string in $O(n)$ time.

During processing, the text string is scanned from left to right, with no backtracking, a symbol at a time. The automaton comprises a finite set of states together with predefined rules governing how it moves from state to state. The latter depend on both the present state of the machine and the particular text symbol currently being inspected.

The automaton starts off in an initial state and moves forward to another for the first text symbol. For subsequent symbols the machine either advances directly to another state or is successively taken back, via a *failure* function, to a previous state until it can once more move forward from that state for the current text symbol. The failure function controlling the reverse state transitions is a generalisation of the Knuth-Morris-Pratt *next* table. The process continues until either the end of the text is reached or an *accepting* state is entered, corresponding to an occurrence of one of the pattern strings having been found.

For cases where the set of pattern strings is fixed — for example, when various texts are to be searched for occurrences of members of the same set of strings — Aoe (1989) has developed an efficient implementation of the Aho-Corasick string-matching automaton. This is based on an adaptation of Johnson's (1975) finite-state-machine data structure.

Commentz-Walter (1979) put forward a procedure combining the Boyer-Moore approach with the above technique, in which an automaton for the set of the reversed keywords is constructed. Although faster in practice for small numbers of pattern strings than the Aho-Corasick algorithm, this method does run in quadratic time in the worst case. However, the worst-case performance is improved to $O(n)$ time in a variation of the algorithm, at the cost of a preprocessing stage running in greater than linear time.

A similar approach involving reversed keywords has been developed by Kim and Shawe-Taylor (1992a), and the Boyer-Moore-Horspool technique has also been employed in this particular application (Baeza-Yates, 1990).

The 'shift-add' algorithm (Baeza-Yates and Gonnet, 1989, 1992) can also be applied to multiple-string searching. This is a flexible numerical approach, which scans the text in $O(\lceil \frac{m}{w} \rceil n)$ time, where w is the computer wordsize in bits. For pattern sets smaller than w, then, the text scan runs in linear time.

It should be noted that the shift-add algorithm is also an efficient method for matching with a single pattern string when that string is small. Its preprocessing and text scanning times for this are $O(\lceil \frac{m}{w} \rceil (m + |C|))$ and $O(\lceil \frac{m}{w} \rceil n)$, respectively, for alphabet C. More detailed discussion of this algorithm is deferred until Chapter 5, where its application to both exact and approximate string matching is examined.

In situations where a fixed text is to be searched repeatedly for occurrences of many different patterns, it is worthwhile constructing an auxiliary text index. For example, Weiner's (1973) index (or equivalents, such as the suffix tree discussed in Chapter 4) may be built in time linear in n, and permits searches for patterns, x, to be performed subsequently in time linear in $|x|$.

2.2 Algorithms in Detail

2.2.1 Brute Force

In the Brute Force approach, x is compared with substrings $y(i, i + m - 1)$ at successive positions, i, in the text string (for $1 \leqslant i \leqslant n - m + 1$), until a match is found or the end of the text is reached.

As a maximum of m symbol comparisons may be performed for each position i in y, $m(n - m + 1)$ comparisons are required in total in the worst case. For this maximum to be incurred, the substring comparison for each position i must either first fail on the last (m^{th}) symbol comparison, or in the case of the final position ($i = n - m + 1$) alternatively provide a successful match. This situation arises in the following example.

$$x \; = \; \text{EEEEW}$$
$$y \; = \; \text{EEEEEEEEEEEEEEEEEEEEEEW}$$

However, this type of case is likely to occur but seldom in practical applications of text searching. The expected performance is therefore about $O(m + n)$, since the majority of the unsuccessful substring matching attempts are likely to fail very early on. The actual performance will, of course, depend on the statistical parameters of the particular pattern and text involved.

An implementation of the Brute Force string-matching algorithm is given in the pseudocode of Figure 2.1. The pattern and text indices are initially both set to point to the start of their respective strings, and are both incremented as long as the symbols to which they point match. In the event of a symbol mismatch, j is reset to point to the start of the pattern, and i to the next potential pattern position in the text. If a match is found, then i is set to the starting position in y of the pattern, otherwise it is reset to zero to indicate that the text search has been unsuccessful.

2.2.2 Knuth-Morris-Pratt

The basic method of the Knuth-Morris-Pratt algorithm is similar to that of the Brute Force approach, except that the text index, i, is never decremented. This is achieved by shifting pattern x forward relative to text y, in the event of a mismatch, by an amount dependent on both the structure of the pattern and the position, j, within x

```
i = 1    — initialise y index
j = 1    — initialise x index
while (i ⩽ n) and (j ⩽ m)
  if x_j = y_i
      i = i + 1
      j = j + 1
  else
      i = i - j + 2
      j = 1
if j > m    — check for successful match
  i = i - m
else
  i = 0
```

Figure 2.1: Brute Force string matching

at which the mismatch occurs. This shift information is obtained from an m-entry, auxiliary table, $next$, precomputed from the pattern before searching the text.

The search algorithm is given in Figure 2.2. In the event of a mismatch between the text and the pattern at positions i and j, respectively, it is known that the previous $j - 1$ text symbols, i.e. substring $y(i - j + 1, i - 1)$, match the first $j - 1$ pattern symbols, i.e. prefix $x(1, j - 1)$. This information is exploited by using the $next$ table, which contains values for the next pattern position, $next_j$, to be used after a mismatch at pattern position j.

In the inner loop, j is set to $next_j$, which is equivalent to shifting the pattern $j - next_j$ symbol positions to the right relative to the text. This is performed repeatedly until either $j = 0$ or $x_j = y_i$. In the former case, none of x matches the current text substring; in the latter, the prefix $x(1, j)$ matches the substring $y(i - j + 1, i)$. The outer loop then resumes by incrementing the text and pattern indices. If a complete match is found, then i is set to the starting position of the occurrence of x in y, otherwise it is reset to 0.

The crucial part of the algorithm is the $next$ table. Before considering it in its final form, we shall first examine a simplified version. This is illustrated in the following example.

$i = 1$ — initialise y index
$j = 1$ — initialise x index
while $(i \leqslant n)$ **and** $(j \leqslant m)$
    while $(j > 0)$ **and** $(x_j \neq y_i)$
        $j = next_j$
    $i = i + 1$
    $j = j + 1$
if $j > m$
    $i = i - m$
else
    $i = 0$

Note that the **and** in the inner loop is a 'conditional and,' which only evaluates its right-hand operand if its left-hand one evaluates to true.

Figure 2.2: Knuth-Morris-Pratt string matching

j	1	2	3	4	5	6	7	8
x_j	A	B	C	D	A	B	C	E
$next_j$	0	1	1	1	1	2	3	4

This shows that if, for example, matching between the above pattern and a given text string fails at $j = 8$, then the next pattern symbol to be compared with the current text symbol is x_4. This situation is shown below.

Match attempt fails at comparison of y_i and x_8

```
                    j = 8
pattern     A B C D A B C E
text    ... A B C D A B C D ...
                            i
```

Next comparison is between y_i and x_4

```
                        j = 4
pattern             A B C D A B C E
text    ... A B C D A B C D ...
                        i
```

The entries of the *next* table may be derived from x as follows. For a mismatch between x_j and y_i, it is known that $x(1, j - 1)$ matches the previous $j - 1$ symbols of y. If there exists a proper prefix of substring $x(1, j - 1)$, of maximal length $k - 1$, say, i.e. $x(1, k - 1)$, equal to a suffix of the same substring, i.e. $x(j - k + 1, j - 1)$, then the next pattern symbol to try is that obtained by shifting the pattern relative to the text until the prefix occupies the space previously occupied by the suffix. The next symbol to be compared with y_i is therefore the one immediately following the prefix, namely x_k. For the case of a mismatch at the first pattern symbol, $next_1$ is given the value of 0 so that the entire pattern is shifted past y_i.

To reiterate, the value of $next_j$ is given by the maximum k, less than j, such that $x(1, k - 1)$ is a suffix of $x(1, j - 1)$, i.e. $x(1, k - 1) = x(j - k + 1, j - 1)$ (note that for the case of the prefix $x(1, k - 1) = \epsilon$, k is taken to be 1). This may be found in the following manner. Compare $x(1, j - 1)$ with itself by sliding one copy over the other from left to right. Start in the position such that the first comparison is between x_1 and x_2, and stop when either all the overlapping symbols match or there is none left. The overlapping characters then define the required prefix, and k is given by the size of this prefix plus 1.

Returning to the previous example pattern, the situation for $next_8$ is shown below.

$$\begin{array}{cc} & \text{A B C D A B C} \\ x(1,7) & \text{A B C D A B C} \end{array}$$

From the above, it may be seen that there are 3 overlapping symbols. In this case, the value of $next_8$ is therefore equal to 4.

Note that in the search procedure, just after it has been incremented, the value of j is the largest integer, less than or equal to i, such that $x(1, j-1) = y(i-j+1, i-1)$. This is exactly the requirement described earlier for the *next* values, when y is replaced by x. The method to generate the *next* table is therefore similar to the actual search procedure, with the exception that the pattern is being matched against itself. The pseudocode for this is given in Figure 2.3.

It was mentioned previously that the above formulation of the *next* table caters for a simplified case. This does not take into account all the available information, and advantage may still be taken of the actual symbol causing a mismatch. Consider the previous example. If there is a mismatch between y_i and x_7 (the second C), say, then the next comparison would be between y_i and x_{next_7}, i.e. x_3 (the first C). However, this comparison will also fail and its *next* value will shift the comparison to x_1. An improved *next* table would take the comparison directly to x_1 in the event of a mismatch at x_7. The modified requirement for $next_j$ is therefore that it is now equal to the greatest k less than j such that $x(1, k - 1) = x(j - k + 1, j - 1)$ and $x_j \neq x_k$, and is equal to 0 if there is no such k. Using this definition, the new *next* table is given below.

$j = 1$
$k = 0$
$next_1 = 0$ — special value for mismatch at x_1
while $j < m$
    while $(k > 0)$ **and** $(x_j \neq x_k)$
      $k = next_k$
    $j = j + 1$
    $k = k + 1$
    $next_j = k$

Note that the **and** in the inner loop is a 'conditional and.'

Figure 2.3: Initialisation of the *next* table (simplified)

j	1	2	3	4	5	6	7	8
x_j	A	B	C	D	A	B	C	E
$next_j$	0	1	1	1	0	1	1	4

This revised requirement is easily accommodated by modifying the $next_j$ assignment in the *next*-table creation algorithm, giving the final version of Figure 2.4. The value of $next_k$ is now assigned to $next_j$ if $x_j = x_k$. This ensures that on a mismatch, a comparison is not next attempted between the current text symbol and another pattern symbol equal to the one just tried.

The search algorithm given in Figure 2.2 has the unusual feature that the total number of times that the assignment "$j = next_j$" in the inner loop is executed never exceeds that of the increment operation of i in the outer loop. The pattern is therefore shifted to the right a total of at most n times by the inner loop, giving a matching time of $O(n)$. Similarly, it may be shown that the *next* table initialisation stage is performed in $O(m)$ time. This gives an overall, worst-case time of $O(m + n)$, which is, incidentally, independent of the size of the symbol alphabet.

The worst-case time is incurred for the task of matching a Fibonacci string pattern. Also, the maximum number of times that the inner loop is executed whilst still at the same position in the text has been shown to be $1 + \log_\phi m$, where ϕ is the golden ratio, equal to $(1 + \sqrt{5})/2 \approx 1.618$ (Knuth, Morris and Pratt, 1977).

The average-case performance of the algorithm for random strings has been analysed by Baeza-Yates (1989b). An upper bound for the expected number of symbol comparisons, A_n, was derived which improves upon an earlier result (Régnier,

```
j = 1
k = 0
next₁ = 0     — special value for mismatch at x₁
while j < m
    while (k > 0) and (xⱼ ≠ xₖ)
        k = nextₖ
    j = j + 1
    k = k + 1
    if xⱼ = xₖ
        nextⱼ = nextₖ
    else
        nextⱼ = k
```

Note that the **and** in the inner loop is a 'conditional and.'

Figure 2.4: Initialisation of the *next* table

1988). This is given below.

$$\frac{A_n}{n} \leqslant 1 + \frac{1}{|C|} + \frac{\left\lceil \log_\phi m \right\rceil - 1}{|C|^3} + O\left(\frac{\log^2 m}{|C|^4}\right) \tag{2.1}$$

for $|C| > \left\lceil \log_\phi m \right\rceil$, where C is the alphabet. To give a numerical value to this bound, consider the case of a pattern length of 10 and an alphabet size of 256. This gives an upper bound for A_n of $\approx 1.004n$. Note that, with the same parameters and for large n, a virtually identical result is obtained for the average case of the Brute Force algorithm, for which the expected value of A_n for random strings is as follows (Baeza-Yates, 1989b):

$$A_n = \frac{|C|}{|C| - 1}\left(1 - \frac{1}{|C|^m}\right)(n - m + 1) + O(1) \tag{2.2}$$

Various implementation efficiency considerations were addressed by Knuth, Morris and Pratt (1977). For example, sentinels may be appended to the ends of the strings in order to reduce the requirement for index-bound checking. Also, the *next* table may be used to compile a finite-state machine matcher for the pattern. Extensions to the problem, such as finding *all* the occurrences of the pattern in the text were also considered.

2.2.3 Boyer-Moore

In the Boyer-Moore search algorithm, the pattern is scanned across the text string from left to right, but the actual symbol comparisons between the pattern and the text are performed from right to left. The first comparison is therefore between x_m and y_m. In the event of a mismatch, if y_m does not occur at all in x, then the pattern may be shifted safely m places to the right. This is due to the fact that the possibility of x occurring in y starting at any of the first m positions has been ruled out. The next comparison would then be between x_m and y_{2m}.

Consider the case of a mismatch occurring between x_m and y_i, say. As mentioned above, if y_i does not appear anywhere in the pattern, then a shift of the pattern m places to the right may be effected. If, on the other hand, y_i does appear in the pattern and its rightmost occurrence is x_{m-s}, then the pattern may be shifted s places to the right, aligning x_{m-s} with y_i. Testing may be resumed by comparing x_m with y_{i+s}, i.e. the text index is incremented by s.

If a match is found between symbols x_m and y_i, then the corresponding preceding symbols from the pattern and the text are compared until either a complete match is obtained or a mismatch occurs. If a mismatch occurs at x_j, say, then the suffix, of length $m-j$, $x(j+1, m)$ will be equal to text substring $y(i-m+j+1, i)$, and $x_j \neq y_{i-m+j}$. If the rightmost occurrence in x of y_{i-m+j} is again x_{m-s}, say, then the pattern may be shifted $j-m+s$ places to the right, lining up x_{m-s} with y_{i-m+j}. Once more, the procedure may be continued by comparing x_m with its corresponding text symbol, in this case $y_{i+j-m+s}$. The increment in the text index from the mismatch position to that of the next comparison is therefore $(i+j-m+s) - (i-m+j) = s$. Note that this increment is the same as that for the case considered previously.

If x_{m-s} happens to be to the right of x_j, giving a negative value for $j - m + s$, there is nothing to be gained by aligning x_{m-s} with y_{i-m+j}, as this would involve a retrograde step. In these circumstances, therefore, the pattern may be shifted one place to the right, with the comparisons being resumed with symbols x_m and y_{i+1}. This requires a text index increment of $(i + 1) - (i - m + j) = m + 1 - j$.

The increments, s, obtained from this *occurrence* heuristic are precomputed and stored in a *skip* table (denoted by $delta_1$ by Boyer and Moore (1977)). During the search, the table is indexed by the text symbol causing a mismatch, so a table the size of the symbol alphabet in use is required. The entry for symbol w is equal to $m - j$, where x_j is the rightmost occurrence of w in x, and equal to m if w does not occur at all in x, i.e.

$$skip[w] = \min\{s \mid s = m \text{ or } (0 \leqslant s < m \text{ and } x_{m-s} = w)\} \qquad (2.3)$$

The *skip* table is simply initialised as follows for alphabet C.

```
for w = 1 to |C|
    skip[w] = m
for j = 1 to m
    skip[x_j] = m - j
```

From the above, it may be seen that the initialisation of the $skip$ table is accomplished in $O(m + |C|)$ time. The following example illustrates the operation of the $skip$ table for the pattern ABCDB.

w	A	B	C	D	E	F	G	H	. . .
$skip[w]$	4	0	2	1	5	5	5	5	. . .

Mismatch occurs at y_i = A

```
pattern         A B C D B
text        . . L M N A B C D B . . .
                          i
```

Next comparison is between x_m and $y_{i+skip[A]}$, i.e. y_{i+4}

```
pattern         A B C D B
text        . . L M N A B C D B . .
                          i       i+4
```

For the case described earlier of a mismatch occurring after a partial match had been obtained, it is possible that a greater shift of the pattern than that given by the occurrence heuristic may be feasible. If this is so, then it is preferable to use the larger shift, which is obtained via the *match* heuristic. This is based on a table similar to that of the Knuth-Morris-Pratt algorithm. The idea behind this is that when the pattern is shifted, it must match all the symbols previously matched, and there must be a change in the pattern symbol at the text position that caused the mismatch. The latter condition was proposed independently by Kuipers (credited in Boyer and Moore (1977)) and by Knuth (in the postscript of Knuth, Morris and Pratt (1977)). It improves over Boyer and Moore's original heuristic in a manner analogous to that of the improvement of the *next* table of the Knuth-Morris-Pratt algorithm.

As mentioned earlier, the particular case under examination is when $x(j + 1, m) = y(i - m + j + 1, i)$ and $x_j \neq y_{i-m+j}$. If the suffix $x(j + 1, m)$ also occurs in x as the substring $x(j + 1 - t, m - t)$, with $x_{j-t} \neq x_j$, and it is the rightmost such occurrence, then the pattern may be shifted t places to the right. This brings $x(j + 1 - t, m - t)$ into alignment with $y(i - m + j + 1, i)$, and the search process may be resumed by comparing x_m with y_{i+t}. A $shift$ table (denoted by $delta_2$ by

Boyer and Moore (1977)) for the t-shift information may be precomputed from the pattern, and is indexed by the position in the pattern at which mismatch occurs. The value of $shift[j]$ is equal to a pattern shift, t, plus the extra shift required to restart the comparisons at the extreme right of the pattern. The value of t is the minimum such that when x_m is aligned with y_{i+t}, then assuming that $x_j \neq y_{i-m+j}$, pattern substring $x(j + 1 - t, m - t)$ will match text substring $y(i - m + j + 1, i)$. Thus, the $shift$ table entries are defined as follows:

$$shift[j] = \min\{t + m - j \mid t \geqslant 1 \text{ and } (t \geqslant j \text{ or } x_{j-t} \neq x_j) \text{ and} \qquad (2.4)$$
$$((t \geqslant k \text{ or } x_{k-t} = x_k) \text{ for } j < k \leqslant m)\}$$

The $shift[j]$ value is therefore equal to the required increment for the text index from the current position, y_{i-m+j}, to the next comparison position, y_{i+t}, i.e. $(i + t) - (i - m + j) = t + m - j$. The following example illustrates the $shift$ values for the pattern ABCDABC.

x_j	A	B	C	D	A	B	C
j	1	2	3	4	5	6	7
$m - j$	6	5	4	3	2	1	0
t	4	4	4	4	7	7	1
$shift[j]$	10	9	8	7	9	8	1

From the definition of $shift[j]$, it may be seen that $shift[j] \geqslant m+1-j$. Thus, in the case described earlier requiring a text-index increment of $m + 1 - j$ rather than the relevant $skip$ value, as the latter would involve a backwards pattern shift, it is sufficient to use the relevant $shift$ table value. In the event of a mismatch while searching, the maximum of the text increments from the two heuristics described above should therefore be used. The algorithm for this method is given in Figure 2.5. The final value of i gives the position of the pattern in the text, with 0 indicating that the pattern was not found.

The $shift$ table may be precomputed from the pattern in $O(m)$ time as shown in Figure 2.6. This is the method presented by Aho (1990), originated by Knuth (Knuth, Morris and Pratt, 1977) and modified by Mehlhorn (Smit, 1982). The intermediate function, f, calculated in the algorithm is defined as follows: $f[m] = m + 1$, and for $1 \leqslant j < m$, $f[j] = \min\{i \mid j < i \leqslant m \text{ and } x(i + 1, m) = x(j + 1, j + m - i)\}$.

Knuth demonstrated that to locate all the occurrences of the pattern, the Boyer-Moore algorithm performs $O(n + rm)$ symbol comparisons, where r is the number of times the pattern appears in the text (Knuth, Morris and Pratt, 1977). He also showed that when the pattern is absent from the text, a total of $6n$ symbol comparisons is required. For large alphabets, the expected performance of the

$i = m$
$j = m$
while $(j > 0)$ **and** $(i \leqslant n)$
  if $y_i = x_j$
    $i = i - 1$
    $j = j - 1$
  else
    — a mismatch
    $i = i + \max\{skip[y_i], shift[j]\}$
    $j = m$
if $j < 1$
  $i = i + 1$
else
  $i = 0$

Figure 2.5: Boyer-Moore string matching

Boyer-Moore algorithm is sublinear, requiring about n/m symbol comparisons on average.

A variant of the Boyer-Moore algorithm developed by Apostolico and Giancarlo (1986) finds all of the occurrences of the pattern, performing at most $2n - m + 1$ symbol comparisons. The attendant preprocessing requirements are slightly more onerous, but are still linear in m. The method employed exploits knowledge of which pattern substrings matched which text substrings at previous trial positions, and uses the simpler form of the $shift$-table definition.

There are many other variations of the Boyer-Moore approach to string matching. One of the more notable of these, the Boyer-Moore-Horspool algorithm, which involves simplified preprocessing, is described in the next section. But before that, we shall first examine a particularly efficient implementation of the Boyer-Moore algorithm.

Fast Skip Loop

In discussing efficiency considerations, Boyer and Moore noted that the part of the algorithm most frequently executed was that concerned with shifting the pattern on immediate mismatches. An alternative implementation of their technique, which has since been much neglected, was then presented. This incorporates a 'fast' skip loop, involving only the occurrence heuristic, to perform the said operation. The fast loop is used to discount non-match positions rapidly, and only after a

---

```
for i = 1 to m
    shift[i] = 2 * m - i
j = m
k = m + 1
while j > 0
    f[j] = k
    while (k ⩽ m) and (x_j ≠ x_k)
        shift[k] = min{shift[k], m - j}
        k = f[k]
    j = j - 1
    k = k - 1
for i = 1 to k
    shift[i] = min{shift[i], m + k - i}
j = f[k]
while k ⩽ m
    while k ⩽ j
        shift[k] = min{shift[k], j - k + m}
        k = k + 1
    j = f[j]
```

Note that the **and** in the second **while** loop is a 'conditional and.'

Figure 2.6: Initialisation of the *shift* table

---

successful match has been found for the first pattern symbol to be tested, i.e. x_m, is a 'slow' loop entered in which the other pattern symbols are compared with the text. If a mismatch occurs at this stage, then the maximum of the two heuristics is used to determine the next trial pattern position, and searching is then resumed using the fast loop.

A version of the fast-skip-loop implementation is shown in Figure 2.7. The auxiliary tables are the same as before except that $skip[x_m]$ is assigned a sentinel value LARGE, which is some value greater than $m + n$. This permits the fast loop to scan swiftly through the text string, searching for an occurrence of symbol x_m without actually performing any explicit symbol comparisons. Only the *skip* table need be employed here as the increment that it provides will always be greater than or equal to that given by $shift[m]$.

The fast loop is exited either when the end of the text has been reached or when $y_i = x_m$ (causing i to be incremented by amount LARGE). In the latter case, the slow

```
i = m
j = m
while (j > 0) and (i ≤ n)
    — fast skip loop
    while i ≤ n
        i = i + skip[yᵢ]
    if i > LARGE
        — xₘ has been found in y
        — set up indices to start comparing preceding symbols
        i = i − LARGE − 1
        j = m − 1
        — slow comparison loop
        while (j > 0) and (yᵢ = xⱼ)
            i = i − 1
            j = j − 1
        if j > 0
            — a mismatch
            if skip[yᵢ] = LARGE
                i = i + shift[j]
            else
                i = i + max{skip[yᵢ], shift[j]}
if j < 1
    i = i + 1
else
    i = 0
```

Note that the **and** in the slow comparison **while** loop is a 'conditional and.'

Figure 2.7: Fast-loop Boyer-Moore string matching

loop is then entered in which the preceding pattern and text symbols are compared until either a complete match is found or an unequal pair of symbols is encountered. On a complete match, the process terminates; otherwise i is incremented by the larger of the two appropriate auxiliary table entries, and scanning is then resumed in the fast loop.

As before, if an instance of the pattern is found in the text, then the final value of i gives its location; otherwise i is set to zero.

Boyer and Moore also discussed certain efficiency concerns for the assembly-level implementation of the fast loop, which they estimated accounted for 80% of the execution time during the text search. Hume and Sunday (1991) also examine the fast-loop form of the algorithm, and discuss implementations in C due to King and Macrakis in 1985 and Woods in 1986.

2.2.4   Boyer-Moore-Horspool

In practice, the match heuristic of the Boyer-Moore algorithm makes only a small contribution to the overall speed of the search. It does provide benefits for highly self-repetitive patterns, but these seldom crop up in actual applications. The inclusion of the heuristic ensures that the theoretical worst-case performance is linear rather than quadratic in time.

Horspool (1980) developed a simplified form of the Boyer-Moore algorithm which dispenses with the match heuristic and relies solely on the occurrence heuristic. This reduces the preprocessing effort required, and also cuts down the space requirements from $O(m + |C|)$ to $O(|C|)$, for alphabet C. As the alphabet is usually fixed, the storage requirements will therefore normally be constant. Although the worst-case performance is now $O(mn)$, this actually occurs only for rare, pathological cases, and the expected performance is comparable to that of the full Boyer-Moore algorithm.

The way in which the $skip$ table is used in the Horspool variant differs from that of the Boyer-Moore algorithm in two important respects. As we shall see below, these involve the value assigned to $skip[x_m]$, and the actual text symbol utilised to index the table.

Recall from the Boyer-Moore $skip$ table definition, (2.3), that the value of $skip[x_m]$ is 0. If a mismatch does occur at position i in the text such that $y_i = x_m$, then the actual text increment used is obtained from the $shift$ table. In the Horspool version, however, the value of $skip[x_m]$ is defined differently in order to provide a non-zero increment. Its value is taken to be m if symbol x_m is unique within the pattern, otherwise it is defined to be s, where x_{m-s} is the penultimate occurrence of the symbol in the pattern. Only a slight modification of the Boyer-Moore table initialisation is required to implement the new value of $skip[x_m]$. The reasoning behind the new definition is explained in a little more detail below.

Firstly, consider the case where symbol x_m occurs only once in the pattern, i.e. at the extreme right-hand end. If this symbol occurs somewhere in the text, at position i, say, then the only possible potential match position involving y_i is such that x_m is aligned with y_i. Thus, if a mismatch occurs at $y_i = x_m$, then the pattern may be shifted all the way past y_i for the next trial. This then aligns x_1 with y_{i+1} and x_m with y_{i+m}, giving a *skip* value of m. This case is illustrated in the following example for pattern ABCDE. A description of the second case, namely that in which x_m does occur more than once in the pattern, shall be postponed until after the other major difference of the Horspool algorithm has been examined.

Pattern = ABCDE

```
w          A B C D E F G H . . .
skip[w]    4 3 2 1 5 5 5 5 . . .
```

Mismatch occurs at $y_i = x_m = $ E

```
pattern            A B C D E
text       . . . . . E D E . . . . . .
                     i
```

Next comparison is between x_m and $y_{i+skip[E]}$, i.e. y_{i+5}

```
pattern                      A B C D E
text       . . . . . E D E . . . . . . .
                     i       i+5
```

In order to overcome a potential difficulty, the actual operation of the Boyer-Moore-Horspool algorithm differs from that depicted above with respect to the text symbol used to index the *skip* table. It was mentioned in the previous section that under certain circumstances, the value obtained from the *skip* table can correspond to a backwards shift of the pattern. This situation is demonstrated in the example given below for pattern ABCDE.

```
w          A B C D E F G H . . .
skip[w]    4 3 2 1 5 5 5 5 . . .
```

Mismatch occurs at $y_i = $ D

```
pattern            A B C D E
text       . . . . . D C D E . . . . .
                     i
```

Next comparison is between x_m and $y_{i+skip[D]}$, i.e. y_{i+1}

```
pattern      A B C D E
text     . . . . . D C D E . . . . .
             i i+1
```

Whereas the Boyer-Moore algorithm avoids this situation by virtue of the *shift* table, Horspool's version does so by always using the text symbol corresponding to the final pattern symbol (x_m) to index the *skip* table. This ensures that the pattern is always advanced forwards by at least one symbol position. That it is possible to do this follows from the fact that in the event of a mismatch, the next pattern position to try may be such that *any* one of the text symbols currently aligned with the pattern is lined up with the rightmost occurrence in the pattern of that specific symbol (or the rightmost but one in the case of symbol x_m). This is illustrated in the following example, which shows two particular possible next trial positions for pattern ABCDE in which either the C's or the A's are brought into alignment.

```
pattern      A B C D E
text     . . . . . A C E . . . . .
```

Aligning the C's:

```
pattern        A B C D E
text     . . . . . A C E . . . . .
```

Aligning the A's:

```
pattern          A B C D E
text     . . . . . A C E . . . . .
```

The Boyer-Moore-Horspool algorithm is depicted in Figure 2.8. Again, the pattern position is given by the final value of i, with 0 indicating that no match was found. Its operation for the previously problematic example involving a negative shift for pattern ABCDE is illustrated below.

```
w         A B C D E F G H . . .
skip[w]   4 3 2 1 5 5 5 5 . . .
```

Mismatch occurs at $y_k = D$

```
pattern      A B C D E
text     . . . D C D E . . . . . . . .
             k       i
```

```
— initialise skip table
for w = 1 to |C|
    skip[w] = m
for j = 1 to m − 1
    skip[x_j] = m − j
— search
i = m
j = m
while (j > 0) and (i ⩽ n)
    k = i
    while (j > 0) and (y_k = x_j)
        k = k − 1
        j = j − 1
    if j > 0
        — a mismatch
        i = i + skip[y_i]
        j = m
    if j < 1
        i = k + 1
    else
        i = 0
```

Note that the **and** in the inner **while** loop is a 'conditional and.'

Figure 2.8: Boyer-Moore-Horspool string matching

Next comparison is between x_m and $y_{i+skip[y_i]}$, i.e. y_{i+5}

```
pattern            A B C D E
text       . . . D C D E . . . . . . . .
           i                 i+5
```

We can now return our attention to the value of $skip[x_m]$ for the case where symbol x_m occurs more than once in the pattern. As hinted at earlier, if y_i matches x_m but a mismatch occurs at y_k, then the next position to try should be that such as to align the second last occurrence within x of symbol x_m with y_i. If the said occurrence is x_{m-s}, then the required $skip$ value is equal to s. This situation is illustrated in the following example for pattern AECDE.

Pattern = AECDE

w A B C D E F G H . . .

$skip[w]$ 4 5 2 1 3 5 5 5 . . .

Mismatch occurs at $y_k = $ A

pattern   A E C D E

text   . . . . . A E . . . . .

              k i

Next comparison is between x_m and $y_{i+skip[E]}$, i.e. y_{i+3}

pattern   A E C D E

text   . . . . . A E . . . . .

            i $i+3$

Baeza-Yates (1989a) has shown that the expected number of symbol comparisons, A_n, performed by the Boyer-Moore-Horspool algorithm for random strings is bounded from below as follows:

$$A_n \geqslant \frac{1 - \frac{1}{|C|^m}}{(|C| - 1)\left[1 - \left(1 - \frac{1}{|C|}\right)^m\right]} (n - m + 1) \qquad (2.5)$$

For a pattern of length 10, the above relation gives lower bounds of 0.17, 0.11, and 0.10 times $(n - m + 1)$ for alphabet sizes of 10, 100, and 256 respectively. This shows that, for large alphabets, the lower bound is close to $(n - m + 1)/m$ in the average case, i.e. about n/m for $n \gg m$.

Later analysis, based on the use of a stationary, stochastic-process model, resulted in the following simpler asymptotic expression for the linearity constant, K, for A_n in the average case (Baeza-Yates and Régnier, 1992).

$$K \sim \frac{1}{|C|} + O(\frac{1}{|C|^2}) \qquad (2.6)$$

In natural language texts, dependencies between successive symbols can influence the performance of symbol comparison strategies. Recall that in the Boyer-Moore-Horspool algorithm, the pattern-symbol comparisons are performed strictly right to left. A pattern ending in a common suffix, such as -ion in English, will thus require, on average, a relatively disproportionate number of symbol comparisons to discount non-match positions following a successful match of the terminal pattern symbol. This observation led Raita (1992) to propose a variation of the Boyer-Moore-Horspool method in which the order of the comparisons is such as to try to minimise the effects of the dependencies from the symbols already tested. In the most effective approach found, the last pattern symbol is tested first of all, followed by the first, and then by the middle one. If all three match their corresponding text symbols, then the internal pattern symbols are tested next from right to left, as before. Using this strategy, a speed-up of about 25% was obtained for searches for randomly selected patterns from a sample English text.

2.2.5 Sunday — Quick Search, Maximal Shift, and Optimal Mismatch

Sunday (1990) observed that in the Boyer-Moore algorithm, for a mismatch occurring when x_m is aligned with text symbol y_i, say, then the *next* text symbol, y_{i+1}, could be used rather than y_i to address the occurrence-heuristic table. This is due to the fact that for the minimum pattern shift, i.e. one place to the right, y_{i+1} is part of the next text substring to be examined. Sunday states that in practice this should result in a shift greater than or equal to that of the Boyer-Moore *skip* value plus 1, on average. The speed advantage offered by this phenomenon, however, diminishes as the length of the pattern increases.

Smith (1991) has pointed out that there are circumstances under which the use of y_i rather than y_{i+1} is advantageous, as demonstrated in the example below for the pattern ABCDE. He therefore proposed using the maximum of the occurrence-heuristic values for text symbols y_i and y_{i+1}.

Boyer-Moore *skip* table for the pattern ABCDE

w	A B C D E F G H . . .
$skip[w]$	4 3 2 1 0 5 5 5 . . .

Mismatch occurs at $y_i = $ T

pattern   A B C D E
text   . . . P Q R S T D U V W X . . .
              i

Next pattern position based on $skip[y_i]$, i.e. $i + skip[\text{T}]$

pattern   A B C D E
text   . . . P Q R S T D U V W X . . .
                  $i + 5$

Next pattern position based on $skip[y_{i+1}]$, i.e. $i + skip[\text{D}] + 1$

pattern   A B C D E
text   . . . P Q R S T D U V W X . . .
             $i + 2$

```
— initialise skip table
for w = 1 to |C|
    skip[w] = m + 1
for j = 1 to m
    skip[xⱼ] = m + 1 - j
— search
i = 1
j = 1
while (j ≤ m) and (i ≤ n - m + 1)
    k = i
    while (j ≤ m) and (yₖ = xⱼ)
        k = k + 1
        j = j + 1
    if j ≤ m
        — a mismatch
        i = i + skip[yᵢ₊ₘ]
        j = 1
if j ≤ m
    i = 0
```

Note that the **and** in the inner **while** loop is a 'conditional and.'

Figure 2.9: Sunday Quick Search

Sunday also noted that the symbol comparisons between the pattern and the current text-substring may be performed in an arbitrary order, and used this fact in an effort to improve the overall matching efficiency. He proposed three different variations of the Boyer-Moore search, all of which use y_{i+1} in the occurrence heuristic, but differ in the way in which the order of the symbol comparisons is determined. Sunday has conjectured that the linear worst-case behaviour of the Boyer-Moore algorithm is preserved when the substring symbols are compared in an arbitrary order.

The simplest of the three variations is the Quick Search algorithm, in which the comparisons are performed strictly from left to right and only the occurrence heuristic is employed. Pseudocode for this method is given in Figure 2.9. Note that the *skip*-table values are initialised to be 1 greater than those of the Boyer-Moore table to take into account the extra place in the pattern shifts.

In the other two methods — the Maximal Shift and the Optimal Mismatch algorithms — an additional array is used to store the pattern indices in the order that the symbol comparisons are performed at each trial pattern position. During the search, this array is therefore accessed sequentially so as to provide the desired order of symbol positions within the pattern.

In the Maximal Shift algorithm, the comparison order is chosen such that the match-heuristic shift values are maximised. This is done by sorting the pattern symbols in descending order of their distance to their next leftward occurrence in the pattern, or, if there is none, to the start of the pattern. Thus, for a pattern containing no repeated symbols, the comparisons are performed in sequential order from right to left.

In the final algorithm, the Optimal Mismatch search, the probability of an early detection of a mismatch is maximised by comparing rarer symbols first. This requires the pattern symbols to be sorted in ascending order of their frequency of occurrence in the text to be searched, necessitating an a priori knowledge of its statistics. Full implementations of the Maximal Shift and Optimal Mismatch algorithms, coded in C, may be found in Sunday (1990).

Sunday found the Optimal Mismatch version to be the fastest of his methods, and reported all three to be superior in average-case performance to the Boyer-Moore algorithm — a speed advantage of 10-20% is reported for the Optimal Mismatch algorithm. The speed differentials, however, decreased with an increase in the pattern length, consistent with the behaviour obtained by using the text symbol following that causing a mismatch.

Sunday's algorithms have also been empirically compared with a simplified Boyer-Moore variant by Pirklbauer (1992). In this study, it was found that for long strings and for the case where preprocessing times were taken into account, the Maximal Shift and Optimal Mismatch procedures fared rather badly. Their preprocessing overheads were found to be significant, especially when searching for only the first occurrence of the pattern. The Quick Search algorithm was, however, recommended on the grounds of its performance, similar to that of the Boyer-Moore variant, and its ease of implementation.

The disadvantage of the Optimal Mismatch method, namely its requirement for foreknowledge of the input-text statistics, has been addressed by Smith (1991). His adaptive approach starts with an arbitrary symbol comparison order, which is modified as the search proceeds. The algorithm dispenses with the match heuristic and relies solely on the occurrence heuristic. This language-independent scheme was found to perform only slightly worse on average than the equivalent static, language-based search, i.e. a version of the Optimal Mismatch algorithm employing only the occurrence heuristic. The method used to adapt the ordering is to move the pattern symbol position that causes a mismatch either up one position or to the top of the ordering list, thereby giving it a higher precedence in future trials. As noted earlier, Smith's method also involves selecting the maximum of two occurrence-heuristic shift values — one for the text symbol aligned with the end of the pattern, and the other for the following text symbol.

2.2.6   Hume and Sunday — Tuned Boyer-Moore and Least Cost

Hume and Sunday (1991) have presented a taxonomy of various cognate algorithms based on the structure of the fast-loop form of the Boyer-Moore search method discussed earlier. Three distinct components of the procedure were considered, namely the fast skip loop, the slow matching loop, and the calculation of the pattern shift to the next trial position in the event of a mismatch whilst in the slow loop.

For each of these three components, various different techniques were considered. For example, initially testing for x_1, x_m, or the least frequent (in terms of the text-symbol statistics) pattern symbol were examined for the skip loop. Various comparison orders were investigated for the matching loop — e.g. left to right, right to left, and Sunday's Maximal Shift and Optimal Mismatch orderings. With the exception of the Optimal Mismatch, these were optionally *guarded* by preceding the full match attempt with a single comparison involving a low-frequency pattern symbol. The tests in the shift-calculation stage involved the use of the Knuth-Morris-Pratt table, the Boyer-Moore heuristics, Sunday's shift tables, and combinations thereof. It was found, however, that the advantages of combining more than one heuristic were outweighed by the overhead incurred by computing the maximum of the different values.

From empirical tests, based on searches of a bible text, the most effective methods for each of the three stages were identified, and two new procedures were proposed, namely the Tuned Boyer-Moore and the Least Cost algorithms. These both use a guarded, left-to-right comparison for the match loop and Sunday's version of the match heuristic for the shift calculation for a mismatch in the match loop. However, they differ in the methods used in the skip loop — the Tuned Boyer-Moore algorithm uses an optimised version of Boyer and Moore's original 'fast' loop, whereas the Least Cost algorithm initially seeks the pattern symbol incurring the lowest search cost. This cost is based on both the text-symbol frequency-distribution and the position of the symbol in the pattern, which influences the size of the pattern shift possible.

Implementations of the two algorithms in C are presented in Hume and Sunday (1991), where details of how full copies of the programs and the data-sets employed may be obtained via internet ftp (by logging in as netlib at research.att.com) or email are also given.

A speed improvement by a factor of 4.5 over the original Boyer-Moore algorithm (not in its 'fast-loop' implementation) has been reported for the Tuned Boyer-Moore and Least Cost search procedures. Note that the latter method relies on a priori information of the text-symbol statistics. Furthermore, it should be pointed out

that, in common with Sunday (1990), the algorithms were compared for the case of
searching for all occurrences of the pattern in the text, the preprocessing costs were
not included in the measurements, and the tests were conducted using relatively
small patterns ($m \leqslant 16$).

2.2.7 Harrison

Although not strictly solving the string-matching problem as defined earlier, Harrison's approach is included here since it can provide an efficient method of eliminat-
ing text strings, with low probabilities of containing a given pattern, when there is
no actual match. Also, note that this technique requires the text to be preprocessed.

The basic idea of this substring decision-procedure involves representing strings
with simpler data objects, which preserve some of their inherent properties. In this
method, a string is represented by the set of its substrings of a fixed length q, say
(its q-grams). A suitable hashing-function is employed that maps the $|C|^q$ possible
distinct q-grams (where C is the alphabet) to integers in the interval $[1, p]$. A binary
string of length p, known as a *hashed q-signature*, may then be used to represent this
set of substrings: the ith bit of the signature is set to 1 only if i is the hashed value
of some member of the set of substrings.

A necessary, but not sufficient, condition for a pattern to occur as a substring
of a text is that the pattern's signature, x_{sig}, is a subset of that of the text, y_{sig}. If
a pattern substring appears nowhere in the text, then the pattern itself cannot be
a substring of the text. This means that if x_{sig} has a 1 in a position where y_{sig}
does not, then it can be concluded that x is not a substring of y. This test may be
performed efficiently using logical operators on the two signatures as follows. A
non-zero result from the bitwise AND of x_{sig} and NOT y_{sig} indicates that there can
be no possible match. On the other hand, however, in the event of a zero result, a
rigorous search is still required to establish whether or not x is present in the text.

The method may therefore be used to rapidly discount text strings where there
can be no match with the pattern. Each line of a large text file could, for example,
be stored together with a hashed k-signature to facilitate later pattern searches.

2.2.8 Karp-Rabin

In the Karp-Rabin algorithm, comparison of m-symbol text-substrings, $y(i, i + m -
1)$, at successive positions, $1 \leqslant i \leqslant n - m + 1$, with the pattern x, proceeds in a
manner similar to that of the Brute Force approach. The difference is that rather than
a direct comparison of $x(1, m)$ with $y(i, i + m - 1)$, it is a single integer-comparison
that is performed. The integers involved are the hash values for the corresponding
m-symbol strings.

The hash values, or signatures, for $x(1, m)$ and $y(1, m)$ are precomputed, and
the use of a carefully selected hash-function permits the signature for $y(i, i + m - 1)$

to be derived easily from that for $y(i-1, i+m-2)$ as the scan of the text proceeds. The actual hash-function used is:

$$h(k) = k \bmod q \qquad (2.7)$$

where q is a large prime. For the calculation, the m-symbol strings are treated as m-digit integers in base c, where $c = |C|$ for alphabet C. The component symbols are therefore the (base c) digits of the integer. Adopting a big-endian convention, the most significant digit comes first. Thus, the number, k_i, corresponding to the text substring at position i is given by:

$$k_i = y_i c^{m-1} + y_{i+1} c^{m-2} + \ldots + y_{i+m-1} \qquad (2.8)$$

The number, k_{i+1}, for the next text-substring, $y(i+1, i+m)$, is derived from k_i as follows:

$$k_{i+1} = (k_i - y_i c^{m-1})c + y_{i+m} \qquad (2.9)$$

The associative property of the mod function, i.e. $(a+b) \bmod c = (a \bmod c + b \bmod c) \bmod c$, allows the remainders to be taken after each stage of the calculation. This keeps the partial results small, and yields the same result as that that would be obtained by performing the mod operation only at the final stage of the calculation.

As the hash-function values are not unique, the equality of two signatures is a necessary, but not sufficient, condition for the equality of their corresponding strings. Therefore, when a potential match is detected, the two strings must then be compared directly, to check for a signature *collision*. For a large hash-table, i.e. a large value of q, the chances of such collisions are slight. One of the algorithms presented by Karp and Rabin (1987) further reduces the probability of a large number of collisions by randomly reselecting the prime q should a collision occur, reinitialising, and then continuing with the search. The theoretical worst case involves m symbol comparisons being forced at each stage, giving an overall execution time of $O(mn)$. In practice, however, the signatures at each stage would be expected, on the whole, to be unequal. In these circumstances, each text position is processed in constant time, giving an $O(m+n)$ expected performance.

The algorithm is given in Figure 2.10. Note that the initial calculation of h_x and h_y may be performed in the following manner.

$$h_x = 0$$
$$\textbf{for } j = 1 \textbf{ to } m$$
$$h_x = (h_x * c + x_j) \bmod q$$

The value of d, used in the incremental signature calculation, may also initially be computed iteratively, again exploiting the associativity of mod. In the calculation of the next signature value, $c * q$ is added to ensure that the partial result

---

— initialisation
$i = 1$
$found = $ **false**
$d = c^{m-1} \bmod q$
$h_x = (x_1 * c^{m-1} + x_2 * c^{m-2} + \ldots + x_m) \bmod q$
$h_y = (y_1 * c^{m-1} + y_2 * c^{m-2} + \ldots + y_m) \bmod q$
— search
while $(i \leqslant n - m + 1)$ **and** (**not** $found$)
  if $(h_x = h_y)$ **and** $(x(1, m) = y(i, i + m - 1))$
    — a successful match
    $found = $ **true**
  else
    — calculate next signature value
    $h_y = (h_y + c * q - y_i * d) \bmod q$
    $h_y = (h_y * c + y_{i+m}) \bmod q$
    $i = i + 1$
if $(i > n - m + 1)$
  $i = 0$

Note that the **and** in the **if** statement is a 'conditional and.'

Figure 2.10: Karp-Rabin string matching

---

remains positive. On completion of the search procedure, i gives the position of the pattern in the text, or is equal to 0 when no match has been found.

The prime number q should be as large as possible, consistent with $(c + 1)q$ not causing arithmetic overflow (this is the maximum partial result in the next-signature computation). Sedgewick (1983) uses a value of 33554393 (for $c = 32$), and Pirklbauer (1992) suggests 8355967 (for $c = 256$).

Gonnet and Baeza-Yates (1991) present an implementation of the algorithm that does away with the mod operations by virtue of the implicit modular arithmetic of the target hardware.

2.3 Further Reading

A recent survey and comparison of string-matching algorithms, including the fairly recent contributions by Sunday (1990), has been conducted by Pirklbauer (1992). A comprehensive comparison of the time and space complexities of various algorithms is also provided by Gonnet and Baeza-Yates (1991). Not to be neglected are the reviews by Aho (1990, 1980), Baeza-Yates (1989c), and Sedgewick (1983).

3

String Distance and Common Sequences

La distance n'y fait rien; il n'y a que le premier pas qui coûte.
(The distance is nothing; it is only the first step that is difficult.)
— Madame du Deffand (1697–1780), *Letter to d'Alembert*, 7 July 1763.

3.1 Overview

In many string-processing applications there is a need to measure the degree of similarity between two strings. This type of requirement arises in a variety of tasks, ranging from the comparison of two text files to the quantification of degrees of homology in genetic sequences. The concept of string distance functions, providing such a measure, shall shortly be discussed. As we shall later see, the use of string distance functions also figures prominently in the area of approximate string matching — the subject of Chapter 5.

Closely related to the problem of evaluating the distance between a pair of strings is that of finding a subsequence of maximal length common to the pair. Methods of solving both of these problems are examined in this chapter — briefly at first and later in greater detail. Also discussed here are other related problems, such as the shortest common supersequence and the heaviest common subsequence problems.

3.1.1   String Distance Measures

The notion of a distance function, or metric, crops up in many diverse fields, and is often employed as a measure of the similarity between two vectors, or n-tuples. This allows the degree of correlation between two entities to be assessed, and, for example, has uses in pattern-recognition applications such as template matching. Formally, a distance metric, d, is a function satisfying the following axioms.

$$
\begin{array}{lll}
\text{Non-negative Property} & d(x,y) \geqslant 0 \ \forall x,y & (3.1) \\
\text{Zero Property} & d(x,y) = 0 \Leftrightarrow x = y & (3.2) \\
\text{Symmetry} & d(x,y) = d(y,x) \ \forall x,y & (3.3) \\
\text{Triangle Inequality} & d(x,z) \leqslant d(x,y) + d(y,z) \ \forall x,y,z & (3.4)
\end{array}
$$

In order to evaluate the distances between sequences, a sequence of length n may be regarded as a vector in $\mathbb{R}^n$. For two vectors of the same dimensionality (i.e. two sequences of the same length), with components of either discrete or continuous numerical values, common metrics are: the chessboard distance ($\max_i |x_i - y_i|$); the city-block distance ($\sum_i |x_i - y_i|$); and the familiar Euclidean distance ($[\sum_i (x_i - y_i)^2]^{1/2}$).

In string-processing applications, however, it is often not appropriate to interpret the component symbols as numerical values, although they are normally assigned such for the convenience of coding; and strings to be compared are often of disparate lengths. The distance metrics employed in this area therefore tend to quantify the minimum cost of transforming one string into the other. In general, cost weights may be assigned to the individual editing operations involved in such a transformation — namely symbol substitution, insertion, and deletion. Note that the latter two operations are sometimes referred to collectively as *indels*.

It is worth noting that not all string distance functions are necessarily metrics. For example, when the cost of the editing operations is a function of the particular symbols involved, the triangle inequality may not necessarily be satisfied.

Hamming, Levenshtein, and Edit Distances

For two strings of equal length, the *Hamming distance* (Hamming, 1982) between them is defined as the number of symbol positions at which they differ. This is equivalent to the minimum cost of transforming the first string into the second, when only substitutions are permitted and are given a unity weighting. When not restricted to comparing equal-length strings, insertions and deletions will also generally be required. When these are given the same weight as a substitution, the minimum total transformation cost is equal to one of the two metrics proposed by Levenshtein (1965). His second metric is equal to the minimum transformation cost when only indels are permitted. This is equivalent to assigning a cost of 1 to an indel and 2 to a substitution, as the latter may be implemented by an insertion-deletion pair. The first metric, involving equal, unit costs, shall henceforth be referred to as the *Levenshtein distance*, and the second as the *edit distance*.

Longest Matches and q-grams[1]

Measures of the similarity between strings may also be based on various other notions. One such idea involves the substrings common to the pair of strings being compared. For example, Baskin and Selfridge (Alberga, 1967) proposed a measure based on the proportion of the larger string matched in a process involving the successive removal of the longest common substring from the pair of strings. Also, Ehrenfeucht and Haussler (1988) put forward a distance function equal to the minimum number of symbols that must be removed from the first string such that intervening portions between these deletions are substrings of the second. A value of 0 for this measure indicates that the first string is a substring of the second.

Another approach involves the use of q-grams. A q-gram is simply a substring of length q. A string x, of length m, thus has, at most, $m - q + 1$ distinct q-grams. The degree of similarity between two strings may be assessed, then, by comparing their respective q-grams — the greater the number they have in common, the greater is their similarity. A decrease in the precision of the comparison for smaller values of q must be balanced against prohibitively large numbers of possible distinct q-grams for higher values (for alphabet C, there are $|C|^q$ possible distinct q-grams). In practice, values for q of 2 or 3 — giving *digrams* and *trigrams*, respectively — are normally employed.

One similarity measure based on q-grams is given by the ratio of the number of q-grams common to a pair of strings to the total number in the strings (Angell, Freund and Willett, 1983; Owolabi and McGregor, 1988). Another is a distance function equal to the sum of the absolute differences between corresponding numbers of occurrences of the q-grams in each string (Ukkonen, 1992a). This may thus be considered to be the city-block distance between vectors associated with the strings; the components of each vector giving the numbers of occurrences in the related string of all $|C|^q$ possible q-grams. Note that for this distance function, a zero value is not a guarantee of string identity: e.g. strings ada and dad are distinct, but nevertheless have digrams identical in number and value, and are consequently separated by a digram distance of 0.

Last to be considered here are measures based on the symbols common to the strings, irrespective of their order or position of occurrence. One early such function was proposed by Faulk (1964) as a measure of 'material similarity' (he also suggested two other measures which did take into account the order and

---

[1] Also known as n-grams.

position of the common symbols). More recently, Bickel (1987) has employed a similarity measure based on common symbols in which more significance is given to statistically rarer symbols: weights are assigned to the symbols in the alphabet according to their relative frequency of occurrence, and the similarity value is calculated by summing the weights associated with the distinct symbols shared by the two strings. The measure was proposed primarily for use in a system that compares an input pattern with a small subset of personal names in a database. Note that in general applications, a maximum value for this measure would be obtained were a pattern to be compared with any of its anagrams or with any string containing all of the symbols in the alphabet.

3.1.2   String Distance and Longest Common Subsequence

The major algorithms developed to solve both the string distance problem — sometimes given under the guise of the file difference problem or the string-to-string correction problem — and the related longest common subsequence problem shall now be considered. A more detailed examination of selected algorithms is presented later on. But before going any further, definitions of these two problems shall first of all be given.

String Distance Problem

Given strings x and y, with $|x| = m$, $|y| = n$, where $m, n > 0$ and $m \leqslant n$, and a generalised Levenshtein string-distance measure, d, find $d(x, y)$. When given as the file difference problem, x and y represent two files, where x_i is the ith line of x and y_j is the jth line of y. The requirement is then to determine a minimal sequence of editing operations necessary to transform x into y.

Longest Common Subsequence Problem

A longest common subsequence of two strings is a subsequence common to both having maximal length, i.e. it is at least as long as any other common subsequence of the strings. Given two strings x and y, with $|x| = m$, $|y| = n$, where $m, n > 0$ and $m \leqslant n$, find $|lcs(x, y)|$, where $lcs(x, y)$ is a longest common subsequence of x and y. It is normally also required to determine an actual $lcs(x, y)$ in addition to its length.

One method of evaluating the distance between two strings, based on a dynamic-programming (Bellman and Dreyfus, 1962) technique, has been discovered independently by many different investigators. Sankoff and Kruskall (1983) credit the following authors with procedures all based on the same underlying principle: Vintsyuk (1968); Needleman and Wunsch (1970); Velichko and Zagoruyko (1970);

Sakoe and Chiba (1970, 1971); Sankoff (1972); Reichert, Cohen and Wong (1973); Haton (1973); Wagner and Fischer (1974); and Hirschberg (1975).

The basic idea of the dynamic-programming method is to evaluate successively the distance between longer and longer prefixes of the two strings until the final result is obtained. These partial results are computed iteratively and are entered into an $(m + 1) \times (n + 1)$ array, leading to $O(mn)$ time and space complexities. In Wagner and Fischer's (1974) method, an lcs may then be derived in a straightforward manner from the completed distance array via a structure known as a *trace*. This may be obtained in $O(m + n)$ time by tracing a path back from position (m, n) in the array.

Hirschberg (1975) modified Wagner and Fischer's technique, preserving the $O(mn)$ time complexity, but reducing the space requirement from a quadratic to a linear characteristic. In this method, it is the length of the lcs of progressively longer string prefixes, rather than the distance between them, that is computed iteratively. Space is saved by holding only two rows of the dynamic-programming array in memory at any given time. However, the loss of the full array leads to a more complicated method of extracting an lcs of the two strings. The 'divide-and-conquer' technique employed is to bisect recursively the first string and obtain an lcs between each half and an appropriate substring of the second string. The recursion is performed until this lcs extraction becomes trivial. The final lcs of the complete strings is then obtained by concatenating those obtained for the recursively sliced string sections.

Hunt and McIlroy (1976) implemented Hirschberg's lcs algorithm for the Unix diff command. This was found to work well for short inputs, but its quadratic running time resulted in a significant deterioration in performance as the lengths of the input files were increased. However, McIlroy later obtained a dramatic improvement by employing the lcs algorithm developed by Hunt and Szymanski (1977).

Hunt and Szymanski's approach to extracting an lcs is equivalent to determining the longest strictly increasing path in the graph composed of vertices (i, j) such that $x_i = y_j$. Whereas previous methods required quadratic time in all cases, their algorithm requires $O((r + n) \log n)$ time for equal-length strings, where r is the total number of ordered pairs of positions at which the two strings match. In the worst case, every element of x can match every symbol in y, resulting in n^2 such ordered pairs and a complexity of $O(n^2 \log n)$. For many applications, however, such as the file difference problem where each line of a file is taken as an atomic symbol, r can be expected to be close to n, giving a performance of $O(n \log n)$ — a significant improvement over the quadratic-time procedures. The space required by the algorithm is $O(r + n)$.

Two important properties of the dynamic-programming, lcs-length matrix are that its entries increase monotonically in i and j, and that adjacent entries differ by at most 1. The table may therefore be contoured into disjoint regions: one for each value, k, say, from 0 up to l, where $l = |\operatorname{lcs}(x, y)|$. Hirschberg (1977) developed an algorithm to find an lcs in $O(ln)$ time by successively producing the k-contours of the table. The algorithm additionally requires $O(n \log n)$ time to preprocess the input strings, and consumes $O(t + n)$ space, where $t \leqslant r$ is the number of *dominant matches* between the two strings. (A k-dominant match is a corner point of the contour of values equal to k in the lcs-length table. Note that finding all the dominant matches is sufficient for the solution of the lcs problem.)

Masek and Paterson (1980, 1983) developed a string-distance algorithm, based on Wagner and Fischer's dynamic-programming approach, which has a subquadratic running time, even in the worst case. The method does, however, require the alphabet to be finite and the cost weights to be integral multiples of a fixed real number. Their algorithm uses the 'Four Russians' technique (Arlazarov, Dinic, Kronod and Faradzev, 1970), and has a worst-case execution time of $O(n^2/\log n)$ for equal-length input strings. The basic idea of this method is to partition the distance matrix into a number of smaller submatrices. The lower and rightmost edges of each submatrix may then be calculated from those of adjacent submatrices, above and to the left of the current one, and from the appropriate substrings of x and y, using a precomputed lookup-table. Although asymptotically faster than the straightforward, dynamic-programming method, Masek and Paterson (1983) point out that their algorithm should only be used for very long strings — for example, it actually computes the distance between two binary strings more quickly only once the string lengths exceed 262418.

Szymanski has shown that alphabets of unrestricted size may be accommodated by a modified version of Masek and Paterson's algorithm, taking time $O(n^2 (\log \log n)^2/\log n)$ (Hirschberg, 1983) — a behaviour still asymptotically better than quadratic.

An alternative lcs algorithm, having a favourable performance for the case of similar strings, has been proposed independently by Ukkonen (1983, 1985a) and Myers (1986a). The underlying principle of their methods is to search for a minimum-cost path in an *edit graph*. This is a graph composed of the vertices of the distance matrix together with horizontal, vertical, and diagonal edges, corresponding to the dependencies between adjacent nodes. The required path in the graph starts at $(0, 0)$ and ends on (m, n).

In Ukkonen's method, unnecessary calculations in the distance matrix are avoided in a threshold test of the distance between the two strings. This process is repeated with successively larger threshold values until the test is successful, yielding the required string distance in $O(md)$ time, where d is the distance between x and y. An actual editing sequence may then be recovered from the computed distance-matrix values as in the Wagner-Fischer algorithm. For the particular case of the Levenshtein distance, Ukkonen developed a more efficient, $O(md)$-time, direct method of computing $d(x, y)$.

Myers' approach is to find the end points of successively longer furthest-reaching paths in the graphs until point (m, n) is reached. In the worst case, this takes $O((m+n)d_e)$ time, but Myers has shown that the expected-case temporal complexity is $O(m + n + d_e^2)$. (Here, d_e is the edit distance between x and y, and is equal to $m + n - 2l$.) This algorithm has also been used in an implementation of the Unix diff program (Miller and Myers, 1985). A linear-space version of the algorithm and a variation with a worst-case time of $O((m+n)\log(m+n) + d_e^2)$ were also developed. The latter is based on *suffix-tree* techniques (McCreight, 1976) and its improved asymptotic behaviour is of theoretical interest. It is not, however, a practicable technique owing to the complex methods involved in its implementation.

A binary representation of the lcs-length table has been proposed by Allison and Dix (1986), in which the positions of the 1s mark out the contours. Their associated algorithm computes the table column by column, using arithmetic/logical operations on the binary strings representing the columns. The lcs length is computed in this way using $O(\lceil \frac{m}{w} \rceil n)$ operations, for a computer wordsize of w and a fixed, finite alphabet, C. Preprocessing of string x is also required, taking $O(\lceil \frac{m}{w} \rceil |C| + m)$ time. If the completed table is stored (using $O(\lceil \frac{m}{w} \rceil n)$ computer words), an actual lcs may then be recovered as in the simple dynamic-programming method in $O(m + n)$ time.

Apostolico and Guerra (1987) have analysed both the Hirschberg (1977) and the Hunt-Szymanski methods of finding a longest common subsequence, and have devised corresponding cognate algorithms with certain improvements. Both of these require $O(n \log |C|)$-time preprocessing. Their version of Hirschberg's algorithm runs in $O(lm \log(\min\{|C|, m, 2n/m\}))$ time. As noted above, the running time of Hunt and Szymanski's algorithm becomes superquadratic in the worst case. The time complexity of Apostolico and Guerra's adaptation, however, is never worse than quadratic. The actual time bound of their revised version of the algorithm is $O(m \log n + t \log(2mn/t))$. The algorithm involves the use of a data structure known as a *characteristic tree*. (The more complicated *finger tree* (Brown and Tarjan, 1978, 1979; Mehlhorn, 1984) was used instead of this in an earlier implementation (Apostolico, 1986).)

Kumar and Rangan (1987) have developed a linear-space lcs algorithm running in $O(n(m - l))$ time. The lcs length is computed first of all; an actual lcs is then obtained using a divide-and-conquer technique, in which the problem is decomposed by recursively cutting each of the two strings into two in an optimal manner. The algorithm improves upon an earlier $O(n(m - l))$-time procedure, due to Nakatsu, Kambayashi and Yajima (1982), which required $O(mn)$ working space.

Another $O(n(m - l))$-time algorithm, this time one to compute edit distances, has been proposed by Wu et al. (1990). This is based on Myers' (1986a) method, but examines fewer vertices in the edit graph by using a path-compression technique developed by Sedgewick and Vitter (1986). The algorithm's expected-case running time is $O(n + d_e(m - l))$, where, once more, d_e is the edit distance between x and y.

Finally, Apostolico, Browne and Guerra (1992) have improved the space requirements for two previous lcs approaches. First, they have developed a linear-space,
$O(n(m - l))$-time algorithm, based on the Hunt-Szymanski method and using a
divide-and-conquer technique similar to that of Kumar and Rangan. Again, the
value of l is determined first of all and an lcs is then found by recursive subdi-
vision of the problem. Second, they have adapted an Apostolico-Guerra (1985)
version of Hirschberg's (1977) algorithm so as to require only linear space, and
to run in $O(lm \log(\min\{|C|, m, 2n/l\}))$ time. This bound is the same as that for
Apostolico and Guerra's (1985, 1987) algorithms based on Hirschberg's method
when $l = \Theta(m)$. The new variant uses finger trees, and again employs the divide-
and-conquer paradigm.

Lower bounds for the time complexity of the lcs problem, for particular computational models, have been the subject of some investigation. Wong and Chandra
(1976) have derived bounds for the calculation of string distance in terms of the
editing cost-function when the symbol comparisons are restricted to only tests of
equality. They have also shown that $\Omega(mn)$ symbol comparisons are required to
find an lcs under this restriction.

Using a similar 'equal/unequal' decision-tree model of computation, Aho,
Hirschberg and Ullman (1976) derived bounds for the lcs problem in terms of
the size of the symbol alphabet. They found that, in general, the worst-case minimum number of comparisons required is $\Theta(n^2)$ for equal-length strings, and is
$\Omega(|C| n)$ for $n \geqslant |C|$, when the alphabet, C, is fixed.

When a lexicographic symbol ordering is employed, allowing 'less-than/equal-
to/greater-than' symbol comparisons to be performed, Hirschberg (1978) has
shown that the minimum number of such comparisons required is $\Omega(n \log n)$ in
the worst case.

3.1.3 Comparative Performance

To sum up, the salient points concerning the performance of the various approaches
to the related string-distance and lcs problems are as follows. The dynamic-
programming method of Wagner and Fischer is very simple to implement, but
is quadratic in both time and space. Although sharing the same asymptotic characteristic, the Allison-Dix approach can provide a useful speed-up for long strings
and small alphabets.

For large applications, though, linear-space techniques are preferable. This
requirement is fulfilled by Hirschberg's early algorithm, but this still has a quadratic
running time. As far as time is concerned, the only known algorithm having a
complexity better than quadratic in the worst case is that of Masek and Paterson.
(Bear in mind that the computational overheads of this method render it more

efficient than the straightforward, dynamic-programming technique only for very long strings.) A range of differing conditions, dependent upon output parameters such as d and l, are, however, better served by various other separate approaches.

When the number of matches, r, is small, for example, the Hunt-Szymanski approach works well. The greater-than-quadratic worst-case running time of the original is overcome in the Apostolico-Guerra (1987) upgrade. Also, the execution time of the latter is dependent upon the number of dominant matches, t, which can be much less than r.

For the case where the two strings are similar, i.e. when d is small, the methods of Ukkonen or Myers become attractive.

When the longest subsequence common to both strings is short, i.e. when l is small, the time complexity of Hirschberg's (1977) algorithm is favourable. And when the two strings differ greatly in length, i.e. when $m \ll n$, faster operation can be obtained from Apostolico and Guerra's (1987) variant of this. For cases where $l = \Theta(m)$, similar performance is delivered by Apostolico, Browne and Guerra's later version — an algorithm having the added attraction of requiring only linear space.

Finally, the $O(n(m - l))$-time algorithms (Nakatsu, Kambayashi and Yajima, 1982; Kumar and Rangan, 1987; Wu et al., 1990; Apostolico, Browne and Guerra, 1992) also perform well when the lcs length is close to m, which is the case when y contains a subsequence similar to x. It is worth remarking that of these methods, those of Kumar and Rangan and of Apostolico, Browne and Guerra are linear-space techniques.

3.1.4   Related Problems

Local Alignments

A related problem, often arising in molecular biology, is that of determining which portions of two sequences are similar, or homologous. This problem is discussed by Sankoff and Kruskall (1983), who expand upon Smith and Waterman's (1981) method of finding such *local alignments*. In addition to trying to minimise the distance between sections of the sequences, some means of maximising the portion length is also required, since a minimum distance of zero will always be possible for trivial substrings. A variation of the dynamic-programming method is therefore used in which matches are rewarded, and substitutions and indels penalised. This is achieved by assigning a positive cost to the former and negative ones to the latter operations. Waterman and Eggert (1987) have also extended this method to find the k best, non-intersecting, local alignments.

The quadratic nature of the simple dynamic-programming method makes it impractical for use with very large sequence databases, though. Certain efforts have consequently been directed at reducing the time and space required to solve the problem.

For example, various fast, heuristic methods have been developed, such as those of Lipman and Pearson (1985); Pearson and Lipman (1988); Karlin et al. (1988); Pearson (1990); and Altschul et al. (1990).

Also, Hirschberg's (1975) divide-and-conquer technique has been applied to finding *global* alignments using only linear space (Myers and Miller, 1988). This method has been taken up, and combined with the Waterman-Eggert approach by Huang, Hardison and Miller (1990) to find the k best, disjoint, local alignments in linear space. But the running time of their algorithm is $O(kmn)$, as a quadratic-time pass of the entire dynamic-programming matrix is made for each of the k alignments. However, Huang and Miller (1991) later improved upon this performance by computing the entire table once and then recomputing only selected submatrices. Although still requiring $O(kmn)$ time in the worst case, their algorithm[2] has an expected-case running time of $O(mn + \sum_{i=1}^{k} l_i^2)$, where l_i is the length of the ith computed alignment. This offers a significant saving, then, when searching for a large number of mostly short local alignments.

Symbol Transpositions

The problem of determining the distance between two strings when transpositions, or swaps, of adjacent symbols are permitted as editing operations in addition to indels and substitutions has also been studied. This case, for example, allows transposition errors occurring during manual keyboard operation to be taken into account when calculating string distances. Despite the significant increase in the difficulty of analysing this situation, the problem is still soluble in quadratic time using an extension of the dynamic-programming method (Lowrance and Wagner, 1975; Wagner, 1975, 1983).

Longest Common Subsequence of N Strings

A generalisation of the lcs problem is the N-lcs problem, where it is required to determine a longest subsequence common to a set of N strings. Denoting the fact that x is a subsequence of y by $x \lhd y$, we may formally state the problem as follows. Given a set of N strings over alphabet C, $X = \{x_1, x_2, \ldots, x_N\}$, find N-lcs(X), where N-lcs(X) is a maximal-length sequence such that $\forall x \in X$ N-lcs$(X) \lhd x$. Under this convention, the lcs problem discussed previously is known as the 2-lcs problem.

For arbitrary N, Maier (1978) has shown that the problem of determining $|N$-lcs$|$ is NP-complete (Karp, 1972) for alphabets of size two and above. In general, the

---

[2]An implementation of the algorithm in C is available via electronic mail from either huang@cs.mtu.edu or webb@cs.psu.edu.

extraction of N-lcs's from sets of strings is therefore not viable for increasing N. For example, Itoga (1981) extended the dynamic-programming approach to the N-lcs problem, computing an N-dimensional table in $O(Nn^N)$ time and space, for strings each of length n.

Although still exponential in the worst case, several algorithms that perform more favourably in the average case have since been developed. For instance, a method due to Hsu and Du (1984), in which all of the common subsequences of the set of strings are represented explicitly in a 'CS-tree,' takes $O(N |C| (n + r))$ time and $O(N |C| n + r)$ space. It is assumed here that each string is of length n; and r denotes the number of matched points between the N strings. The value of r is at worst equal to, but often much less than, n^N.

Improvements in the time and space requirements to $O(N |C| n \log n + r)$ and $O((N + |C|)n + r)$, respectively, were obtained by Baeza-Yates (1991) for an automaton-based method. A partial deterministic, finite-state automaton, known as a Directed Acyclic Subsequence Graph (DASG), which can recognise all the subsequences of the strings in X, is built. During its construction, each of its edges is labelled with the number of strings sharing the corresponding transition. The lcs's of X may then be recovered by searching the graph for maximal sequences of edges labelled with N. The DASG can be built in $O(N |C| n \log n)$ time and $O((N + |C|)n)$ space. The graph may be traversed in $O(r)$ time, and at most $O(r)$ extra space is required to obtain the set of lcs's of the strings.

Hakata and Imai (1992) have developed an algorithm for use when $N \geqslant 3$ and the alphabet is small. Their approach is based on an lcs algorithm due to Chin and Poon (1990), in which the k-dominant matches are computed from the $(k - 1)$-dominant ones, for k up to the length, l, of the lcs. In Hakata and Imai's algorithm, a set of candidates for the dominant matches at each stage is generated, from which redundant matches are then removed. The running time is $O(N |C| (n + t(\log^{N-3} n + \log^{N-2} |C|)))$, where $t \leqslant r$ is the number of dominant matches.

Dominant matches are also found iteratively in a generalisation of the Hunt-Szymanski lcs algorithm developed by Irving and Fraser (1992). The temporal and spatial complexities for this are both $O(N(|C| n + l(n - l)^{N-1}))$. Irving and Fraser also proposed another algorithm, based on straightforward dynamic-programming, in which unnecessary calculations are avoided in a manner reminiscent of Ukkonen's and Myers' lcs algorithms. In practice, though, this was found to improve upon simple dynamic-programming only when l is close to n. Its time and space requirements are $O(Nn(n - l)^{N-1})$.

Shortest Common Supersequences and Superstrings

Maier (1978) has also addressed the N-scs problem. This is the problem of finding the shortest common supersequence of a set of N strings. If $x \lhd y$, then y is said to be a supersequence of x, equivalently denoted by $y \triangleright x$. The N-scs problem may thus be stated as follows. Given a set of N strings over alphabet C, $X = \{x_1, x_2, \ldots, x_N\}$, find N-scs(X), where N-scs(X) is a minimal-length sequence such that $\forall x \in X$ N-scs$(X) \triangleright x$. Maier found that, for alphabet sizes $\geqslant 5$, the problem of finding $|N$-scs$|$ is NP-complete, and conjectured that this might also be the case for alphabet sizes $\geqslant 3$. The result has, in fact, been extended to strings over alphabets of size $\geqslant 2$ by Räihä and Ukkonen (1981).

Timkovskii (1989) suggested solving the N-scs problem by adopting a *tournament* approach. This involves repeatedly solving the 2-scs problem (which may be done via an lcs). Shortest common supersequences are first of all found for pairs of strings from X; scs's are then found for pairs of these supersequences; and so on, until an scs for the entire set X is obtained. However, Bradford and Jenkyns (1991) have shown that, in general, this method is not sufficient, for there exist instances of the problem where no ordering of tournament operations can render a correct scs.

Similar to the N-scs problem is the shortest common superstring problem. This involves finding a minimal-length string, y, say, such that each member of X is a substring, rather than a subsequence, of y, i.e. $\forall x \in X$ $y = u_x x v_x$ for some strings u_x and v_x. Again, this problem has been found to be NP-complete (Maier and Storer, 1977; Gallant, Maier and Storer, 1980; Gallant 1982).

The problem is, however, of great practical significance in, for example, molecular biology. There, owing to limitations on the size of molecules that can be sequenced, long molecules must first be cut into very much shorter segments. (Whereas the human genome comprises 3×10^9 base pairs, current techniques allow segments of only up to about 500 pairs to be sequenced.) Once many random, sample segments have been sequenced, the problem then remains of reassembling their representative strings into a superstring corresponding to the whole molecule. It is often the shortest common superstring of the segment strings that is sought in this respect. The determination of good approximate solutions to the problem in polynomial time has thus become the focus of some attention. Besides the complexity of the computation, another important measure of the performance of such methods is the actual length of the superstring obtained with reference to the minimum value possible.

One approach, put forward independently by Tarhio and Ukkonen (1986; 1988) and Turner (1986; 1989), uses a *greedy* approximation algorithm (Gallant, 1982). In this method, the pair of strings in X having the greatest overlap (i.e. the longest common substring occurring as a prefix of one string and a suffix of the other) is successively replaced in the set by the string formed by merging the pair, until only one string remains — a superstring of the original elements of X.

In Tarhio and Ukkonen's implementation, the Knuth-Morris-Pratt string matching approach is employed to find the lengths of the maximal overlaps for all possible pairs of strings from X. A common superstring is then found by applying greedy heuristics to the search for a longest Hamiltonian path in the weighted, directed graph representing the pairwise string-overlaps. The overall procedure is accomplished in $O(Nm)$ time, where m is the sum of the lengths of the strings in X, i.e. $m = \sum_{x \in X} |x|$.

Turner's approach involves the use of suffix trees and, when dealing with large alphabets, *lexicographic splay trees* (Sleator and Tarjan, 1985). It runs in the asymptotically more favourable $O(m \log N)$ time for alphabets sufficiently small to permit indexing over their symbols to be implemented directly (and in $O(m \log m)$ time otherwise). However, Ukkonen (1990) further improves on this, achieving time linear in m for small alphabets and $O(m \cdot \min\{\log N, \log |C|\})$ for larger alphabets, C. This is accomplished by firstly constructing an augmented Aho-Corasick pattern-matching machine to evaluate the maximal overlaps. Greedy heuristics are then applied to a traversal of the states of the augmented automaton to obtain an approximate longest Hamiltonian path, and hence an approximate shortest common superstring.

It has been conjectured, on the strength of the empirical evidence, that the length of the superstring obtained by greedy approximation never exceeds $2n$, where n denotes the optimal superstring length. Blum et al. (1991) have proven an upper bound of $4n$ for the greedy algorithm, and have developed a modified version of the procedure guaranteed to yield a superstring of length at most $3n$. The $2n$ conjecture for the greedy algorithm, however, still remains open.

An alternative approximation approach — the first for which an upper bound for the superstring length has been proven — has been developed by Li (1990). Again, pairs of strings are merged successively, but this time the idea is to try to merge large groups of strings at once. This is attempted at each step by carefully selecting the two strings so that many others might become substrings of the newly formed, merged string. The degree to which advantage is taken of the overlap whilst merging the two strings can vary between two extremes: from deleting all of the common affix from one string, to simply concatenating the two strings intact. The actual pair of strings selected at each stage and the manner in which they are merged are determined by minimising a cost function, given by the ratio of the length of the composite string to the sum of the lengths of its substrings occurring in X.

An upper bound on the length of the superstring obtained by this method of $n \log n$ has been proven, and a tighter bound of $2n$ conjectured. One advantage of this method is that the algorithm is easily extended, without adverse effects on the $n \log n$ bound, to cater for a generalised problem involving negative examples. Such a situation arises when, in addition to the sample strings, certain other strings are also given which must *not* occur as substrings of the computed superstring. The computation inherent in this method is nevertheless relatively expensive, apparently with a running time cubic in the size of the set of input strings.

Shortest Common Non-Subsequence of N Strings

The N-scns problem has applications in mechanical engineering and was posed by Timkovskii (1989). The problem involves finding the shortest string over alphabet C that is not a subsequence of any of a set of N strings over C. It may thus be stated as follows. Given a set of N strings over alphabet C, $X = \{x_1, x_2, \ldots, x_N\}$, find N-scns(X), where N-scns(X) is a minimal-length sequence such that $\forall x \in X$ N-scns$(X) \not\triangleleft x$.

Middendorf (1993) has shown the decision version of the problem — i.e. that of determining whether $|N$-scns$(X)|$ is less than a given threshold value — to be NP-complete for alphabets of size $\geqslant 2$.

Heaviest Common Subsequence

The problem of obtaining a heaviest common subsequence (hcs) of two strings has been examined by Jacobson and Vo (1992). An hcs(x, y) is a subsequence common to x and y having a maximal sum of weights for its component symbols for a given weight function. In general, this function may depend on both the symbols themselves and also on their positions in the original strings.

The determination of an hcs finds application in, for example, the updating of CRT screens. The line indels required to transform one screen into another may be derived from an lcs of the two screens. In the interests of minimising screen disruption, however, it is preferable to give precedence to closely aligned pairs of matched lines. A minimal-distance weight function, which diminishes as the distance between the positions in their respective sequences of matching symbols increases, may therefore be employed to obtain an appropriate hcs. The computation of an hcs may be performed using an adaptation of the dynamic-programming lcs algorithm, which has been used, for example, in the curses screen-update library distributed with System V Unix (Vo, 1986).

Jacobson and Vo (1992) present an hcs algorithm derived from one to compute a heaviest increasing subsequence (his). This, in turn, was derived from the Robinson-Schensted (Schensted, 1961) method of computing a longest increasing subsequence (lis). An lis is a maximal-length subsequence whose components are strictly increasing, given some linear ordering of the alphabet, and an his is an increasing subsequence with maximal weight. Their algorithm is a generalisation of the Hunt-Szymanski method, and has the same temporal complexity. For position-independent weight functions, a specialised form of the hcs procedure becomes a generalisation of the Apostolico-Guerra (1987) lcs algorithm.

3.2 Algorithms in Detail

3.2.1 Wagner-Fischer

In the dynamic-programming method of computing the distance between two strings, the distances between longer and longer prefixes of the strings are successively evaluated from previous values until the final result is obtained. The precise details of this procedure are given below.

Let the distance between the prefixes of strings x and y, of lengths i and j, respectively, be denoted by $d_{i,j}$, i.e.

$$d_{i,j} = d(x(1,i), \ y(1,j)) \tag{3.5}$$

Further, let the weighting for the cost of transforming symbol a into symbol b be denoted by $w(a, b)$. Thus, $w(a, b)$ is the cost of a symbol substitution if $a \neq b$, $w(a, \epsilon)$ is the cost of deleting a, and $w(\epsilon, b)$ is the cost of inserting b. Note that when d is the Levenshtein distance, we have the following:

$$
\begin{aligned}
w(a, \epsilon) &= 1 \\
w(\epsilon, b) &= 1 \\
w(a, b) &= \begin{cases} 1 & \text{if } a \neq b \\ 0 & \text{if } a = b \end{cases}
\end{aligned}
\tag{3.6}
$$

During the calculation procedure, the values of $d_{i,j}$ are recorded in an $(m+1) \times (n+1)$ array, and are computed using the following recurrence relation.

$$d_{i,j} = \min\{d_{i-1,j} + w(x_i, \epsilon), \ d_{i,j-1} + w(\epsilon, y_j), \ d_{i-1,j-1} + w(x_i, y_j)\} \tag{3.7}$$

This relationship is derived as follows. If the cost of transforming $x(1, i-1)$ into $y(1, j)$ is known, then that of transforming $x(1, i)$ into $y(1, j)$ may be obtained by adding the cost of deleting x_i. Similarly, if the cost of transforming $x(1, i)$ into $y(1, j-1)$ is known, then that of transforming $x(1, i)$ into $y(1, j)$ may be obtained by adding the cost of inserting y_j. Finally, if the cost of transforming $x(1, i-1)$ into $y(1, j-1)$ is known, then that of transforming $x(1, i)$ into $y(1, j)$ may be obtained by adding the cost of replacing x_i by y_j. Recalling that the distance $d_{i,j}$ is the minimum cost of transforming $x(1, i)$ into $y(1, j)$, we can see that it is necessary to select the cheapest of the results of the three operations described above to arrive at the correct value for $d_{i,j}$.

Before the $d_{i,j}$ calculations are performed, the array boundary conditions must be set up. For the zeroth column of the array, the value of $d_{i,0}$ is equal to the sum of the costs of deleting the first i symbols of x. Similarly, for the zeroth row, the value of $d_{0,j}$ is given by the sum of the costs of inserting the first j symbols of y. Thus, we have the following:

$$d_{0,0} = 0 \qquad (3.8)$$

$$d_{i,0} = \sum_{k=1}^{i} w(x_k, \epsilon) \text{ for } 1 \leqslant i \leqslant m$$

$$d_{0,j} = \sum_{k=1}^{j} w(\epsilon, j_k) \text{ for } 1 \leqslant j \leqslant n$$

For the case of the Levenshtein distance, it therefore follows that $d_{i,0} = i$ and $d_{0,j} = j$. The calculation procedure is demonstrated in the following example which shows the array produced in the evaluation of the Levenshtein distance between the strings preterit and zeitgeist. From this, it may be seen that the distance between these strings, i.e. $d_{8,9}$, is equal to 6.

j		0	1	2	3	4	5	6	7	8	9
i			z	e	i	t	g	e	i	s	t
0		0	1	2	3	4	5	6	7	8	9
1	p	1	1	2	3	4	5	6	7	8	9
2	r	2	2	2	3	4	5	6	7	8	9
3	e	3	3	2	3	4	5	5	6	7	8
4	t	4	4	3	3	3	4	5	6	7	7
5	e	5	5	4	4	4	4	4	5	6	7
6	r	6	6	5	5	5	5	5	5	6	7
7	i	7	7	6	5	6	6	6	5	6	7
8	t	8	8	7	6	5	6	7	6	6	6

The algorithm to compute the distance array, as developed by Wagner and Fischer, is given in Figure 3.1. It may be seen that the border-initialisation stage comprises $1 + m + n$ assignments, and that the main loop is iterated mn times. The time complexity of the method is therefore $O(mn)$.

The editing sequence taking x to y may be obtained by way of a structure known as a *trace*. A trace from x to y may be visualised as comprising string x placed above string y, with edges joining symbols in x to symbols in y, such that any symbol is touched by at most one edge and no two edges cross each other. Representing the edge from x_i to y_j by the ordered pair of integers (i,j), we may formally define a trace from x to y as a set of such ordered pairs satisfying the following conditions.

$(a) \quad 1 \leqslant i \leqslant m, \ 1 \leqslant j \leqslant n \qquad (3.9)$

$(b) \quad$ for distinct edges (i_1, j_1), (i_2, j_2)

$$i_1 \neq i_2 \text{ and } j_1 \neq j_2, \ i_1 < i_2 \iff j_1 < j_2$$

An editing sequence may be obtained from a trace as follows. Symbols in x untouched by edges are deleted, whereas those untouched in y are inserted. For

---

— initialise array borders
$d_{0,0} = 0$
for $i = 1$ **to** m
   $d_{i,0} = d_{i-1,0} + w(x_i, \epsilon)$
for $j = 1$ **to** n
   $d_{0,j} = d_{0,j-1} + w(\epsilon, y_j)$
— calculate $d_{i,j}$
for $i = 1$ **to** m
   for $j = 1$ **to** n
      $d_{i,j} = \min\{d_{i-1,j} + w(x_i, \epsilon),\ d_{i,j-1} + w(\epsilon, y_j),\ d_{i-1,j-1} + w(x_i, y_j)\}$

Figure 3.1: Wagner and Fischer string-distance calculation

---

an edge, (i, j), in the trace, if $x_i \neq y_j$, then x_i is replaced by y_j, otherwise no edit is required. Returning to the previous example, a least-cost trace from `preterit` to `zeitgeist` is given below.

```
i       1 2 3 4 5 6 7 8
x_i     p r e t e r i t
        |  /  |  \  |  \
y_j     z e i t g e i s t
j       1 2 3 4 5 6 7 8 9
```

A minimal-cost trace, and hence a least-cost editing sequence, from x to y may be obtained from the completed distance array. An algorithm to print out the ordered pairs of the trace is given in Figure 3.2. The procedure starts with $d_{m,n}$ and works back until either i or j equals 0. The method is to determine from which of its neighbours $d_{i,j}$ was derived, and to move to that position in the array. If $d_{i,j}$ was derived from $d_{i-1,j-1}$, then the ordered pair (i, j) is output — corresponding to an edge in the trace, i.e. either a substitution or a match depending on whether $x_i \neq y_j$ or not, respectively. No output is produced for the case where $d_{i,j}$ was derived from either $d_{i-1,j}$ or $d_{i,j-1}$, as deletions and insertions correspond to symbols untouched by edges in the trace. Since either i or j, or both, is decremented on each pass of the loop, the maximum number of iterations is $m + n$. The least-cost trace is thus determined in $O(m + n)$ time.

Returning once more to the previous example, the above procedure yields the following trace, T (in reverse order from that output by the algorithm).

$$T = \{(1,1),\ (3,2),\ (4,4),\ (5,6),\ (7,7),\ (8,9)\}$$

$$i = m$$
$$j = n$$
while $(i > 0)$ **and** $(j > 0)$
    if $d_{i,j} = d_{i-1,j} + w(x_i, \epsilon)$
      $i = i - 1$
    else if $d_{i,j} = d_{i,j-1} + w(\epsilon, y_j)$
      $j = j - 1$
    else
      print (i, j)
      $i = i - 1$
      $j = j - 1$

Figure 3.2: Wagner and Fischer least-cost trace computation

Note that it is now a fairly straightforward matter to obtain an $\mathrm{lcs}(x, y)$ from the least-cost trace from x to y. The components of $\mathrm{lcs}(x, y)$ are the x_i symbols, or, equivalently, the y_j symbols, such that $(i, j) \in T$ and $x_i = y_j$. So, for our example, we have:

$$\mathrm{lcs}(x, y) = x_3 x_4 x_5 x_7 x_8 = y_2 y_4 y_6 y_7 y_9 = \texttt{eteit}$$

A particular point made by Wagner and Fischer worth noting here is that for spelling correction applications, it might be useful to have a cost function for the edit $a \rightarrow b$, $w(a, b)$, dependent on the particular symbols a and b. For the standard qwerty keyboard, for example, it is much more likely that an e would be miskeyed as a w than would, say, a p. With this criterion, wast would, for example, be deemed to be closer to east than to past.

Symbol Transpositions

The above dynamic-programming method may be adapted to include the interchange of a pair of adjacent symbols as a basic editing operation — allowing for transposition errors. Lowrance and Wagner (1975) developed an $O(mn)$ time and space algorithm to compute the distance between two strings in such a case, provided that the cost assigned to a transposition is $\geq (w(\epsilon, a) + w(a, \epsilon))/2$.

In particular, the Levenshtein distance (given by the edit costs of (3.6)) may be generalised by allocating a unit cost to a transposition. The dynamic-programming computation may then be modified as follows to take this into account.

The minimum cost of transforming $x(1, i - 2)$ into $y(1, j - 2)$ is given by $d_{i-2,j-2}$. If the next two symbols of x occur in reverse order as the next two symbols of y (i.e. if $x_{i-1}x_i = y_j y_{j-1}$), then the minimum cost of transforming $x(1, i)$ into $y(1, j)$, i.e. $d_{i,j}$, is equal to $d_{i-2,j-2}+1$. In this case, $w(x_{i-1}, y_j) = w(x_i, y_{j-1}) = 0$. Transpositions may therefore be accommodated by augmenting the minimisation in the $d_{i,j}$ recurrence relation, (3.7), with the following term:

$$d_{i-2,j-2} + w(x_{i-1}, y_j) + w(x_i, y_{j-1}) + 1 \qquad (3.10)$$

The revised distance calculation is illustrated in the following example, which shows the distance matrix for the strings ABCD and ACBD. Since the term $d_{i-2,j-2}$ is now involved in the computation, extra boundary values for $i = -1$ and $j = -1$ are required: values of ∞ prevent transpositions that would involve symbols from before the start of the strings from being considered. (In practice, any large value $\geqslant n - 1$, where $n \geqslant m$, will suffice in place of ∞.)

	j	-1	0	1	2	3	4
i				A	C	B	D
-1		∞	∞	∞	∞	∞	∞
0		∞	0	1	2	3	4
1	A	∞	1	0	1	2	3
2	B	∞	2	1	1	1	2
3	C	∞	3	2	1	1	2
4	D	∞	4	3	2	2	1

The distance between ABCD and ACBD, $d_{4,4}$, is thus equal to 1. At the position of the transposition, $(3,3)$, $w(x_2, y_3) = w(x_3, y_2) = 0$. Distance value $d_{3,3}$ is therefore arrived at by adding 1 to $d_{1,1}$, as this result is lower than those that would be obtained for an insertion, deletion, or substitution.

3.2.2 Hirschberg

The space requirement of Wagner and Fischer's method is $O(mn)$. In order to avoid potential storage problems when dealing with long strings, Hirschberg (1975) developed a linear-space version of the algorithm.

Hirschberg's objective was to determine an lcs(x, y) of two strings x and y. Rather than the string distances, it is therefore the lengths of longest common subsequences of progressively longer string prefixes that are evaluated in the dynamic-programming table. Let this quantity be denoted by $l_{i,j}$, i.e.

$$l_{i,j} = |\text{lcs}(x(1, i), y(1, j))| \qquad (3.11)$$

For a given metric, there is a fixed relationship between $l_{i,j}$ and $d_{i,j}$. Consider, for example, the edit distance, defined by the following costs.

$$w(a, \epsilon) = 1 \tag{3.12}$$
$$w(\epsilon, b) = 1$$
$$w(a, b) = \begin{cases} 2 & \text{if } a \neq b \\ 0 & \text{if } a = b \end{cases}$$

From a minimal-cost trace from x to y, we can see that the edit distance, $d(x, y)$, is related to $|\text{lcs}(x, y)|$ as derived below, where *del*, *ins* and *sub* are the numbers of symbol deletions, insertions and substitutions, respectively.

$$\begin{aligned} d(x, y) &= del + ins + 2sub \\ &= m - (|\text{lcs}(x, y)| + sub) + n - (|\text{lcs}(x, y)| + sub) + 2sub \\ &= m + n - 2\,|\text{lcs}(x, y)| \end{aligned} \tag{3.13}$$

In this case, the relationship between $l_{i,j}$ and $d_{i,j}$ is therefore as follows:

$$l_{i,j} = (i + j - d_{i,j})/2 \tag{3.14}$$

Employing this transformation, the dynamic-programming procedure for $l_{i,j}$ may be derived from that for $d_{i,j}$, and is given in Figure 3.3. Since the length of an lcs of any string and the empty string is 0, the array border values are given by $l_{i,0} = l_{0,j} = 0$. As with the $d_{i,j}$ calculations, the values of $l_{i,j}$ are built up from previous results. When at position (i, j), i.e. when considering prefixes $x(1, i)$ and $y(1, j)$, if $x_i = y_j$ then we obtain a new lcs by appending this symbol to the current lcs of $x(1, i - 1)$ and $y(1, j - 1)$, and thus $l_{i,j} = l_{i-1,j-1} + 1$. Otherwise the length of the current partial lcs is simply the maximum of the previous neighbouring values.

The storage requirements of the above algorithm may be reduced by noting that only row $i - 1$ of the matrix is required in the evaluation of row i. This fact is exploited in the algorithm given in Figure 3.4. This returns vector ll as output, where $ll_j = l_{m,j}$. A $2 \times (n+1)$ array, h, is employed, whose rows 0 and 1 act as rows $i - 1$ and i of array l, respectively. Row 1 is therefore shifted up into row 0 prior to each new 'row i' calculation.

As before, the if statement is executed exactly mn times, giving a time complexity of $O(mn)$. The input and output arrays require $m + n + (n + 1)$ locations, with $2(n + 1)$ storage locations allocated to array h. The space complexity is therefore $O(m+n)$. This method may be used in an algorithm to determine an actual $\text{lcs}(x, y)$ in linear space, as described below.

The general idea is to divide recursively string x in half, and for each half, $x1$ and $x2$, find a corresponding prefix and suffix, $y1$ and $y2$, of y such that the lcs of $x1$ and $y1$ concatenated with that of $x2$ and $y2$ is equal to an lcs of the complete strings x and y, i.e.

$$\text{lcs}(x1, y1) \cdot \text{lcs}(x2, y2) = \text{lcs}(x, y) \tag{3.15}$$

— initialise array borders
$l_{0,0} = 0$
for $i = 1$ **to** m
  $l_{i,0} = 0$
for $j = 1$ **to** n
  $l_{0,j} = 0$
— calculate $l_{i,j}$
for $i = 1$ **to** m
  for $j = 1$ **to** n
    if $x_i = y_j$
      $l_{i,j} = l_{i-1,j-1} + 1$
    else
      $l_{i,j} = \max\{l_{i-1,j},\ l_{i,j-1}\}$

Figure 3.3: Calculation of $|\operatorname{lcs}(x, y)|$

$lcs\_length(m,\ n,\ x,\ y,\ ll)$
  — initialise
  for $j = 0$ **to** n
    $h_{1,j} = 0$
  — calculate $h_{1,j}$
  for $i = 1$ **to** m
    — shift row up
    for $j = 0$ **to** n
      $h_{0,j} = h_{1,j}$
    for $j = 1$ **to** n
      if $x_i = y_j$
        $h_{1,j} = h_{0,j-1} + 1$
      else
        $h_{1,j} = \max\{h_{1,j-1}, h_{0,j}\}$
  — copy result to output vector
  for $j = 0$ **to** n
    $ll_j = h_{1,j}$

Figure 3.4: Reduced-space calculation of $|\operatorname{lcs}(x, y)|$

The problem may thus be decomposed recursively until trivial subproblems are obtained.

Let the length of an lcs of the suffixes $x(i+1,m)$ and $y(j+1,n)$ be denoted by $l^*_{i,j}$, i.e.

$$l^*_{i,j} = |\text{lcs}(x(i+1,m), y(j+1,n))| \qquad (3.16)$$

For $0 \leqslant j \leqslant n$, values of $l_{i,j}$ are the lengths of lcs's of the prefix $x(1,i)$ and various prefixes of y. Similarly, for $0 \leqslant j \leqslant n$, values of $l^*_{i,j}$ are the lengths of lcs's of the reversed suffix $x_R(m, i+1)$ and various prefixes of the reversed string y_R. The following theorem, (3.17)–(3.18), permits the appropriate prefix and suffix of y to be found when x is bisected, i.e. when i is taken to be $\lfloor m/2 \rfloor$. The theorem states that when x is divided into two parts at any point, then the maximum value, over all divisions of y into two sections, of the sum of the lengths of an lcs of the first sections of x and y and that of the latter sections is equal to the length of an lcs of the complete strings x and y.

$$M_i = l_{m,n} \quad \text{for } 0 \leqslant i \leqslant m \qquad (3.17)$$
$$\text{where} \quad M_i = \max_{0 \leqslant j \leqslant n} \{l_{i,j} + l^*_{i,j}\} \qquad (3.18)$$

This may be proved as follows. First of all, let: $M_i = l_{i,j} + l^*_{i,j}$ for $j = j_0$, say; s_{i,j_0} be any $\text{lcs}(x(1,i), y(1,j_0))$; and s^*_{i,j_0} be any $\text{lcs}(x(i+1,m), y(j_0+1,n))$. String $c = s_{i,j_0} \cdot s^*_{i,j_0}$ is thus a common subsequence of x and y, and has length M_i. So,

$$l_{m,n} \geqslant M_i \qquad (3.19)$$

Let $s_{m,n}$ be any $\text{lcs}(x,y)$; then $s_{m,n}$ is a subsequence of y that is equal to $s1 \cdot s2$, where $s1$ is a subsequence of $x(1,i)$ and $s2$ is a subsequence of $x(i+1,m)$. So, there exists a value of j, j_1, say, such that $s1$ is a subsequence of $y(1,j_1)$ and $s2$ is a subsequence of $y(j_1+1,n)$. The lengths of $s1$ and $s2$ satisfy the following:

$$
\begin{aligned}
|s1| &\leqslant |\text{lcs}(x(1,i), y(1,j_1))| \\
&\leqslant l_{i,j_1} \quad \text{from (3.11)} & (3.20) \\
|s2| &\leqslant |\text{lcs}(x(i+1,m), y(j_1+1,n))| \\
&\leqslant l^*_{i,j_1} \quad \text{from (3.16)} & (3.21)
\end{aligned}
$$

Thus we have:

$$
\begin{aligned}
l_{m,n} &= |s_{m,n}| \\
&= |s1| + |s2| \\
&\leqslant l_{i,j_1} + l^*_{i,j_1} \quad \text{from (3.20) and (3.21)} \\
&\leqslant M_i \quad \text{from (3.18)} & (3.22)
\end{aligned}
$$

$lcs(m, n, x, y, c)$
  — trivial case
if $n = 0$
  $c = \epsilon$
else if $m = 1$
  if $\exists j,\ 0 \leqslant j \leqslant n$, such that $x_1 = y_j$
    $c = x_1$
  else
    $c = \epsilon$
  — non-trivial case; split the problem
else
  $i = \lfloor m/2 \rfloor$
  — calculate $l_{i,j}$ and $l_{i,j}^*$ for $0 \leqslant j \leqslant n$
  $lcs\_length(i, n, x(1,i), y(1,n), l1)$
  $lcs\_length(m - i, n, x_R(m, i+1), y_R(n, 1), l2)$
  — find j such that $l_{i,j} + l_{i,j}^* = l_{m,n}$
  $M = \max_{0 \leqslant j \leqslant n}\{l1_j + l2_{n-j}\}$
  $k = \min j$ such that $l1_j + l2_{n-j} = M$
  — solve simpler problems
  $lcs(i, k, x(1,i), y(1,k), c1)$
  $lcs(m - i, n - k, x(i+1, m), y(k+1, n), c2)$
  — concatenate results to produce output
  $c = c1 \cdot c2$

Figure 3.5: Hirschberg calculation of $lcs(x, y)$

And from inequalities (3.19) and (3.22), we have the final result: $M_i = l_{m,n}$.

Figure 3.5 gives the overall algorithm, incorporating the above theorem, to determine $lcs(x, y)$. String c is returned as output, and is equal to an lcs of input strings x and y. The procedure returns with either the empty string or a single-symbol lcs for a trivial problem. Otherwise, string x is sliced in half and the lengths of the lcs of its lower half and varying-length prefixes of y, and that of its upper half and varying-length suffixes of y are found. The theorem is then employed in order to find the first position in y, denoted here by k, such that the lcs of the first half of x and $y(1, k)$ concatenated with that of the second half of x and $y(k + 1, n)$ is equal to the desired $lcs(x, y)$. It thus only remains to use this value of k in two recursive calls to the procedure to obtain the required subproblem lcs's, and then to concatenate them to provide the output.

The linear-space characteristic of this algorithm may be demonstrated as follows. Strings x and y may be held in global storage, and substring parameters may be passed by transferring as arguments pointers to the start and end of the relevant substrings. As shown earlier, calls to *lcs_length* require temporary storage proportional to m plus n. Not counting recursive calls, the storage requirement of procedure *lcs* is constant. It can be shown that during execution, there is a total of $2m - 1$ calls to *lcs*. The overall storage requirement of this method is therefore $O(m+n)$. Hirschberg (1975) also analysed the execution time of the algorithm, and has shown this to be $O(mn)$.

3.2.3 Hunt-Szymanski

Hunt and Szymanski's method of extracting an lcs from two input strings, x and y, is equivalent to finding a maximal, strictly increasing path in the graph composed of points (i, j) such that $x_i = y_j$. This will be illustrated here by an example once the actual method has been described.

For convenience, it shall be assumed that the lengths of the input strings are equal, i.e. $|x| = |y| = n$. The final algorithm may, however, be modified easily in order to accommodate strings with unequal lengths. The number of ordered pairs of positions within x and y at which the respective symbols match, i.e. the cardinality of the set $\{(i, j) \mid x_i = y_j\}$, shall be denoted by r.

Crucial to the method is an array of $k_{i,l}$ values, defined as follows, where $l_{i,j}$ is defined in (3.11).

$$k_{i,l} = \min j \text{ such that } l_{i,j} = l \qquad (3.23)$$

The value of $k_{i,l}$ thus gives the shortest length of prefix of y having a subsequence of length l in common with the prefix of x of length i. This is illustrated by considering the case where $x = $ preterit and $y = $ zeitgeist, for example, for which $k_{5,1} = 2$; $k_{5,2} = 4$; $k_{5,3} = 6$; and $k_{5,4}$ and $k_{5,5}$ are not defined.

Since, by definition, $k_{i,l}$ is a minimal value, it follows that the last symbol of a subsequence of length l common to the prefixes $x(1, i)$ and $y(1, k_{i,l})$ is equal to $y_{k_{i,l}}$. Thus, the length of the lcs of $x(1, i)$ and $y(1, k_{i,l} - 1)$ is equal to $l - 1$. Consequently, $k_{i,l-1} \leqslant k_{i,l} - 1$, i.e. $k_{i,l-1} < k_{i,l}$. This shows that the values of $k_{i,l}$ in each row of the array must be strictly increasing.

The values of k may be computed iteratively from previous values in the array. In particular, the value of $k_{i+1,l}$ may be derived from those of $k_{i,l-1}$ and $k_{i,l}$. But before it is shown how this is done, the range of values within which $k_{i+1,l}$ must fall shall first be examined.

If $x(1, i)$ and $y(1, k_{i,l})$ have a common subsequence of length l, then so too will $x(1, i + 1)$ and $y(1, k_{i,l})$. Thus:

$$k_{i+1,l} \leqslant k_{i,l} \qquad (3.24)$$

By definition, $x(1, i+1)$ and $y(1, k_{i+1,l})$ have an lcs of length l. The lcs of prefixes one symbol shorter, namely $x(1, i)$ and $y(1, k_{i+1,l} - 1)$, will therefore be shorter than l by at most one symbol. Thus, $k_{i,l-1} \leqslant k_{i+1,l} - 1$, or:

$$k_{i,l-1} < k_{i+1,l} \tag{3.25}$$

Combining (3.24) and (3.25) gives the following bounds for $k_{i+1,l}$:

$$k_{i,l-1} < k_{i+1,l} \leqslant k_{i,l} \tag{3.26}$$

The actual rule for calculating $k_{i+1,l}$ from $k_{i,l-1}$ and $k_{i,l}$ is given below.

$$k_{i+1,l} = \begin{cases} \min j \text{ such that } x_{i+1} = y_j \text{ and } k_{i,l-1} < j \leqslant k_{i,l} \\ k_{i,l} \text{ if no such } j \text{ exists} \end{cases} \tag{3.27}$$

This may be shown to be correct as follows. Firstly, consider the case for which no suitable j exists. Since $k_{i+1,l}$ is a minimal value, the last component of any length-l subsequence common to $x(1, i+1)$ and $y(1, k_{i+1,l})$ must be equal to $y_{k_{i+1,l}}$. Since $k_{i+1,l}$ must lie within the bounds given in (3.26), it follows that $y_{k_{i+1,l}} \neq x_{i+1}$, otherwise $k_{i+1,l}$ would be the required value of j. It then follows that the same length-l subsequence is common to $x(1, i)$ and $y(1, k_{i+1,l})$, implying that $k_{i,l} \leqslant k_{i+1,l}$. Combining this with (3.26) gives the result that, when no suitable j exists, $k_{i+1,l} = k_{i,l}$.

Secondly, consider the case where there is a j such that $x_{i+1} = y_j$ and $k_{i,l-1} < j \leqslant k_{i,l}$. String prefixes $x(1, i+1)$ and $y(1, j)$ will have a common subsequence of length l equal to the one of length $l-1$, common to $x(1, i)$ and $y(1, k_{i,l-1})$, with symbol x_{i+1} appended to the end (since $x_{i+1} = y_j$). Thus, $k_{i+1,l} \leqslant j$. It now remains to determine whether, as is desired, the equality holds, or whether the value of $k_{i+1,l}$ is actually less than our value of j. By assuming the latter and obtaining a contradiction, the former may be proven. We proceed as follows. Assume that $k_{i+1,l} < j$. Again, the last symbol of the length-l subsequence common to $x(1, i+1)$ and $y(1, k_{i+1,l})$ must be $y_{k_{i+1,l}}$. Since both $k_{i+1,l}$ and j are constrained to lie in the same interval (from (3.26) and (3.27)), we know that $y_{k_{i+1,l}} \neq x_{i+1}$, as j is the minimum value in the permitted range such that $y_j = x_{i+1}$ and we are assuming that $k_{i+1,l} < j$. It then follows that $x(1, i)$ and $y(1, k_{i+1,l})$ also have a common subsequence of length l, implying that $k_{i,l} \leqslant k_{i+1,l}$. Taken in conjunction with (3.26), this means that $k_{i,l} = k_{i+1,l}$. Our assumption was that $k_{i+1,l} < j$. Thus, from (3.27), $k_{i+1,l} < k_{i,l}$, which obviously contradicts the previous result. This shows that our value of j is, in fact, equal to the required $k_{i+1,l}$.

An algorithm to determine $|\mathrm{lcs}(x, y)|$ using the $k_{i,l}$ values is given in Figure 3.6. Vector kk is used as the ith row of array k. Thus, at the start of each iteration of i, $kk_l = k_{i-1,l}$ for $0 \leqslant l \leqslant n$, and, on completion of the iteration, $kk_l = k_{i,l}$ for $0 \leqslant l \leqslant n$. Note that at the outset, kk_0 is initialised to 0 and the rest of kk to $n+1$, signifying

---

— initialise
$kk_0 = 0$
for $l = 1$ **to** n
   $kk_l = n + 1$
— calculate $|\text{lcs}(x, y)|$
for $i = 1$ **to** n
   for $j = n$ **downto** 1
      if $x_i = y_j$
         find l such that $kk_{l-1} < j \leqslant kk_l$
         $kk_l = j$
print $\max l$ such that $kk_l \neq n + 1$

Figure 3.6: Hunt-Szymanski calculation of $|\text{lcs}(x, y)|$

---

undefined values of $k_{i,l}$. Only a single row is required for the calculations, since the values down a column either remain unaltered or are decreased and the values along a row remain in a monotonically increasing order.

It is important that the j-loop counts down from n to 1. Consider the case where x_i matches several symbols in y — y_{j_1}, y_{j_2}, ..., y_{j_p}, say — such that $k_{i-1,l-1} < j_1 < j_2 < \ldots < j_p \leqslant k_{i-1,l}$. From (3.27), it can be seen that the correct value for $k_{i,l}$ is therefore j_1. By iterating downwards for j, $k_{i,l}$ will be assigned successively smaller values j_p, j_{p-1}, ..., j_1, ending in the final assignment of the required value. If, however, the iteration for j were carried out forwards, then $k_{i,l}$ would first of all be given the correct value but then $k_{i,l+1}$ would be set to j_2, $k_{i,l+2}$ to j_3, and so on up to $k_{i,l+p-1}$, which would not be correct.

At the end of the procedure, the value of $|\text{lcs}(x, y)|$ is given by the maximum l for which $k_{n,l}$ is defined. As the values in kk increase monotonically, the 'find' operation may be implemented in $O(\log n)$ time by performing a binary search. Since the **if** statement is executed exactly n^2 times, it follows that the algorithm runs in $O(n^2 \log n)$ time in the worst case. Note that for unequal-length strings, the bounds for the kk initialisation and the outer i-loop would be set to m rather than n, where $m < n$. The results of the procedure are demonstrated below, which shows the $k_{i,l}$ values for $x = $ preterit and $y = $ zeitgeist. It may be seen from the final row that $|\text{lcs}(\text{preterit}, \text{zeitgeist})| = 5$.

		0	1	2	3	l 4	5	6	7	8
1	p	0	10	10	10	10	10	10	10	10
2	r	0	10	10	10	10	10	10	10	10
3	e	0	2	10	10	10	10	10	10	10
i 4	t	0	2	4	10	10	10	10	10	10
5	e	0	2	4	6	10	10	10	10	10
6	r	0	2	4	6	10	10	10	10	10
7	i	0	2	3	6	7	10	10	10	10
8	t	0	2	3	4	7	9	10	10	10

The exhaustive testing for matching symbols in the above algorithm is rather inefficient and may be avoided by preprocessing the strings to obtain a prior record of the positions at which they match. An array of pointers to linked lists, $matchlist$, may thus be constructed such that $matchlist[i]$ provides a linked list of positions, j, in descending order, at which $x_i = y_j$. The same physical list may be used for repeated instances of a symbol in x. For example, the actual lists for the case of $x =$ preterit and $y =$ zeitgeist are as follows:

$matchlist[1] = ()$
$matchlist[2] = ()$
$matchlist[3] = (6, 2)$
$matchlist[4] = (9, 4)$
$matchlist[5] = matchlist[3]$
$matchlist[6] = ()$
$matchlist[7] = (7, 3)$
$matchlist[8] = matchlist[4]$

The final algorithm, which incorporates this improvement and which also extracts an lcs of the two strings, is given in Figure 3.7. The lcs is recovered by using a backtracking device employed whilst calculating the successive kk values. Whenever kk_l is defined, $link_l$ is set to point to the head of a list of (i, j) pairs defining a common subsequence of length l. This is implemented using the $newnode$ procedure, which creates a new node, containing the current (i, j) pair together with a pointer to the previous node in the list, and returns a pointer to the node just created.

The preprocessing stage may be implemented by sorting the symbols of each string, keeping note of their original positions, and then merging the sorted strings to create the $matchlist$'s. Using the heapsort algorithm, this phase may be performed in $O(n \log n)$ time and $O(n)$ space. The initialisation stage takes $O(n)$ time. During the calculation of the kk values, the inner loop is iterated a total of r times.

— create linked lists
for $i = 1$ to n
    $matchlist[i] = (j_1, j_2, \ldots, j_p)$ such that $j_1 > j_2 > \cdots > j_p$
    and $x_i = y_{j_q}$ for $1 \leqslant q \leqslant p$
— initialise
$kk_0 = 0$
for $l = 1$ to n
    $kk_l = n + 1$
$link_0 =$ null
— calculate successive kk values
for $i = 1$ to n
    for j in $matchlist[i]$
        find l such that $kk_{l-1} < j \leqslant kk_l$
        if $j < kk_l$
          $kk_l = j$
          $link_l = newnode(i, j, link_{l-1})$
— extract lcs in reverse order
$l = \max l$ such that $kk_l \neq n + 1$
$pointer = link_l$
while $pointer \neq$ null
    print (i, j) pair pointed to by $pointer$
    advance $pointer$

Figure 3.7: Hunt-Szymanski calculation of $\text{lcs}(x, y)$

For each iteration, a binary search and a few constant-time operations are performed. This stage therefore takes $O(r + r \log n)$ time and involves the creation of at most r new nodes. Finally, the actual extraction of an lcs takes $O(|\text{lcs}(x, y)|)$ time, which is $O(n)$. The overall time and space complexities of the algorithm are therefore $O((r + n) \log n)$ and $O(r + n)$, respectively. Again, the more general case of unequal-length strings is easily catered for by setting the bounds for the kk initialisation and the i-loops to m rather than n.

For our example of computing $\text{lcs}(\texttt{preterit}, \texttt{zeitgeist})$, the above procedure produces the following list of (i, j) pairs for the lcs (in reverse order).

$$(8, 9), \ (7, 7), \ (5, 6), \ (4, 4), \ (3, 2)$$

This is illustrated below, where the nodes indicate the points (i, j) such that $x_i = y_j$. The lcs is formed by the symbols corresponding to the filled-in nodes, namely eteit, and is thus equivalent to a maximal, strictly increasing path in the graph.

	j	1	2	3	4	5	6	7	8	9
i		z	e	i	t	g	e	i	s	t
1	p									
2	r									
3	e		●				o			
4	t				●					o
5	e	o					●			
6	r									
7	i			o				●		
8	t				o					●

Dominant Matches

Apostolico and Guerra (1987) have developed a variation of the Hunt-Szymanski algorithm, which overcomes the latter's degradation in behaviour to worse than quadratic in the worst case. Their variant has a running time of $O(m \log n + t \log(2mn/t))$, which is at worst $O(mn)$, and requires $O(n \log |C|)$-time preprocessing. Here $t \leqslant r$ is the number of *dominant* matches between the strings. A k-dominant match is an ordered pair (i, j) such that $x_i = y_j$, $l_{i,j} = k$, and it is the only such point occurring in the submatrix $l_{(1,\ldots,i),(1,\ldots,j)}$ ($l_{i,j}$ is defined in (3.11)). (An ordered pair (i, j) is said to *dominate* ordered pair (i', j') if $i \leqslant i'$ and $j \leqslant j'$.) A match (i, j) is thus dominant if the occurrences in $x(1, i)$ and $y(1, j)$ of every $\text{lcs}(x(1, i), y(1, j))$ have x_i and y_j, respectively, as their final symbols. Apostolico and Guerra's variant efficiently finds the dominant matches, and employs characteristic trees to represent the various lists that it requires to do so.

An upper bound, formalised by Jacobson and Vo (1992), for the total number of dominant matches, t, between two strings, is obtained as follows. The k-dominant matches may be sorted in increasing order of i to give $\{(i_1, j_1), (i_2, j_2), \ldots, (i_{t_k}, j_{t_k})\}$, where t_k denotes the number of k-dominant matches, and $i_1 < i_2 < \cdots < i_{t_k}$, $j_1 > j_2 > \cdots > j_{t_k}$. Since the i's and j's are strictly increasing and decreasing, respectively, we have the following inequalities, where $1 \leqslant p \leqslant t_k$.

$$i_p - i_1 \geqslant p - 1$$
$$j_p - j_{t_k} \geqslant t_k - p \tag{3.28}$$

The edit distance between prefixes $x(1, i_p)$ and $y(1, j_p)$, and the length of their lcs are related as follows:

$$\begin{aligned} d_{i_p, j_p} &= i_p + j_p - 2l_{i_p, j_p} \quad \text{from (3.13)} \\ &= i_p + j_p - 2k \end{aligned} \tag{3.29}$$

Since the match (i_1, j_1) is k-dominant, we have that $i_1 \geqslant k$, and also since match (i_{t_k}, j_{t_k}) is k-dominant, we have that $j_{t_k} \geqslant k$. Combining this with (3.29) gives the following:

$$
\begin{aligned}
d_{i_p, j_p} &\geqslant i_p + j_p - (i_1 + j_{t_k}) \\
&\geqslant (i_p - i_1) + (j_p - j_{t_k}) \\
&\geqslant (p - 1) + (t_k - p) \quad \text{from (3.28)} \\
&\geqslant t_k - 1 \tag{3.30}
\end{aligned}
$$

Let the value of k having the greatest number of k-dominant matches be denoted by k'. An $\mathrm{lcs}(x, y)$ built using only dominant matches must incorporate one of these k'-dominant matches, (i_p, j_p), say. The distance between the complete strings x and y must then be greater than or equal to that between the prefixes $x(1, i_p)$ and $y(1, j_p)$, i.e.

$$
\begin{aligned}
d_{m,n} &\geqslant d_{i_p, j_p} \\
\Rightarrow d_{m,n} + 1 &\geqslant t_{k'} \quad \text{from (3.30)} \tag{3.31}
\end{aligned}
$$

Since $t_{k'}$ is a maximal number of dominant matches, i.e. $t_{k'} \geqslant t_l$ for $1 \leqslant l \leqslant l_{m,n}$, we have the following:

$$
t \leqslant l_{m,n} \cdot t_{k'} \tag{3.32}
$$

Combining this with inequality (3.31) gives the following final result for the upper bound for the total number of dominant matches.

$$
t \leqslant l_{m,n}(d_{m,n} + 1) \tag{3.33}
$$

The number of dominant matches can be much less than the total number of matches, especially when the distance between the strings is small. The worst-case bound for t is obtained as follows. Substituting for $d_{m,n}$, from (3.13), gives the following:

$$
t \leqslant l_{m,n}(m + n - 2l_{m,n} + 1) \tag{3.34}
$$

In the case of equal-length strings, this bound is maximised when the lcs length is $(2n + 1)/4$, with a corresponding value of $(2n + 1)^2/8$. Recall that the maximum number of matches is n^2. It may thus be seen that, in the worst case, the bound for the total number of matches is asymptotically twice that for the dominant matches.

3.2.4 Masek-Paterson

Masek and Paterson (1980) applied the approach of Arlazarov, Dinic, Kronod and Faradzev (1970) — the 'Four Russians' — to Wagner and Fischer's string-distance procedure to obtain an $O(n^2/\log n)$-time algorithm. Their resulting technique is described below.

The distance matrix, d, is broken up into a number of square submatrices with overlapping edge vectors. The (i, j, p) submatrix shall be defined as the $(p + 1) \times$

$(p + 1)$ submatrix whose top-left element is $d_{i,j}$. From the definition of the entries in the d matrix, (3.7), it may be seen that the values in an (i, j, p) submatrix are derived from its relevant substrings, $x(i + 1, i + p)$ and $y(j + 1, j + p)$, and from its initial vectors, i.e. its top row $(d_{i,j}, d_{i,j+1}, \ldots, d_{i,j+p})$ and its leftmost column $(d_{i,j}, d_{i+1,j}, \ldots, d_{i+p,j})$.

The first stage of the algorithm is to calculate the values in the final vectors, i.e. the bottom row and the rightmost column, of all the possible (i, j, p) submatrices of any d matrix for a given alphabet and cost function. This involves enumerating all the submatrices, requiring all the combinations of possible substrings and initial vectors to be listed. In order to enumerate all the length-p substrings, we must assume that the alphabet is finite. Furthermore, attempting to enumerate every possible initial vector may be prohibitive. However, we may restrict the edit costs to be integral multiples of some real number. This then results in there being only a finite number of differences between consecutive values of d for all distance matrices using the same alphabet and cost function. It is thus more practical to use these differential values, rather than the absolute distances. Let a *step* be defined as the difference between any two horizontally or vertically adjacent matrix-elements. We then have the following corollary of the rule for calculating $d_{i,j}$, (3.7).

$$
(d_{i,j} - d_{i-1,j}) = \min \left\{ \begin{array}{l} w(x_i, \epsilon), \\ d_{i,j-1} - d_{i-1,j} + w(\epsilon, y_j), \\ d_{i-1,j-1} - d_{i-1,j} + w(x_i, y_j) \end{array} \right\} \tag{3.35}
$$

$$
= \min \left\{ \begin{array}{l} w(x_i, \epsilon), \\ w(\epsilon, y_j) + (d_{i,j-1} - d_{i-1,j-1}) - (d_{i-1,j} - d_{i-1,j-1}), \\ w(x_i, y_j) - (d_{i-1,j} - d_{i-1,j-1}) \end{array} \right\}
$$

$$
(d_{i,j} - d_{i,j-1}) = \min \left\{ \begin{array}{l} d_{i-1,j} - d_{i,j-1} + w(x_i, \epsilon), \\ w(\epsilon, y_j), \\ d_{i-1,j-1} - d_{i,j-1} + w(x_i, y_j) \end{array} \right\}
$$

$$
= \min \left\{ \begin{array}{l} w(x_i, \epsilon) + (d_{i-1,j} - d_{i-1,j-1}) - (d_{i,j-1} - d_{i-1,j-1}), \\ w(\epsilon, y_j), \\ w(x_i, y_j) - (d_{i,j-1} - d_{i-1,j-1}) \end{array} \right\}
$$

Each submatrix may thus be derived from the appropriate substrings, $x(i+1, i+p)$ and $y(j+1, j+p)$, a starting value $d_{i,j}$, and its initial step vectors — the top row $(d_{i,j+1} - d_{i,j}, \ldots, d_{i,j+p} - d_{i,j+p-1})$ and the first column $(d_{i+1,j} - d_{i,j}, \ldots, d_{i+p,j} - d_{i+p-1,j})$. All the possible submatrices may be enumerated by listing all pairs of length-p strings over our finite alphabet, C, and all pairs of length-p step vectors.

The algorithm to precompute all the submatrices is given in Figure 3.8. The enumeration of the length-p strings and the length-p step vectors is in lexicographic order, assuming fixed orderings on C and on the finite set of possible step values. A

---

for each pair of strings $u, v \in C^p$
  for each pair of length-p step vectors T, L
    — initialise initial step vectors
    for $i = 1$ **to** p
      $V_{i,0} = L_i$
      $H_{0,i} = T_i$
    — calculate step-matrix entries
    for $i = 1$ **to** p
      for $j = 1$ **to** p

$$V_{i,j} = \min \left\{ \begin{array}{l} w(u_i, \epsilon), \\ w(\epsilon, v_j) + V_{i,j-1} - H_{i-1,j}, \\ w(u_i, v_j) - H_{i-1,j} \end{array} \right\}$$

$$H_{i,j} = \min \left\{ \begin{array}{l} w(u_i, \epsilon) + H_{i-1,j} - V_{i,j-1}, \\ w(\epsilon, v_j), \\ w(u_i, v_j) - V_{i,j-1} \end{array} \right\}$$

    — save results
    $R = (V_{1,p}, V_{2,p}, \ldots, V_{p,p})$
    $B = (H_{p,1}, H_{p,2}, \ldots, H_{p,p})$
    $store(R,\ B,\ L,\ T,\ u,\ v)$

Figure 3.8: Masek-Paterson submatrix preprocessing

---

step submatrix is evaluated for each pair of strings, u and v, and each pair of initial step vectors, T and L, according to (3.35). To facilitate later retrieval, a procedure *store* saves the final step vectors, B and R, of the submatrix determined by u, v, T and L. Two matrices of steps are computed during the procedure — V comprises the vertical step values, and H the horizontal ones.

As the innermost loop takes constant time and is iterated exactly p^2 times for each pair of strings and step vectors, each submatrix is computed in $O(p^2)$ time. The number of pairs of length-p strings over alphabet C is equal to $|C|^{2p}$. If s is the cardinality of the set of possible step values, which we will assume to be finite, then there are s^{2p} distinct pairs of length-p step vectors. There is therefore a total of $(s\,|C|)^{2p}$ different submatrices, giving an overall preprocessing time of $O(p^2(s\,|C|)^{2p})$.

It was previously stated that, for the restriction on the cost function, the set of possible step values was finite. This will now be examined a little more closely. It may be seen from the rule for $d_{i,j}$ and the boundary conditions, (3.7)–(3.8), that the step values are bounded, independently of the actual strings involved, as shown below.

$$-I \leqslant (d_{i,j} - d_{i-1,j}) \leqslant D$$
$$-D \leqslant (d_{i,j} - d_{i,j-1}) \leqslant I$$
$$\text{where } D = \max\{w(a, \epsilon) \mid a \in C\},$$
$$I = \max\{w(\epsilon, b) \mid b \in C\} \tag{3.36}$$

The cost function is said to be *sparse* if every member of the set of cost values, namely $\{w(a, \epsilon) \mid a \in C\} \cup \{w(\epsilon, b) \mid b \in C\} \cup \{w(a, b) \mid a, b \in C\}$, is an integral multiple of some constant. It can be shown that, for finite alphabets, if the cost function is sparse, then the set of step values obtained in the submatrices is finite irrespective of the particular strings involved, thereby justifying this earlier assumption.

The algorithm to compute the string distance from the preprocessed submatrices is given in Figure 3.9. Assuming that $m \bmod p = n \bmod p = 0$, i and j step through the submatrices vertically and horizontally, respectively. P is a matrix of length-p step-submatrix column vectors, such that $P_{i,j}$ is the rightmost column of submatrix (i, j), which is equal to the leftmost one of submatrix $(i, j + 1)$, since adjacent $(p + 1) \times (p + 1)$ submatrices share a common border. Similarly, Q is a matrix of length-p step-submatrix row vectors, such that $Q_{i,j}$ is the bottom row of submatrix (i, j), equal to the top row of submatrix $(i+1, j)$. The 0th column and row, respectively, of P and Q are initialised with the steps corresponding to the distance-array boundary conditions given in (3.8). Procedure $fetch$ returns the rightmost column and the bottom row of submatrix (i, j) by retrieving the precomputed values addressed by the leftmost column and top row of the submatrix together with the relevant substrings. Finally, the absolute distance between the two input strings, $d_{m,n}$, is obtained by accumulating the distance differences along a path from $d_{0,0}$ to $d_{m,n}$. Function sum, employed during this stage, returns the sum of the components of the vector supplied as its argument.

The initialisation stage of this algorithm runs in linear time, as does the final summation of the differences to obtain the required distance value. The main calculation stage involves $2mn/p^2$ length-p vector lookups and assignments, and thus takes $O(mn/p)$ time. It was noted earlier that the submatrix precomputations require $O(p^2 c^{2p})$ time, where $c = s \mid C \mid$. If p is taken as $\lfloor (\log_c m)/2 \rfloor$, then the preprocessing time is asymptotically less than that required for the main computation. The overall distance calculation, including the preprocessing, therefore takes $O(mn/p)$ time. This bound is still valid when m and n are not exact multiples of p. This case is handled by appending dummy symbols not in the strings, α, say, to x and y to bring their lengths up to integral multiples of p. The edit costs involving α are then set as follows:

— initialise first column of the leftmost step-submatrices
for $i = 1$ **to** m/p
    $P_{i,0} = (w(x_{(i-1)p+1}, \epsilon), \ w(x_{(i-1)p+2}, \epsilon), \dots, \ w(x_{ip}, \epsilon))$
— initialise top row of the uppermost step-submatrices
for $j = 1$ **to** n/p
    $Q_{0,j} = (w(\epsilon, y_{(j-1)p+1}), \ w(\epsilon, y_{(j-1)p+2}), \dots, \ w(\epsilon, y_{jp}))$
— lookup final step vectors for the submatrices
for $i = 1$ **to** m/p
    for $j = 1$ **to** n/p
        $P_{i,j}, Q_{i,j} = fetch(P_{i,j-1}, \ Q_{i-1,j}, \ x((i-1)p+1, ip), \ y((j-1)p+1, jp))$
— sum the distance increments to obtain $d_{m,n}$
$d = 0$
for $i = 1$ **to** m/p
    $d = d + sum(P_{i,0})$
for $j = 1$ **to** n/p
    $d = d + sum(Q_{m/p,j})$

Figure 3.9: Masek-Paterson string-distance calculation

$$
\begin{aligned}
w(\alpha, \epsilon) &= 0 \\
w(\epsilon, \alpha) &= 0 \\
w(a, \alpha) &= w(a, \epsilon) \quad \forall a \in C \\
w(\alpha, b) &= w(\epsilon, b) \quad \forall b \in C
\end{aligned}
\tag{3.37}
$$

An actual minimal-cost edit sequence from x to y may be found in a manner similar to the backtracking technique of Wagner and Fischer. Obtaining the required distance values for this involves either recalculating the submatrices crossed by the optimal edit path, or storing the complete submatrices during the preprocessing stage. Adopting the latter approach allows the edit sequence to be determined from the completed P and Q matrices and the precomputed submatrices in linear time, and requires $O(n \log^2 n)$ space for submatrix storage. Note that the P and Q matrices each require $(1 + m/p) \times (1 + n/p) \times p$ storage locations, which is $O(n^2/\log n)$. The overall space complexity of this method is therefore also $O(n^2/\log n)$.

The algorithm may also be applied to the problem of determining $\mathrm{lcs}(x, y)$, by employing the cost function of the edit distance, given by (3.12). The relationship between $d(x, y)$ and $|\mathrm{lcs}(x, y)|$ given in (3.13) then permits the length of the lcs to be computed in $O(n^2/\log n)$ time. An actual lcs may then be recovered using a technique similar to that used to obtain an optimal edit sequence.

The computation of string distances using this method has been shown to be asymptotically faster than the quadratic method of Wagner and Fischer. Practical savings are, however, only obtained for very long strings. To illustrate this point, Masek and Paterson (1983) calculated that, for a binary alphabet and the edit-distance cost function, superior performance is achieved only for strings with lengths in excess of 262418.

3.2.5 Ukkonen

Ukkonen's (1985a) method of calculating the distance between two strings and ob-taining a minimal edit sequence is based on the dynamic-programming approach, but requires $O(md)$ time and space, where d is the distance between strings x and y and m is the smaller of the two string lengths. The method is thus attractive when the inter-string distance is small, i.e. when the two strings are similar. The basic idea of the algorithm is to find the cheapest-cost path in a directed graph in the $d_{i,j}$ matrix. Unnecessary $d_{i,j}$ calculations are avoided during this process.

In the following description, it is assumed, as before, that $m \leqslant n$. Recall that in the dynamic-programming method, $d_{i,j}$ is derived from a minimisation involving its previously computed neighbours using relation (3.7). On completion of the calculation of $d_{m,n}$, a minimal-cost edit sequence is obtained by tracing a path — composed of transitions that resulted in the minimum for the values of $d_{i,j}$ — through the matrix.

The dependencies between the elements of the d matrix may be represented by directed arcs — an arc exists from (i, j) to (i', j') only if $d_{i',j'}$ has been obtained from $d_{i,j}$. The resulting *dependency graph* is a subgraph of the larger graph composed of all the nodes (i, j) and the vertical, horizontal, and (top-left to bottom-right) diagonal arcs connecting adjacent nodes. These arcs correspond to deletions, insertions, and substitutions or matches, respectively. The costs of these operations may therefore be associated with the relevant arcs, and the value of $d_{i,j}$ is thus given by the sum of the costs on any path from $(0, 0)$ to (i, j). The arcs and their associated costs are as follows:

$$d_{i-1,j} \quad \rightarrow \quad d_{i,j} \quad : \quad w(x_i, \epsilon)$$
$$d_{i,j-1} \quad \rightarrow \quad d_{i,j} \quad : \quad w(\epsilon, y_j)$$
$$d_{i-1,j-1} \quad \rightarrow \quad d_{i,j} \quad : \quad w(x_i, y_j)$$

The terminal values on a path from (i, j) to (i', j') in the dependency graph are related as follows, where d is the sum of the costs of the arcs in the path.

$$d_{i',j'} = d_{i,j} + d \tag{3.38}$$

The distance between the two strings, $d_{m,n}$, is thus the minimum total cost for a path from $d_{0,0}$ to $d_{m,n}$ in the dependency graph.

Dijkstra's algorithm could be used to find the cheapest path (Aho, Hopcroft and Ullman, 1974) in $O(mn \log mn)$ time. However, the topology of the graph lends itself to more efficient solutions, such as the dynamic-programming method. It is further shown below how the number of entries of the d array that need be calculated may be reduced.

Only entries $d_{i,j}$ on some path from $(0,0)$ to (m,n) are relevant for the value of $d_{m,n}$. Note that this value is $O(n)$, since any such path has at most $m+n$ arcs. Consider the problem of ascertaining whether or not $d_{m,n}$ exceeds some threshold, h, say. From (3.7), it may be seen that the values of $d_{i,j}$ increase monotonically along any path in the dependency graph. Thus, if $d_{m,n} \leqslant h$, and if some $d_{i,j} > h$, then that $d_{i,j}$ cannot possibly be part of any path to (m,n).

Let w_{min} denote the minimum cost of all indels, that is:

$$w_{min} = \min\{w(a, \epsilon), w(\epsilon, a) \mid a \in C\} \tag{3.39}$$

for alphabet C. For non-zero, positive weights, $w_{min} > 0$. Also, let the diagonals of the distance matrix be numbered with integers, $p \in [-m, n]$, such that diagonal p consists of elements (i, j) for which $j - i = p$.

Consider any path from (i, j) to (i', j') in the dependency graph. Element (i, j) lies on diagonal $p = j - i$, and (i', j') on diagonal $p' = j' - i'$. If $p' - p \leqslant 0$, then the path contains at least $|p' - p|$ deletions (vertical arcs), and if $p' - p \geqslant 0$, at least $|p' - p|$ insertions (horizontal arcs). From (3.38), we then have the following:

$$d_{i',j'} \geqslant d_{i,j} + |(j' - i') - (j - i)| \cdot w_{min} \tag{3.40}$$

Thus, $d_{i,j} \geqslant |j - i| \cdot w_{min}$ for every (i,j) on a path from $(0,0)$ to (m,n). Also, since $d_{i,j} \leqslant d_{m,n}$ for every (i,j) on the path, we have the following:

$$|j - i| \leqslant d_{i,j}/w_{min} \leqslant d_{m,n}/w_{min} \tag{3.41}$$

It is thus sufficient to consider elements (i, j) in the diagonal band $-d_{m,n}/w_{min} \leqslant j - i \leqslant d_{m,n}/w_{min}$ in order to calculate $d_{m,n}$. This band may, in fact, be further narrowed as shown below.

Consider a path from $(0,0)$ to (m,n) in the dependency graph. This may be decomposed into the subsidiary paths from $(0,0)$ to (i,j) and from (i,j) to (m,n). From (3.40) we have the following:

$$d_{m,n} \geqslant d_{0,0} + |j - i| \cdot w_{min} + |(n - m) - (j - i)| \cdot w_{min}$$
$$\Rightarrow d_{m,n} \geqslant (|j - i| + |(n - m) - (j - i)|) \cdot w_{min} \tag{3.42}$$

There are two cases for the relative sizes of i and j to consider, namely when $j \leqslant i$ and when $j \geqslant i$. For the former case, (3.42) becomes:

$$d_{m,n} \geqslant (-(j - i) + n - m - (j - i))w_{min}$$
$$\Rightarrow d_{m,n}/w_{min} - (n - m) \geqslant -2(j - i) \tag{3.43}$$

Taken together with the fact that $j - i$ is an integer $\leqslant 0$, this gives the following:

$$- \left\lfloor \left(\frac{d_{m,n}}{w_{min}} - (n - m) \right) /2 \right\rfloor \leqslant j - i \leqslant 0 \qquad (3.44)$$

For the case where $j \geqslant i$, there are two further possibilities to consider, namely when $n - m \geqslant j - i$ and when $n - m \leqslant j - i$. For the former case, (3.42) becomes:

$$d_{m,n} \geqslant (j - i + n - m - (j - i))w_{min}$$
$$\Rightarrow d_{m,n}/w_{min} \geqslant n - m \qquad (3.45)$$

and for the latter case:

$$d_{m,n} \geqslant (j - i + j - i - (n - m))w_{min}$$
$$\Rightarrow d_{m,n}/w_{min} - (n - m) \geqslant 2(j - i) - 2(n - m) \qquad (3.46)$$

Taken together with the fact that, in this case, $j - i$ is an integer $\geqslant 0$, this gives the following:

$$\left\lfloor \left(\frac{d_{m,n}}{w_{min}} - (n - m) \right) /2 \right\rfloor + (n - m) \geqslant j - i \geqslant 0 \qquad (3.47)$$

Combining (3.44) and (3.47) gives the following bounds for $j - i$ at points (i, j) lying on some path from $(0, 0)$ to (m, n) in the dependency graph.

$$-q \leqslant j - i \leqslant n - m + q \qquad (3.48)$$
$$\text{where } q = \left\lfloor \left(\frac{d_{m,n}}{w_{min}} - (n - m) \right) /2 \right\rfloor$$

A consequence of (3.48) is that, when testing whether $d(x, y) \leqslant h$, the computation of $d_{i,j}$ values may be restricted to the diagonal band between the diagonals $-q$ and $n - m + q$, where $q = \lfloor (h/w_{min} - (n - m)) /2 \rfloor$.

An algorithm to perform this threshold test is given in Figure 3.10. The procedure returns a negative value if the test fails, and returns the value of $d_{m,n}$ if this is less than or equal to the threshold value. The test fails in the trivial case given by (3.45), as the distance must at least be equal to the difference in length of the strings times the minimum indel cost. For the non-trivial case, $d_{i,j}$ values are evaluated in the diagonal strip defined by (3.48). On completion of these computations, the final value of $d_{m,n}$ is compared with the threshold value.

For each of the $m + 1$ rows, the number of matrix elements evaluated is at most $n - m + 2q + 1$, which is $O(h)$, as shown below.

$$q = \lfloor (h/w_{min} - (n - m)) /2 \rfloor$$
$$\Rightarrow 2q \leqslant h/w_{min} - (n - m)$$
$$\Rightarrow n - m + 2q + 1 \leqslant 1 + h/w_{min}$$
$$= O(h) \qquad (3.49)$$

$distance\_test(h)$
  if $h/w_{min} < n - m$
    — trivial case
    return(-1)
  else
    — initialise
    $q = \lfloor (h/w_{min} - (n - m))/2 \rfloor$
    $d_{0,0} = 0$
    for $j = 1$ **to** $\min\{n, n - m + q\}$
      $d_{0,j} = d_{0,j-1} + w(\epsilon, y_j)$
    — calculate $d_{m,n}$
    for $i = 1$ **to** m
      for $j = \max\{0, i - q\}$ **to** $\min\{n, i + n - m + q\}$
        if $j = 0$
          $d_{i,0} = d_{i-1,0} + w(x_i, \epsilon)$
        else
          $d_{i,j} = \min\{d_{i-1,j} + w(x_i, \epsilon),\ d_{i,j-1} + w(\epsilon, y_j),\ d_{i-1,j-1} + w(x_i, y_j)\}$
    if $d_{m,n} \leqslant h$
      return$(d_{m,n})$
    else
      return(-1)

Figure 3.10: Ukkonen string-distance threshold test

$h = (n - m + 1)w_{min}$
while $(d = distance\_test(h)) < 0$
  $h = 2h$

Figure 3.11: Ukkonen string-distance calculation

The threshold test therefore executes in $O(hm)$ time, and requires $O(hm)$ space if only the $d_{i,j}$ values in the diagonal band are stored. Note that if only the value of the string distance is required, then the space requirement could be reduced to $O(h)$ locations, as only the previous row is required in the computation of the current one (cf. Hirschberg's linear-space algorithm).

In order to determine the actual distance between the two strings, the threshold-test procedure may be called with successively increasing values of h until the test succeeds, as shown in Figure 3.11. The threshold is initially set to the minimum possible value of the distance plus w_{min}, and is successively doubled as long as the threshold test fails. On completion, the distance between the two strings is given by d.

If we denote the initial value of h by h_0, then the next value, h_1, equals $2h_0$, and the one after that, h_2, equals $2^2 h_0$, and so on. Thus, the rth value, h_r, is equal to $2^r h_0$. If $r + 1$ calls to $distance\_test$ are required to determine $d(x, y)$, then the total time required is $O(m \sum_{k=0}^{r} h_k)$, i.e. $O(m(2h_r - h_0))$ which is $O(mh_r)$. Since $d > h_r/2$, the overall time complexity is thus $O(md)$. An actual editing sequence from x to y may be obtained from the computed $d_{i,j}$ values on completion as in the Wagner-Fischer method.

Ukkonen also considered the special case when all the editing-operation costs are equal (i.e. the calculation of the Levenshtein distance), for which the storage requirements may be reduced and a more efficient, $O(md)$-time, direct method of computing $d(x, y)$ may be employed.

3.2.6 Heaviest Common Subsequence

Jacobson and Vo's (1992) heaviest common subsequence (hcs) algorithm, derived from the Robinson-Schensted longest increasing subsequence (lis) algorithm (Schensted, 1961), is described below. The algorithms presented here are in a slightly modified form so that the construction of the directed graphs used in the procedures is correct.

Firstly, the weight of a subsequence, s, common to strings x and y may be defined thus:

$$W(s) = \sum_{p=1}^{|s|} f(i_p, j_p, s_p) \tag{3.50}$$

where (i_p, j_p) is a matched pair for x and y, i.e. $x_{i_p} = y_{j_p} = s_p$, and f is a weight function.

The dynamic-programming method of computing an lcs may be adapted to evaluate an hcs. Let $W(\text{hcs}(x(1, i), y(1, j)))$ be denoted by $W_{i,j}$. The recurrence relation for $W_{i,j}$ is then given by:

$$W_{i,j} = \max\{W_{i-1,j}, W_{i,j-1}, W_{i-1,j-1} + f_{i,j}\} \qquad (3.51)$$

$$f_{i,j} = \begin{cases} 0 & \text{if } x_i \neq y_j \\ f(i,j,x_i) & \text{if } x_i = y_j \end{cases}$$

The above follows from the method of calculating the l matrix (see section 3.2.2). When at position (i,j), i.e. when considering prefixes $x(1,i)$ and $y(1,j)$, if $x_i = y_j$, then a new common subsequence may be obtained by appending this symbol to the current common subsequence of $x(1,i-1)$ and $y(1,j-1)$. The weight of this new subsequence is obtained by adding the weight of this match to that of the previous subsequence. Otherwise, position (i,j) does not alter the previous result. The weight for position (i,j) is thus given by the heaviest of the previous neighbouring positions and, if applicable, the newly derived weight.

The Robinson-Schensted algorithm to compute an lis of string y is given in Figure 3.12. L is an ordered list of pairs (a,k), where a is a string symbol and k is its position in the string. The following operations may each be performed in $O(\log n)$ time when L is implemented using a balanced tree structure.

$insert(L, a)$	— insert object a into list L
$delete(L, a)$	— delete object a from list L
$next(L, a)$	— return the least object in L strictly greater than a
$prev(L, a)$	— return the greatest object in L strictly less than a
$max(L)$	— return the greatest object in L
$min(L)$	— return the least object in L

When not defined, procedures $next$, $prev$, max and min all return a null value. The operations $next(L, \text{null})$ and $prev(L, \text{null})$ are taken to be equivalent to $min(L)$ and $max(L)$, respectively.

For each symbol in y, y_i, a is the symbol in L to which y_i may be appended whilst preserving the strictly increasing nature of the list. The element after a in L is then replaced by y_i. A directed graph of string symbols is created using array *node*. The elements of *node* are pointers to nodes, created by procedure *newnode*, containing a symbol, its position in the string, and the address of a previous node. On completion, an lis of y may be recovered by tracing back through the graph, starting from the maximal component of L.

In order to calculate a heaviest increasing subsequence (his), it is necessary to keep track of the cumulative weights of the his's of the successively longer string prefixes as the computation progresses. The components of list L may thus be made triples (a,u,k), where a is a symbol of the input string, u is the total weight of the his ending with a, and k is the position of a in the string. L remains strictly monotonic in all three elements of its component triples. The ordering of L may

---

— initialise list L
$L = $ null
— calculate lis
for $i = 1$ to n
$\quad (a, k) = prev(L, (y_i, 0))$
$\quad (b, l) = next(L, (a, k))$
$\quad$ if $b \neq$ null
$\quad\quad delete(L, (b, l))$
$\quad insert(L, (y_i, i))$
$\quad node_i = newnode((y_i, i), node_k)$

Figure 3.12: Robinson-Schensted lis calculation

---

therefore be maintained with reference to the lexicographic ordering of the first element of each triple.

The algorithm to compute an his, based on the lis algorithm, is given in Figure 3.13. Again, a gives the largest symbol in L less than y_i, so that the latter may be appended to any increasing subsequence ending with a to form a new increasing subsequence. If there is no such a, then u is taken to be 0. The **while** loop ensures that the strict monotonicity of the second element of the component triples of L is maintained. The new triple is then inserted into L if this is consistent with the preservation of the strict increase of the first element of the triples. Array $node$ is employed to construct a linked structure for the recovery of an actual his on completion of the process.

Consider the state of list L at the end of each iteration, denoted by L_i. For each component, (a, u, k) of L_i, an increasing subsequence of prefix $y(1, i)$ ending in a may be recovered by tracing back from a through the directed graph. It will be shown below that for every increasing subsequence, $s(1, k)$, of prefix $y(1, i)$, there exists an element of L_i, $b \leqslant s_k$, terminating an increasing subsequence in the graph at least as heavy as $s(1, k)$. The maximal symbol of L_i, together with the graph, thus provides an his of prefix $y(1, i)$. Consequently, the maximal element of L on completion of the process defines an his for the complete string y.

The above proposition is clearly true for $i = 1$. We may thus assume it to be true for iteration $i - 1$ and analyse the situation for iteration i. Let $s(1, k)$ be an increasing subsequence of prefix $y(1, i)$. From the foregoing, if $s_k = y_i$, then there is an element $b \leqslant s_{k-1}$ in L_{i-1} defining an increasing subsequence at least as heavy as $s(1, k - 1)$. Now, element b cannot be deleted from the list on this iteration, as $b < y_i$. At the end of the ith iteration, y_i will either have been inserted into the list or will have already been present. Recalling that the cumulative weights in L

— initialise list L
$L = $ null
— calculate his
for $i = 1$ **to** n
   $(a, u, k) = prev(L, (y_i, 0, 0))$
   $(b, v, l) = next(L, (a, u, k))$
   while $((b, v, l) \neq$ null$)$ **and** $(u + f(i, y_i) \geqslant v)$
      $delete(L, (b, v, l))$
      $(b, v, l) = next(L, (b, v, l))$
   if $((b, v, l) = $ null$)$ **or** $(y_i < b)$
      $insert(L, (y_i, u + f(i, y_i), i))$
      $node_i = newnode((y_i, u + f(i, y_i), i), node_k)$

Note that the **and** in the **while** loop is a 'conditional and,' which only evaluates
its right-hand operand if its left-hand one evaluates to true.

Figure 3.13: Jacobson-Vo his calculation

---

are strictly increasing, we may see that the increasing subsequence defined by y_i
satisfies the proposition.

Turning our attention to the situation where $s_k \neq y_i$, there are two cases to
consider, namely when $s_k < y_i$ and when $s_k > y_i$. The proposition holds for the
former case since the portion of the list preceding y_i is not altered by the ith iteration.
Thus only the case where $s_k > y_i$ remains to consider. Sequence $s(1, k)$ must then
also be an increasing subsequence of $y(1, i - 1)$. There will thus exist an increasing
subsequence defined by some b in L_{i-1} at least as heavy as $s(1, k)$. If b is extant
in L_i, then clearly the proposition holds. Otherwise, b must have been eliminated
from the L during the ith iteration, for which case the weight condition of the **while**
loop ensures that the sequence defined by y_i is at least as heavy as that previously
defined by b. The above proposition has thus been shown to be valid under all
circumstances, and the algorithm therefore correctly calculates an his of the input
string.

The main loop of the algorithm is iterated a total of n times, and each of its
component operations takes at most $O(\log n)$ time. Note that the total number of
iterations of the inner **while** loop is at most n, since each of the n elements of y may
be inserted into, and deleted from, list L once at most. The temporal complexity of
the his algorithm is therefore $O(n \log n)$.

The operation of the method may be illustrated by way of an example. The
(a, u) components of the triples of list L for each step i are shown below for the

case of y = zeitgeist. Note that the lis of this string is egist. However, the weights have been chosen to be equal to 1 for the first occurrence of a symbol in the string, and equal to 2 for the second occurrence. Under these conditions, increasing subsequence eist using the second e and i is as heavy as lis egist. On completion, the maximal element of L, (t,7), is used to recover the path e ← i ← s ← t from the directed graph.

i	1	2	3	4	5	6	7	8	9
y_i	z	e	i	t	g	e	i	s	t
$f(i, y_i)$	1	1	1	1	1	2	2	1	2
L_i	(z,1)	(e,1)	(e,1)	(e,1)	(e,1)	(e,2)	(e,2)	(e,2)	(e,2)
			(i,2)	(i,2)	(g,2)	(t,3)	(i,4)	(i,4)	(i,4)
				(t,3)	(t,3)			(s,5)	(s,5)
									(t,7)

Directed graph

$$\text{null} \longleftarrow (\text{z},1)$$

$$\text{null} \longleftarrow (\text{e},1) \longleftarrow (\text{i},2) \longleftarrow (\text{t},3)$$
$$\uparrow$$
$$(\text{g},2)$$

$$\text{null} \longleftarrow (\text{e},2) \longleftarrow (\text{i},4) \longleftarrow (\text{s},5) \longleftarrow (\text{t},7)$$

If the matches (i, j) between strings x and y are listed in increasing order of i, and decreasing order of j for equal i values, then every common subsequence of x and y maps to an increasing subsequence of the sequence of j values. Conversely, a common subsequence may be derived from an increasing subsequence of j values. The descending order of j for constant i prevents multiple symbols of y, matching a single symbol of x, from being included in a subsequence. The example given below is for the strings preterit and zeitgeist. The underlined match-indices show the lis of the j sequence, corresponding to the lcs of the two strings.

i	1 2 3 4 5 6 7 8		
x_i	p r e t e r i t		
	- - - - -	Matches	
		i	3 3 4 4 5 5 7 7 8 8
j	1 2 3 4 5 6 7 8 9	j	6 2 9 4 6 2 7 3 9 4
y_j	z e i t g e i s t		- - - - -
	- - - - -		

— construct ordered lists of positions of symbols in y
for $i = 1$ **to** n
 $insert(position_{y_i}, i)$
— initialise list L
$L = $ null
— calculate hcs
for $i = 1$ **to** m
 $j = max(position_{x_i})$
 while $j \neq$ null
  $(a, u) = prev(L, (j, 0))$
  $(b, v) = next(L, (a, u))$
  while $((b, v) \neq$ null$)$ **and** $(u + f(i, j, x_i) \geq v)$
   $delete(L, (b, v))$
   $(b, v) = next(L, (b, v))$
  if $((b, v) = $ null$)$ **or** $(j < b)$
   $insert(L, (j, u + f(i, j, x_i)))$
  $j = prev(position_{x_i}, j)$

Note that the **and** in the **while** loop is a 'conditional and'

Figure 3.14: Jacobson-Vo hcs calculation

In the above ordering of the matches, corresponding weights, $f(i, j, x_i)$, may be associated with the j values. An hcs of the strings may thus be computed by calculating an his of this sequence of j values. The method to do this, given in Figure 3.14, is a generalisation of the Hunt-Szymanski lcs algorithm. Note that only the (a, u) components of the triples of list L are shown here for clarity.

Array *position* contains ordered lists of the positions of the symbols occurring in y. This is thus similar to the *matchlist* of the Hunt-Szymanski algorithm. The latter was in descending order, whereas the lists of *position* are in ascending order. However, the correct ordering of the matches is achieved by stepping backwards through the j positions in $position_{x_i}$ for each i. The his algorithm is applied to the resulting sequence of j values. The corresponding hcs(x, y) may then be recovered on completion of the process from the directed graph, the construction of which has also been omitted from the algorithm for clarity.

The total length of the sequence of j values is equal to the number of matches, r. Taking the construction of the position lists into account, the overall running time of the procedure is $O((r + n) \log n)$.

The following example serves to illustrate the computation of an hcs. As mentioned earlier in the overview, a minimal-distance weight function may be applied to give preference in the selection of common subsequences to closely aligned matches. Consider the pair of strings warfare and forewarn. The longest common subsequences of this pair are shown below, together with their weights for the minimal-distance weight function $8 - |i - j|$, which favours closely aligned matches. The total lcs weights are given in parentheses.

```
i          1 2 3 4 5 6 7
xᵢ         w a r f a r e

yⱼ         f o r e w a r n
j          1 2 3 4 5 6 7 8
```

x_i	w a r		w a r		w a r	
i	1 2 3		1 2 6		1 5 6	
j	5 6 7		5 6 7		5 6 7	
$8 - \|i - j\|$	4 4 4	(12)	4 4 7	(15)	4 7 7	(18)

x_i	r a r		f a r		f r e	
i	3 5 6		4 5 6		4 6 7	
j	3 6 7		1 6 7		1 3 4	
$8 - \|i - j\|$	8 7 7	(22)	5 7 7	(19)	5 5 5	(15)

It may thus be seen that rar is the heaviest lcs. The state of list L after each stage, i, in the computation of hcs(warfare, forewarn) for the above weight function is shown below, together with the resulting directed graph. Once again, for simplicity, only the (a, u) components of the list triples are given.

i	1	2	3	4	5	6	7
x_i	w	a	r	f	a	r	e
L_i	(5,4)	(5,4)	(3,8)	(1,5)	(1,5)	(1,5)	(1,5)
		(6,8)	(7,12)	(3,8)	(3,8)	(3,10)	(3,10)
			(7,12)	(6,15)	(6,15)	(4,15)
					(7,22)	(7,22)

Directed graph

null $\longleftarrow$ (5,4) $\longleftarrow$ (6,8) $\longleftarrow$ (7,12)

null $\longleftarrow$ (3,8) $\longleftarrow$ (6,15) $\longleftarrow$ (7,22)

null $\longleftarrow$ (1,5) $\longleftarrow$ (3,10) $\longleftarrow$ (4,15)

On completion, the maximal element in L, namely (7,22), is used to retrieve path $3 \leftarrow 6 \leftarrow 7$ from the directed graph of j index values, corresponding to the subsequence rar.

A special case of the hcs problem is when the weights are position-independent, i.e. when f is a function only of the symbols. The hcs algorithm may be adapted to take advantage of this special case as discussed below.

When the weight function does not depend on position, the weights associated with the positions j in list $position_{x_i}$ are all equal. Consider the case of a given j being inserted into list L after a. Recall that the j values from the position list are processed in descending order. If the next value of j tried is also greater than a, then the old j will be deleted from L and the new one inserted in its place, since they both have the same weight. This inefficiency may be avoided by going directly to the least j in $position_{x_i}$ greater than a. So, j may be assigned the value of $next(position_{x_i}, a)$ after the assignments of (a, u) and (b, v).

If j is already in list L, then b is assigned the value of j. If the entry in L immediately preceding j is the same as that when j was inserted, then the algorithm will simply delete j from L and then reinsert it at the same point. Thus, when an element j is inserted into L, it may then be deleted from $position_{x_i}$ in order to avoid any unnecessary duplication of effort. It must, however, be reinstated in its position list should it be removed from L or its predecessor in L be changed.

Finally, the condition for inserting j into L is not required when the weights are position-independent. The value of b cannot be less than j, since a is the greatest value in L less than j. Thus, $b \geqslant j$. For the case where $b > j$, j may be inserted into L between a and b without upsetting the list's monotonicity. If $b = j$, then j may safely replace b, since their weights are also the same. This then shows that j may be inserted unconditionally into L.

The hcs algorithm incorporating the above enhancements for the special case of position-independent weights is given in Figure 3.15, which, for clarity, again omits the construction of the directed graph and only depicts the (a, u) pairs of the component triples of list L. When the weights for all the symbols in the alphabet are equal, this reduces to the Apostolico-Guerra (1987) adaptation of the Hunt-Szymanski lcs algorithm.

— construct ordered lists of positions of symbols in y
for $i = 1$ **to** n
   $insert(position_{y_i}, i)$
— initialise list L
$L = $ null
— calculate hcs
for $i = 1$ **to** m
   $j = max(position_{x_i})$
   while $j \neq$ null
      $(a, u) = prev(L, (j, 0))$
      $(b, v) = next(L, (a, u))$
      $j = next(position_{x_i}, a)$
      while $((b, v) \neq$ null$)$ **and** $(u + f(x_i) \geqslant v)$
         $delete(L, (b, v))$
         $(b, v) = next(L, (b, v))$
         $insert(position_{y_b}, b)$
      $insert(position_{y_b}, b)$
      $insert(L, (j, u + f(x_i)))$
      $delete(position_{x_i}, j)$
      $j = prev(position_{x_i}, j)$

Note that the **and** in the **while** loop is a 'conditional and'

Figure 3.15: Jacobson-Vo hcs calculation for position-independent weights

3.3   Further Reading

A comprehensive discussion of a host of application milieux, from molecular biology to speech processing, employing string distance functions is given by Sankoff and Kruskall (1983). A recent review of the string-distance and longest common subsequence problems may be found in Aho (1990), and an overview of complexity results for common-subsequence problems is presented by Hirschberg (1983).

4

Suffix Trees

Grau, teurer Freund, ist alle Theorie und grün des Lebens goldner Baum.
(All theory, dear friend, is grey, but the golden tree of actual life springs ever green.)

— Johann Wolfgang von Goethe (1749–1832).

4.1 Overview

A *suffix tree* (McCreight, 1976) is a very useful data structure that embodies a compact index to all the distinct, non-empty substrings of a given string (i.e. the string's *vocabulary*). As we shall see, recourse shall be made to this data structure in several of the algorithms discussed in the forthcoming chapters dealing with approximate string matching and searching for repetitions within strings.

The suffix tree is one particular manifestation of a certain type of substring index. An early, implicit form is to be found in Morrison's (1968) *Patricia tree* (Practical Algorithm To Retrieve Information Coded In Alphanumeric). But it was Weiner (1973) who initially proposed the explicit index. The index has also been the focus of some attention in various other forms, such as the *position tree* (Aho, Hopcroft and Ullman, 1974) and the *complete inverted file* (Blumer et al., 1984a, 1984b, 1985, 1987).

Various approaches to the problem of building the substring index in linear time have been developed, such as the techniques of Pratt (1973) and Slisenko (1983). Chen and Seiferas (1985) also put forward a clean construction of Weiner's index, and McCreight's suffix-tree construction algorithm yields a structure functionally equivalent to Weiner's, but one that is more space efficient. Majster and Reiser's

(1980) on-line construction allows the index to be built as the input string is read in a symbol at a time from left to right, but does so in greater than linear time. Ukkonen (1992b, 1993) has, however, recently developed a linear-time, on-line, suffix-tree construction algorithm.

In contrast to these linear-time techniques, the straightforward, brute-force method of suffix-tree construction requires quadratic time in the worst case. Its time complexity has, however, been shown to be $O(n \log n)$ in the expected case (Apostolico and Szpankowski, 1992).

Before specific suffix-tree construction strategies are examined, a general description of the data structure itself shall firstly be given, starting off with a discussion of the related *suffix trie*.

4.1.1   Suffix Tries

A *trie* is a type of digital search tree (Knuth, 1973), and thus represents a set of pattern strings, or keys, over a finite alphabet. The term was coined by Fredkin (1959, 1960) from 'information re*trie*val' for a table-based implementation, and the structure was also independently proposed, in a form employing linked lists, by de la Briandais (1959).

For a set of strings over a finite alphabet C, each edge of the trie for the set represents a symbol from C, and sibling edges must represent distinct symbols. The maximum degree of any node in the trie is thus equal to $|C|$. As an example, the trie for the keywords EDGE, END, ENDING, WARP, and WASP is shown in Figure 4.1. The shaded nodes correspond to complete keywords, spelt out by the sequence of symbols represented by the edges comprising the path from the root to the node in question.

Note in passing that the Aho-Corasick pattern-matching automaton employed in multiple-string searching (as discussed in Chapter 2) may be represented by the trie of the pattern strings. The nodes of the trie correspond to the states of the automaton, and the edges to the forward state-transitions. In particular, the root represents the initial state of the automaton, and the shaded nodes the accepting states. In order to realise the state machine, a failure function is additionally required to control the reverse state-transitions. In the event of an input symbol being encountered for which there corresponds no edge leaving the current node in the trie, it is this function that dictates the state (corresponding to a node closer to the root than the current one) next entered by the automaton.

Having given an informal description of the trie structure, we now turn our attention to the specific case of the suffix trie, which is also sometimes referred to as a position tree or a non-compact suffix tree. This is a trie whose set of keywords comprises the suffixes of a single string, y, say. Furthermore, it is required that each suffix is represented by a distinct terminal node, or leaf, of the trie. If any suffix of string y happens to be a proper prefix of another, then we could be in for trouble in

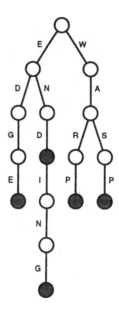

Figure 4.1: Trie for the keywords EDGE, END, ENDING, WARP, WASP

this respect. (Compare this with the case shown in Figure 4.1, where keyword END is a prefix of keyword ENDING.) In order to avoid such a situation arising, it may be assumed that the terminal symbol of y is unique within the string, in which case no suffix of y may be a prefix of any other. If y does not naturally satisfy this criterion, then a special end marker symbol, $, say, not belonging to the alphabet in question, may be appended to y. It shall henceforth be assumed that the length of y, $|y| = n$, includes this end marker if necessary.

An example suffix trie, for the string $y =$ ABCABC$, is depicted in Figure 4.2. Each leaf of the trie has been labelled with an integer value, $1 \leqslant i \leqslant n$, corresponding to the suffix, $y(i, n)$, that it represents. Again, the actual string represented by a leaf may be obtained by concatenating the symbols associated with the edges on the path in the trie from the root to the particular leaf.

Note that there exists a one-to-one correspondence between the nodes of a string's suffix trie and its distinct substrings, with the root corresponding to the empty substring, ϵ. In the worst case, the total number of nodes, and hence edges, required for a suffix trie may be quadratic in n. This situation can arise, for instance, when the paths representing the suffixes are all disjoint, as is the case for strings ABC, ABCD, ABCDE, and so on, for example. In such cases, the total number of edges is given

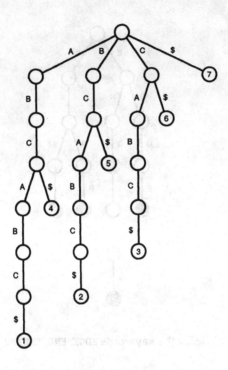

Figure 4.2: Suffix trie for string ABCABC$

by the sum of the lengths of all the suffixes, i.e. $\sum_{i=1}^{n} |y(i,n)| = (n^2 + n)/2$. The length of this type of string is obviously bounded by the cardinality of the alphabet in use. But even for restricted alphabets there exist families of strings having quadratic numbers of distinct substrings, and hence having quadratic numbers of nodes, and edges, in their respective suffix tries. (Consider, for example, strings of the form $A^m B^m \$$, which are of length $2m + 1$ and each have $m^2 + 4m + 2$ distinct substrings.) As we shall see below, however, a modification of the trie results in an improvement to a linear bound on the number of edges necessary.

4.1.2 From Suffix Trie to Suffix Tree

The number of edges necessary in a suffix trie may be reduced by collapsing paths containing unary nodes, i.e. those nodes having only a single child node. This process yields the structure known as the suffix tree, which is sometimes referred to more specifically as the compact suffix-tree. Figure 4.3 shows the result of

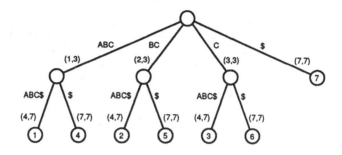

Figure 4.3: Suffix tree for string ABCABC$

converting the suffix trie of Figure 4.2 in this manner. Note that 'Patricia tree' is the general term referring to a compact trie, i.e. one possessing no unary nodes.

Again, the leaves have been labelled with the start positions in y of the suffixes that they represent. This time, the suffixes may be obtained by concatenating the *substrings* associated with the edges of the paths from root to leaf. In practice, these substrings need not be stored explicitly; it suffices to represent a substring associated with an edge by an ordered pair of integers indexing its start and end positions in the original string, as is additionally shown in the figure.

The description of the suffix-tree data structure may be formalised as follows. First of all, the suffix tree for string y shall be denoted by Y. As outlined earlier, the length of y is taken to be n, and it is assumed that symbol y_n occurs nowhere else in the string.

Y is a rooted, digital search tree constructed from the suffixes of y, $y(i, n)$ for $1 \leqslant i \leqslant n$, and is unique up to isomorphism of graphs. It has exactly n leaves, each uniquely defining a position i within y, corresponding to a distinct suffix $y(i, n)$.

Associated with each edge of Y is a non-empty substring of y, $y(k, l)$, where $k \leqslant l$. The substring corresponding to an edge may succinctly be represented by the appropriate ordered pair of indices, (k, l), to a common, randomly-accessible copy of string y.

Internal nodes of the tree are of degree $\geqslant 2$ (with the exception of the root of a trivial suffix-tree), and represent substrings of y which are longest common prefixes of the string's suffixes. If $y(i, i + p)$ is the longest common prefix of two suffixes $y(i, n)$ and $y(j, n)$, i.e. $y(i, i + p) = y(j, j + p)$ and $y_{i+p+1} \neq y_{j+p+1}$, then substring $y(i, i + p)$ defines an internal node of the tree.

The string represented by any node in Y may be obtained by concatenating those associated with the edges on the unique path from the root to the particular node in question — a method similar to that noted earlier for the suffix trie.

Given two distinct nodes in Y, if one is an ancestor of the other, then the string represented by the ancestor is a prefix of that represented by the descendant. Further, the *least common ancestor* (LCA) of a set of nodes (i.e. the node which is an ancestor of each member of the set and which is furthest from the root) represents the longest common prefix of the strings represented by the members of the given set of nodes. Thus, if two nodes represent strings a and b, where $b = ac$, for some non-empty string c, then they are connected by an edge only if a is the longest prefix of b represented by a node in the tree. Note also that the strings associated with sibling edges must therefore start with different symbols.

The total number of nodes in the suffix tree is constrained due to two facts: there are exactly n leaves; and the degree of any internal node is at least 2. The maximum number of leaf parents, p, say, is thus $\lceil n/2 \rceil$, and the maximum number of leaf grandparents $\lceil p/2 \rceil$, and so on back up to the root. There are therefore at most $n - 1$ internal nodes in the tree. That the maximum number of nodes, and hence edges, is linear in n, in conjunction with the fact that each edge label requires constant storage space — its substring being represented by a pair of indices (or pointers) — results in the overall space requirement for Y also being linear in the length of y.

4.2 Algorithms in Detail

4.2.1 Brute Force

An intuitive method of constructing the suffix tree, Y, for a given string, y, is to start with a tree consisting of only a single node and successively to add to it paths corresponding to the suffixes of y. Starting with the longest and progressing to the shortest, i.e. suffixes $y(i, n)$ in order $i = 1, \ldots, n$, we thus have the following procedure.

$$\text{for } i = 1 \text{ to } n$$
$$Y_i = insert(Y_{i-1}, y(i, n))$$

In the above, Y_i represents the suffix tree at stage i of its creation, and the *insert* operation inserts a path corresponding to suffix $y(i, n)$ into tree Y_{i-1}.

Before we embark upon a more detailed description of this process, we must first equip ourselves with some further definitions. Employing McCreight's terminology for this purpose, we have the following:

- *locus* of a string — the node representing the string in the suffix tree

- *extension* of string u — any string having u as a prefix

- *extended locus* of string u — the locus of the shortest extension of u that is represented in the suffix tree

- *contracted locus* of string u — the locus of the longest prefix of u that is represented in the suffix tree

- $head_i$ — the longest prefix of $y(i,n)$ which is also a prefix of $y(j,n)$ for some $j < i$. That is, $head_i$ is the longest prefix of $y(i,n)$ whose extended locus exists within Y_{i-1}.

- $tail_i$ — the string such that $y(i,n) = head_i tail_i$. The requirement for the $ terminator ensures that $tail_i$ is non-empty.

Returning now to the construction process, consider stage i, in which suffix $y(i,n)$ is to be inserted into the tree. In order to do this, the extended locus of $head_i$ in Y_{i-1} is first located. If the string represented by this node is not equal to $head_i$, then the node's incoming edge is broken and a new internal node corresponding to $head_i$ inserted there. Finally, a new edge representing $tail_i$ is added from the locus of $head_i$ to a new leaf representing suffix $y(i,n)$.

The above process is illustrated in Figure 4.4, which shows the various stages involved in the construction of the suffix tree for the string ABAB$. For clarity, the edges have been labelled with their respective explicit substrings instead of the ordered pairs of string indices. The construction of Y_4, for example, proceeds as follows. The new suffix, $y(4,5)$, is B$; $head_4$ is B — a prefix of previous suffix BAB$; and $tail_4$ is thus $. The edge connecting the root to the locus of BAB$, i.e. the extended locus of B, in Y_3 is split and a new node for B inserted. Lastly, an edge representing $ is added from this new node to a new leaf representing suffix B$.

Once the extended locus of $head_i$ in Y_{i-1} has been found, the necessary modification of the tree at step i may be performed in constant time. It is thus finding the extended locus that is critical to the overall performance of the algorithm. A straightforward, brute-force search approach involves starting from the root and thence tracing the edges on the path that represents the extended locus, involving an effort proportional to $|head_i|$. This can, in the worst case, lead to an overall quadratic-time construction. Consider, for example, strings like AAAAAAAA$. For such strings, the length of $head_i$ is equal to $n - i$ for $1 < i < n$. The search at each stage i, other than the first and last, of the construction thus involves $n - i$ symbol comparisons — giving a total over all stages of $\Theta(n^2)$.

As noted earlier, Apostolico and Szpankowski (1992) have shown that in the average case, the brute-force construction requires $O(n \log n)$ time. This follows from the result that the maximum length, over all pairs of suffixes of a string, of the longest common prefix of two suffixes is $O(\log n)$ on average. The analysis whence this result was derived was based on a Bernoulli probabilistic model, in which the symbols of a string are independent and randomly selected from an alphabet according to a given probability distribution.

We shall now see below how the suffix-tree data structure may be augmented with certain auxiliary 'short-cut' links, permitting the extended-locus search to be

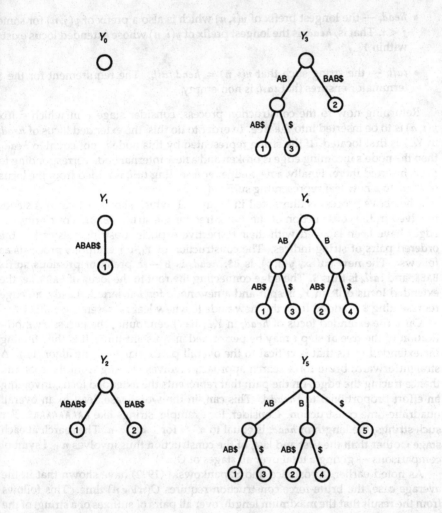

Figure 4.4: Stages in the construction of the suffix tree for string ABAB$

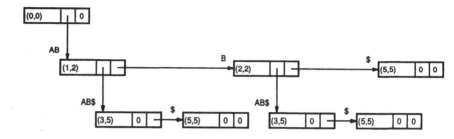

Figure 4.5: Implementation of suffix tree for string ABAB$

performed in constant time (when averaged over all the stages). This then results in the overall time required to build the tree being linear in n.

4.2.2 McCreight

The operation of the short-cut search in McCreight's construction algorithm relies on the relationship that exists between successive values of $head_i$. This shall be examined presently. But first we consider how the suffix-tree structure might actually be implemented.

A suffix tree may be represented by a set of node structures, each comprising a pair of substring indices corresponding to its incoming edge label, together with two pointers — one pointing to the node's first child, the other to its next sibling. This 'left-child, right-sibling' arrangement for the example tree for ABAB$ is illustrated in Figure 4.5, where null pointers are represented by 0. Although not actually stored, the substring for each edge has also been included in the figure for convenience.

Figure 4.6 depicts the same implementation, but this time augmented with the auxiliary *suffix links* that facilitate the faster extended-locus search. Although efficient in space, this tree implementation is slow to search. As a compromise between space requirement and amenability to be searched rapidly, McCreight suggests an implementation in which the edges of the tree are encoded as entries in a hash table (using Lampson's hashing algorithm (see exercise 6.4.13 of Knuth, 1973)). When the alphabet is small enough, the tree may alternatively be implemented by directly indexing the child pointers.

The use of the suffix links in the extended-locus search relies on the following relationship between $head_{i-1}$ and $head_i$. If $head_{i-1} = az$, for some symbol a and some (possibly empty) string z, then z is a prefix of $head_i$. This may be proved as follows. If $head_{i-1} = az$, then $\exists j < i$ such that az is a prefix of both $y(i-1, n)$

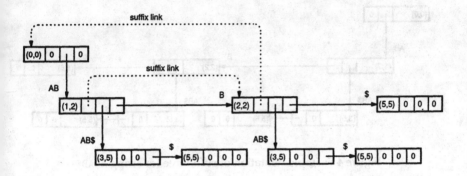

Figure 4.6: Implementation of suffix tree for string ABAB$ showing the suffix links

and $y(j-1,n)$. String z is then a prefix common to $y(i,n)$ and $y(j,n)$, and is, by definition, therefore a prefix of $head_i$.

A suffix link is added in the tree from each internal node, which is the locus of az (for some symbol a and string z), to the locus of z. Note that the latter is never within the subtree rooted at the former, since any descendant of the locus of string az must represent an extension of this string. These auxiliary links allow a short-cut search to be performed at stage i for the extended locus of $head_i$ starting from the locus of $head_{i-1}$, which will have been found at the previous stage. The suffix links shown in the figure emanate from the tree's internal nodes (with the exception of the root), i.e. the loci of AB and B.

We are now in a position to describe the algorithm itself. Two important properties of this are: (1) in Y_i, only the locus of $head_i$ can fail to have a valid suffix link, and that (2) in step i, the contracted locus of $head_i$ in Y_{i-1} (i.e. the locus of the longest prefix of $head_i$ in Y_{i-1}) is visited. At the outset, when $i = 1$, these two requirements obviously hold. At stage i of the algorithm, the following three substeps are carried out.

I three strings u, v and w are found such that:

   (a) $head_{i-1} = uvw$

   (b) if the contracted locus of $head_{i-1}$ in Y_{i-2} is not the root, then it is the locus of uv. Otherwise, $v = \epsilon$

   (c) $|u| \leqslant 1$, $u = \epsilon$ iff $head_{i-1} = \epsilon$

Since $head_{i-1} = uvw$, then, as shown earlier, vw is a prefix of $head_i$ (by (c), u is at most a single symbol). Thus, $head_i$ is given by vwz, for some (possibly empty) string z. A test on the emptiness of v is now performed, with the following appropriate actions:

- $v = \epsilon$ — the root node is designated as c (the locus of v), and the algorithm proceeds to II.

- $v \neq \epsilon$ — from (b), the locus of uv must have already existed in Y_{i-2}. From (1), the suffix link of this internal node must be defined in Y_{i-1}, since the node must have been added prior to step $i - 1$. From (2), this node will have been visited in stage $i - 1$. Its suffix link is then traversed to an internal node c (the locus of v) and the algorithm proceeds to II.

II ('rescanning') It was shown above that $head_i$ is given by vwz. By definition, the extended locus of vw thus exists in Y_{i-1}. There is therefore some downward sequence of edges from c (the locus of v) leading to the locus of some extension of vw. To rescan w, the child of c, e, say, such that e is the locus of an extension, vp, say, of v appended with the first symbol of w is found. If $|p| < |w|$, then a recursive rescan of q, where $w = pq$, is started from node e. If, on the other hand, $|p| \geqslant |w|$, then w is a prefix of p, and the extended locus of vw has been found, completing the rescan and taking time linear in the number of nodes visited. A new internal node is created as the locus of vw if one does not already exist (a new node is added only if $z = \epsilon$, in which case $head_i = vw$). The locus of vw is designated as d, and the algorithm proceeds to III.

III ('scanning') If the suffix link of the locus of uvw (i.e. $head_{i-1}$) is currently undefined, then it is set to point to node d, ensuring the truth of (1). A downwards search starting from d to find the extended locus of vwz (i.e. of $head_i$) is then initiated. While rescanning, the length of w is already known as it has previously been scanned, whereas in scanning, the length of z is unknown. The downward search is thus dictated by the symbols of $tail_{i-1}$ (of which z is a prefix) one at a time from left to right. The extended locus of vwz is then found when this downward excursion may proceed no further. The previous node encountered on this journey is the contracted locus of $head_i$, ensuring the truth of (2). If necessary, a new internal node is created to be the locus of vwz (i.e. $head_i$). A new edge representing $tail_i$ is then added from the locus of vwz to a new leaf representing suffix $y(i, n)$, thus completing stage i.

McCreight gives the following example to illustrate the above process. Consider step 14 in the construction of the suffix tree for $y = $ BBBBBABABBBAABBBBB\$. The tree Y_{13} is shown in Figure 4.7. The relevant suffix links have been included, and ordered pairs of string indices have also been given where long edge label substrings have been abbreviated. At step 14, suffix $y(14, 19)$, namely BBBBB\$, is to be inserted into Y_{13}. Initially, uv is set to AB as this is the string represented by the contracted locus of $head_{13}$ in Y_{12} (from I(b)), so $u = $ A and $v = $ B. The value of $head_{13}$ (uvw) is equal

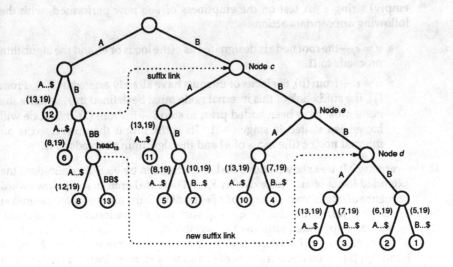

Figure 4.7: Y_{13} for string BBBBBABABBBAABBBBB$

to ABBB, so w must be BB. In **I**, v is non-empty, so the suffix link from the locus of uv (AB) is traversed to node c (the locus of B). From here, w is rescanned in **II**, encountering one intermediate node e and ending up at node d, the locus of BBB. In **III** a new suffix link is added from the locus of $head_{13}$ to node d, and the downward scan from d is then started using the symbols of $tail_{13}$ (BB$), finding that $z = $ BB. A new internal node is then created as the locus of vwz ($head_{14}$), which in this case is BBBBB, and inserted into the incoming edge of the extended locus of vwz (the leaf for $y(1, 19)$). Finally, a new edge is added from the locus of BBBBB to a new leaf representing suffix $y(14, 19)$.

It now remains to show that the running time of the algorithm is linear in n. For stage i, let res_i denote the shortest suffix (i.e. $wz \cdot tail_i$) involved in the rescanning operation. For every intermediate node e visited whilst rescanning w, p is a non-empty string occurring in res_i, but not in res_{i+1}. For each intermediate node, p has a minimum length of 1; thus the maximum length of res_{i+1} is $|res_i| - int_i$, where int_i is the number of intermediate nodes encountered during the rescan of stage i. So, $int_i = |res_i|_{max} - |res_{i+1}|_{max}$. The overall total number of intermediate nodes visited during rescanning is thus $\sum_{i=1}^{n} int_i$, which is bounded from above by n, as the maximum possible value of any $|res_i|$ is obviously n. Also, in stage i, the number of symbols which must be scanned in order to locate $head_i$, i.e. $|z|$, is equal to at most $|head_i| - |head_{i-1}| + 1$, since $|head_{i-1}| = |uvw|$, $|head_i| = |vwz|$, and $|u| \leqslant 1$. Summing over the complete algorithm gives $\sum_{i=1}^{n} |head_i| - |head_{i-1}|$

$+1 = |head_n| - |head_0| + n = n$.

The above shows that the rescanning and scanning operations of the overall process consume at most time linear in n. It has also previously been shown that each of the n stages of the algorithm takes constant time, excluding that required for rescanning and scanning. The time taken by the entire algorithm is therefore linear in n. The running time of the algorithm is also linear in the size of the alphabet of y, as each node may have up to $|C|$ children, for alphabet C.

4.2.3 Ukkonen

Ukkonen's (1992b, 1993) suffix-tree algorithm is based on an on-line suffix-trie construction (Ukkonen and Wood, 1993). An incremental approach is employed in which suffix trees for successively longer prefixes of the input string are built, in overall time linear in the length of the string. In the construction, the symbols of the string are thus examined one at a time, from left to right. This approach is in contrast to that of McCreight. Recall that in the latter, progressively shorter suffixes are added to the tree starting with the longest one first. As a prelude to describing Ukkonen's algorithm itself, the suffix-trie construction upon which it is based shall first be examined.

Suffix Tries

The suffix trie to be constructed for input string y shall be denoted here by Y'. The trie itself is equivalent to that defined earlier, with the addition of a special node, $\star$, use of which will be made in the suffix-tree algorithm. Suffix links are also included in the structure and are utilised in its construction. (Note in passing that the suffix links of a suffix trie correspond to the failure transitions, mentioned in section 4.1.1, of an Aho-Corasick automaton for the set of suffixes of a string.)

Recall that the root of the trie is the locus of the empty string, ϵ. It is also taken to be the child of node $\star$, with the intervening edge representing *any* symbol from the alphabet in use, C. Node $\star$ thus corresponds to the inverse, a^{-1}, of all the symbols, a, belonging to C (since $a^{-1}a = \epsilon$). The suffix link from the root is set to point at $\star$; that from $\star$ itself is left undefined.

The construction proceeds in an iterative manner, building the suffix tries for increasing prefixes, $y(1, i)$, $0 \leqslant i \leqslant n$, at successive stages. The prefix of y at $i = 0$ is taken to be ϵ. (In general, ϵ will be represented here by substring $y(k, l)$ whenever $k = l + 1$.) At stage i, the suffixes of $y(1, i)$ may be obtained from those of $y(1, i - 1)$ by appending symbol y_i to each one, and also adding to their number the empty suffix, ϵ.

The suffix trie for $y(1, i)$, Y_i', may correspondingly be generated from that of previous prefix $y(1, i - 1)$. The general method for doing this is as follows. The loci of the suffixes of $y(1, i - 1)$, including the root, which represents the empty suffix, are examined. For each one, if there does not already exist an edge representing y_i, then one is added from that node to a new leaf. Note that the previous stipulation for the final symbol of the string to be unique cannot, in general, also be imposed on successive prefixes of the string. Suffixes may therefore also be represented in an intermediate suffix-tree by internal nodes as well as by its leaves.

The stages in the construction of the suffix trie for string ABAB\$ are depicted in Figure 4.8. Use of the suffix links, shown as broken arrows in the figure, facilitate the necessary examination of the suffix loci. In trie Y_{i-1}', these may be found by following the *boundary path* — the chain of suffix links starting from the locus of $y(1, i-1)$ and ending at node $\star$. The suffix links comprising the boundary path at each stage of the construction are shown as long dashed arrows in the figure.

As outlined above, in the creation of Y_i', successive nodes on the boundary path of Y_{i-1}' are visited. At each one, representing string u, say, if there is no outgoing edge representing symbol y_i, then a new edge is added from the locus of u to a new leaf representing string uy_i. The newly created nodes are linked together with new suffix links to form the boundary path of Y_i', starting from the locus of $y(1, i)$.

The above process is terminated as soon as a node on the boundary path is found already to have the requisite child. For this to obtain at the node representing a string u, string uy_i must have appeared before as a suffix at some earlier stage. Therefore, successive suffixes of uy_i will also have been defined previously in the trie. Consider, for example, the creation of Y_4' from Y_3' for string ABAB\$, as shown in Figure 4.8. Following the boundary path of Y_3', new edges representing symbol B leading to new leaves are added to the loci of ABA and BA; but not to those of A and ϵ, since an edge for B is already defined from the locus of A. Note that using only this criterion, the process is guaranteed to stop, as the edge from node $\star$ — the final node on a boundary path — is defined for all the symbols in C. Adopting this approach ensures that only constant time is required for the addition of each node to the trie.

The construction algorithm is given in Figure 4.9. The suffix trie starts life as Y_0', which comprises nodes *root* and $\star$, together with the edge and suffix link joining them.

At each stage i, only string symbol y_i is used in the transformation of Y_{i-1}' into Y_i'. Variable *top* denotes the locus of $y(1, i-1)$. This is the starting point of r, which subsequently traverses the boundary path of Y_{i-1}' until a node having a y_i child is encountered.

During this traversal, a new edge labelled y_i is created from r to a new leaf r'. This leaf is remembered as *oldr'* so that a suffix link may thence be added to the next new leaf created in the traversal. The reason for this is as follows. If node r represents string au, say, where $|a| = 1$, then r' is the locus of auy_i. The next node on the traversal is arrived at by following the suffix link from r; it thus represents string u, and the next new leaf represents string uy_i — the required suffix of the previous new leaf.

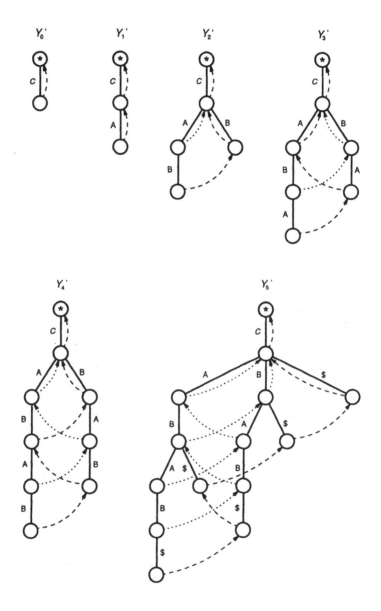

Figure 4.8: Stages in the construction of the suffix trie for string ABAB$

---

initialise Y_0'
$top = root$
for $i = 1$ to n
    $r = top$
    while r has no outgoing edge labelled y_i
        create new leaf r'
        create new edge labelled y_i from r to r'
        if $r \neq top$
            create new suffix link from $oldr'$ to r'
        $oldr' = r'$
        $r =$ node pointed to by suffix link from r
    create new suffix link from $oldr'$ to the y_i child of r
    $top =$ the y_i child of top

Figure 4.9: Suffix-trie construction

Once the journey along the boundary path has been completed, a new suffix link is then inserted from the last leaf added to its appropriate suffix node, which will already be defined in the trie. Finally, stage i is completed by setting top to the correct value for the next iteration.

It may be seen that the above procedure requires time proportional to the size of the suffix trie generated. Recall that there is a one-to-one correspondence between the nodes of a string's suffix trie and its distinct substrings. As we have seen before, the number of these can, in the worst case, be quadratic in n: the above algorithm thus runs in $O(n^2)$ time.

Suffix Trees

The suffix-tree construction based on the above trie algorithm proceeds in a vein similar to that of the latter. Intermediate trees, Y_i, are built successively from their predecessors, Y_{i-1}, until the final tree for the full string has been constructed. The stages in the construction of the suffix tree for the example string ABAB$ are illustrated in Figure 4.10.

As with the suffix trie, the suffix tree is augmented with the special node $\star$. This time, suffix links are only defined for internal nodes of the tree: again, that from the root points at $\star$, and that from $\star$ is not defined.

Recall that a suffix tree may be obtained by condensing paths that contain unary nodes in the corresponding suffix trie. It is convenient to consider such loci as still existing, albeit implicitly, in the tree. In order to refer to a specific locus, r — either

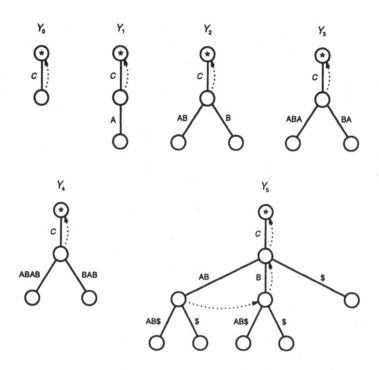

Figure 4.10: Construction of the suffix tree for string ABAB$

implicit or explicit — in the tree, it may be represented by a *reference pair* (s, w), where s is an explicit ancestor of r, and w is the string which, when appended to that represented by s, yields the string corresponding to r. A reference pair is said to be *canonical* if s is the nearest ancestor of r, i.e. if s is the contracted locus of the string represented by r. As a substring of the input string y, w may be represented by the ordered pair of indices (k, l), such that $y(k, l) = w$. Thus, the reference pair (s, w) may be written as $(s, (k, l))$.

A set of procedures comprising the suffix-tree construction shall be presented in due course. Before proceeding with this, however, we must first consider in some detail the circumstances in which new edges are added to nodes in the boundary path during the construction of the corresponding trie. Inspection of the operation of the algorithm described above reveals that there are two distinct settings wherein this happens. In the first, a y_i edge is added to a leaf of Y'_{i-1}, and thus extends an existing branch of the trie. In the second, a y_i edge is added to an internal node of

Y'_{i-1}, and thus creates the start of a new branch in the trie.

The first node visited on the boundary path for which the second situation obtains, namely the first internal node encountered on the traversal, is referred to as the *active point*. (Although not strictly an internal node in the initial tree, the root is taken to be the active point of Y'_0.) Furthermore, the *end point* is defined as being the first node on the boundary path for which a y_i edge already exists. As an example, the active and end points of trie Y'_4 in Figure 4.8 are the locus of AB and node ∗, respectively. The corresponding points in the matching tree, Y_4 (Figure 4.10), are the implicit locus ($root$, AB) and the explicit node ($∗, \epsilon$).

The boundary path of Y'_{i-1} comprises $i + 1$ nodes, $s_1, \ldots, s_{i+1}$, where s_1 is the locus of $y(1, i - 1)$, s_i is the root, and s_{i+1} is node ∗. We shall denote the active and end points on the boundary path by s_j and $s_{j'}$ respectively. Index j is thus the minimum value such that s_j is an internal node, and j' the minimum such that $s_{j'}$ has an edge labelled y_i. Note that s_1 is, perforce, a leaf, and that s_{i+1} is an internal node possessing a y_i edge. Both indices are therefore well defined, with $j \leqslant j'$. It may now be stated that in the construction of trie Y'_i, a y_i edge is added to each node, s_h, on the boundary path of Y'_{i-1}, where $1 \leqslant h < j'$. Furthermore, for $1 \leqslant h < j$, the edges added are of the first type, i.e. they extend existing branches past their current termini; for $j \leqslant h < j'$, the edges added are of the second type, i.e. they create new branches from internal nodes.

The implementation of analogous operations in the construction of the suffix tree Y_i may now be considered, starting with the former situation. It may be seen that a branch ending in a leaf will be extended with successive y_i edges up to the one for the final string symbol, y_n. An edge leading to a leaf may therefore be labelled with the pair of indices (k, ∞), where ∞ indicates that the edge may be extended indefinitely, or, in practice, up to the end of string y. The right-hand substring index for such an edge thus need not explicitly be updated when y_i is added to the branch. On completion of the construction, the ∞ indices should be replaced by n.

So it is only the y_i edges of the second type that need be added explicitly to transform Y_{i-1} into Y_i. It is therefore necessary to find the active point, and thence to add y_i edges to the loci s_h ($j \leqslant h < j'$) — which may not yet necessarily be explicit — up to, but not including, the end point.

Assume first of all that the active point, s_h for $h = j$, has been found. Its canonical reference pair may be denoted by $(s, (k, i - 1))$ for some $k \leqslant i$, since s_h is the locus in trie Y'_{i-1} of some suffix of $y(1, i - 1)$. If the current locus, $(s, (k, i - 1))$, is not the end point, then a new branch must be created from there for y_i. If $(s, (k, i - 1))$ is not already explicit, then such a node must first be inserted into the edge containing the implicit locus. A new edge, labelled (i, ∞), may then be added from s_h to a new leaf. If not already in existence, the suffix link from node s_h must next be added.

$update(s, k, i)$
— $(s, (k, i - 1))$ is the canonical reference pair of the active point
$oldr = root$
while (**not** $end\_point(s, (k, i - 1), y_i)$)
    $r = create\_node(s, (k, i - 1))$
    create new leaf r'
    create new edge labelled (i, ∞) from r to r'
    if $oldr \neq root$
        create new suffix link from $oldr$ to r
    $oldr = r$
    s = node pointed to by suffix link from s
    $(s, k) = canonise(s, (k, i - 1))$
if $oldr \neq root$
    create new suffix link from $oldr$ to s
return(s, k)

Figure 4.11: Procedure $update$

The above procedure is repeated for successive loci s_h, until the end point is reached. The locus s_h was given above by the reference pair $(s, (k, i - 1))$. Thus, s_h represents the string corresponding to s concatenated with $y(k, i - 1)$. The suffix of this obtained by deleting its first symbol is therefore the string represented by s_{h+1}, the next locus on the boundary path. This locus, explicit or implicit, may be found, then, by following the suffix link from s to node s', say, and then finding the canonical reference pair for $(s', (k, i - 1))$.

The process described above of producing Y_i from Y_{i-1} is performed by procedure $update$, given in Figure 4.11. Successive loci on the boundary path, starting from the active point, are visited in the loop. For each one, procedure end_point is called to determine whether or not the end point has been reached. If it has not, then procedure $create\_node$ is invoked, which checks to see whether the current locus, $(s, (k, i - 1))$, is explicit or implicit. If it is implicit, then $create\_node$ splits the appropriate edge and inserts a new node corresponding to $(s, (k, i - 1))$. The new y_i edge, leaf, and, if necessary, suffix link are then added. The next locus on the boundary path is then found by calling procedure $canonise$. Once the loop has been exited, a final suffix link is added and the procedure returns the node and left index of the canonical reference pair of the end point of Y_{i-1} (the right index need not explicitly be mentioned as it is constant at $i - 1$ for all the loci on the boundary path).

$end\_point(s, (k, l), a)$
  — $(s, (k, l))$ is the canonical reference pair of a locus on the
  — boundary path of Y_{i-1}; a is symbol y_i
  if $k \leqslant l$
    $b = y_k$
  else
    — $y(k, l)$ is equal to ϵ
    $b = a$
  if there is no edge from s for a string starting with symbol b
    return(false)
  else
    let string starting with b on edge from s be denoted by $y(k', l')$
    if $y_{k'+(l-k+1)} = a$
      return(true)
    else
      return(false)

Figure 4.12: Procedure end_point

The procedures upon which *update* depends shall now be described, commencing with *end_point*, which is given in Figure 4.12. This procedure determines whether or not the canonical reference pair $(s, (k, l))$ represents the end point in Y_{i-1}, i.e. whether or not this locus would have a y_i edge in the corresponding trie, Y'_{i-1}. If $(s, (k, l))$ is the end point, then there will be an edge in Y_{i-1} from node s labelled with some extension of $y(k, l)y_i$, since $(s, (k, l))$ is canonical. Denoting the first symbol of $y(k, l)y_i$ by b, the end-point question may thus be decided by looking for and inspecting the edge from s representing a string starting with symbol b. Symbol y_i is passed to *end_point* as parameter a. If $y(k, l)$ is non-empty, then b is set to the first symbol of this string; otherwise it is set to y_i. If there is an edge from s representing a substring, $y(k', l')$, starting with symbol b, and if it contains symbol y_i at a position corresponding to the final symbol of $y(k, l)y_i$, then $(s, (k, l))$ does, in fact, represent the end point.

Procedure *create_node*, shown in Figure 4.13, returns the explicit node represented by reference pair $(s, (k, l))$. If this locus is already explicit, then node s is simply returned. Otherwise, a new node, r, is created and inserted into the appropriate edge from s.

Procedure *canonise* is shown in Figure 4.14. The reference pair, $(s, (k, l))$, for some locus r is passed to the procedure, which returns node s' and left index

---

$create\_node(s, (k, l))$
  if $l < k$
    — $y(k, l) = \epsilon$; locus $(s, (k, l))$ is thus already explicit
    return(s)
  else
    find edge from s representing extension $y(k', l')$ of $y(k, l)$
    $s' =$ node at end of this edge
    remove edge labelled (k', l')
    create new node r
    create new edge labelled $(k', k' + (l - k))$ from s to r
    create new edge labelled $(k' + (l - k) + 1, l')$ from r to s'
    return(r)

Figure 4.13: Procedure $create\_node$

---

k' such that $(s', (k', l))$ is the canonical reference pair for r. Node s' is thus the nearest explicit ancestor of r, or r itself if this is an explicit locus; and so the string represented by the edge from s' to r must be a suffix of that represented by the path from s to r, i.e. $y(k, l)$. During canonisation, the right index is therefore not altered, but the left one may be incremented past its original value.

The actual mechanism of the procedure is somewhat reminiscent of the 'scanning' operation in McCreight's algorithm, in which extended and contracted loci of a string are sought.

If the string of the reference pair is empty, then $(s, (k, l))$ refers to explicit node s, and the reference pair is therefore already canonical. Otherwise, *canonise* follows the downward sequence of edges from s that spells out string $y(k, l)$, or the shortest extension thereof. In the former case, locus $(s, (k, l))$ is explicit and is therefore canonically represented by (s', ϵ) — or $(s', (k', l))$ where $k' > l$ — where s' is the final node visited in the downward excursion from s. On the other hand, however, the locus is implicit in the latter case. It is then represented by the canonical reference pair $(s', (k', l))$, where s' is the penultimate node visited on the downward journey and $y(k', l)$ is the string remaining when the prefix spelt out by the edges on the path from s to s' is taken away from $y(k, l)$.

We are now almost in a position to present the overall suffix-tree construction algorithm. Recall, however, that procedure *update* converts one intermediate tree into the next, but in order to do so it requires the active point of the former to be known beforehand. The way that this may be determined is considered below.

Again, the situation may be analysed by taking recourse to an inspection of the

---

```
canonise(s, (k, l))
    if l < k
        — y(k, l) = ε; the reference pair represents an explicit node,
        — and is therefore already canonical
        return(s, k)
    else
        — follow the downward sequence of edges from s spelling out
        — string y(k, l), or the shortest extension thereof
        find edge from s representing string y(k', l') such that y_{k'} = y_k
        s' = node at the end of this edge
        while l' − k' ≤ l − k
            k = k + l' − k' + 1
            s = s'
            if k ≤ l
                find edge from s representing string y(k', l') such that y_{k'} = y_k
                s' = node at the end of this edge
        return(s, k)
```

Figure 4.14: Procedure *canonise*

---

corresponding suffix trie. In the construction of Y_i', all the nodes on the boundary path of Y_{i-1}' before the end point have y_i-child leaves added. These new nodes then become the leaves of the boundary path of Y_i'. It follows that the active point of Y_i', i.e. the first non-leaf node in its boundary path, must therefore be the y_i child of the first node on the boundary path of Y_{i-1}' for which no new y_i was added: namely, the y_i child of the end point of Y_{i-1}'. Note that this is necessarily an internal node in Y_i': if it was an internal node in Y_{i-1}', then so too will it be in Y_i'; if it was a leaf in Y_{i-1}', then it will have had a y_i child added in the construction of Y_i'. For the case of the suffix tree, it may equivalently be stated that if the end point in Y_{i-1} is given by reference pair $(s, (k, i − 1))$, then $(s, (k, i))$ is a reference pair, not necessarily canonical, of the active point in Y_i.

Making use of the above observation, we then have the overall suffix-tree construction algorithm shown in Figure 4.15. This starts off by constructing the initial tree Y_0. In the first iteration of the main loop, the values of s, k, and i are initially such that $(s, (k, i − 1))$ canonically refers to the active point of Y_0, namely $(root, ε)$. At stage i, procedure *update* creates Y_i from Y_{i-1}, and returns the node and left-hand index of the reference pair of the end point of Y_{i-1}, $(s, (k, i − 1))$. The canonical reference pair for the active point of Y_i, to be used by *update* in the next iteration,

---

— initialise Y_0
create node *root*
create node $\star$
for $j = 1$ to n
    create new edge labelled (j, j) from $\star$ to *root*
    create new suffix link from *root* to $\star$
— initialise active point of Y_0
$s = root$
$k = 1$
— create successive trees $Y_1, \ldots, Y_n$
for $i = 1$ to n
    $(s, k) = update(s, k, i)$
    $(s, k) = canonise(s, (k, i))$

Figure 4.15: Ukkonen suffix-tree construction algorithm

---

is then determined from $(s, (k, i))$. The process is repeated in this way until suffix tree Y_n has been built, thus completing the construction.

To round off the description of the algorithm, it now only remains to show that its running time is linear in n. To this end, we first of all neglect, for the time being, the total time consumed by calls to *canonise*. The remainder of the algorithm comprises the repeated traversal of the boundary path from active point to end point, performed by *update*. The operations carried out at each locus so visited — the test for the end point and the addition of a new edge, leaf, and, possibly, suffix link — may be accomplished in constant time (provided that $|C|$ is finite and not dependent on n). The time taken by the remainder is thus proportional to the total number of loci visited, which may be shown to be linear in n as follows.

Recall that the active point at one stage is reached by following a y_i transition from the end point of the previous stage. Denoting the active point of Y_i, $0 \leqslant i \leqslant n$, by r_i, we may see that the loci visited between r_{i-1} and r_i lie on a path comprising suffix links and one y_i transition. The *depth* of a locus may be defined as the length of the string spelt out by the path from the root to the locus. Taking a y_i transition thus increases the depth by one, whereas traversing a suffix link decreases it by one. If there are vl visited loci between the active and end points inclusive, then $depth(endpoint_{i-1}) = depth(r_{i-1}) - (vl - 1)$. Also, moving from the end point to the next active point gives: $depth(r_i) = depth(endpoint_{i-1}) + 1$. Combining and rearranging these relations yields the following expression for vl: $vl = depth(r_{i-1}) - depth(r_i) + 2$. The total number of visited loci is thus $\sum_{i=1}^{n} depth(r_{i-1}) - depth(r_i) + 2 =$

$2n + depth(r_0) - depth(r_n) = 2n$, since $depth(r_0) = depth(r_n) = 0$. (Note that the requirement for y_n to be unique in the string ensures that r_n is the root, as the end point in Y_{n-1} must be node $\star$.) The time taken by the algorithm, excluding that consumed during canonisation, is therefore $O(n)$.

To complete the analysis, the time that was neglected above must now be taken into consideration. It may be seen that, disregarding the while loop, each execution of *canonise* requires constant time, and that constant time is also required for each iteration of the loop itself. The overall time taken is thus proportional to the total number of calls and the total number of iterations of the while loop over all these calls. Procedure *canonise* is invoked once for each visited locus — from *update* for the active point up to the locus immediately preceding the end point, and from the main algorithm for the end point itself. The total number of calls to *canonise* is therefore $O(n)$. During each iteration of the while loop, a non-empty prefix is removed from the string which starts off at the start of *canonise* as $y(k, l)$. The right-hand index, l, is only ever increased by one place at a time, for $i = 1, \ldots, n$, by the final step in the loop that creates successive trees in the main algorithm. The total number of iterations of the while loop over all calls is therefore at most n, since this is the maximum number of non-empty prefix deletions possible. The overall time taken for canonisation is thus $O(n)$, as must then also be that taken by the entire construction process.

4.3   Further Reading

As mentioned previously, suffix trees find application in algorithms for approximate string matching and finding longest repeated substrings. These two areas are covered in more detail in Chapters 5 and 6 respectively.

A variety of other suffix-tree applications are discussed by Apostolico (1985) and also by Apostolico and Szpankowski (1992). These include algorithms for determining longest common substrings; sequentially compressing data; ascertaining whether or not a given string is square-free, which is the case if none of its substrings is a square; and calculating the number of distinct, non-overlapping occurrences of a string's substrings.

It is worthwhile noting in passing that Apostolico and Szpankowski also highlight certain situations in which it can be preferable to construct a suffix tree via the brute-force method rather than one of the available linear-time algorithms. This type of situation can arise in the solution of certain string problems involving suffix trees, such as the above mentioned test for square-freedom and evaluation of non-overlapping substring-statistics. Operations effecting the solution of problems such as these may easily be incorporated into the brute-force construction, but would otherwise necessitate rather elaborate postprocessing of the suffix tree.

5

Approximate String Matching

> It is the nature of all greatness not to be exact...
> — Edmund Burke (1729–1797).

5.1 Overview

A generalisation of the string-matching problem is the *Approximate String-Matching Problem,* which involves finding substrings of a text string similar to a given pattern string. This variation of the problem is important when errors are being taken into consideration, and, for example, finds application in the field of molecular biology. The approximate string-matching problem may be stated as follows.

> Given a pattern string x, with $|x| = m$, text string y, with $|y| = n$, where $m, n > 0$ and $m \leqslant n$, an integer $k \geqslant 0$, and a distance function d, find all the substrings, s, of y such that $d(x, s) \leqslant k$.

The task is thus to determine all the text substrings having a distance of at most k from the pattern, for the given distance function. When d is the Hamming distance, the problem is known as string matching with k *mismatches*; and when d is the Levenshtein distance, it is known as string matching with k *differences* (or sometimes k *errors*).

In this chapter, the major approaches to both of these problems shall be discussed, and mention made of the problem of string matching with *don't-care* symbols. Various parallel hardware architectures and algorithms for string-processing applications are also surveyed in this overview.

5.1.1   String Matching with k Mismatches

The $O(mn)$-time, brute-force string-matching algorithm may be adapted easily to cater for the k-mismatches problem by allowing up to k mismatches in the comparisons at each substring position within the text. However, as with the exact string-matching problem, various more efficient approaches to both the k-mismatches and the k-differences problems have been devised.

Landau and Vishkin (1985, 1986a) developed an algorithm for the k-mismatches problem running in $O(k(m \log m + n))$ time. Their approach is similar to the Knuth-Morris-Pratt string-matching technique in that a table derived from preprocessing the pattern is employed as the text string is examined from left to right, and known information is exploited to reduce the number of symbol comparisons required. The preprocessing contributes $O(km \log m)$ time, and the text-scanning stage $O(kn)$ time, to the overall total. The extra space required by the algorithm is $O(k(m + n))$, which can be significant for large texts.

Landau and Vishkin remarked that an earlier k-mismatches algorithm due to Ivanov (1984), which has a temporal complexity of $O(f(k)(m + n))$, is faster than their algorithm for the case of very small k and comparable values of m and n. However, they highlighted the abstruse nature of the function f and have established that it is bounded from below by 2^k. Excepting the above case, their algorithm is thus faster than Ivanov's, and furthermore has the appeal of its relative simplicity — they state that Ivanov's algorithm required in excess of forty journal pages to describe.

A variant of Landau and Vishkin's k-mismatches algorithm with improved pattern preprocessing has been developed by Galil and Giancarlo (1986, 1988). The overall time complexity of their version is $O(m \log m + kn)$, and its space requirement is $O(m)$. The improvement in the asymptotic running time is, however, at the cost of a large constant hidden in the 'O' formula.

An alternative approach has been suggested by Grossi and Luccio (1989). This involves firstly finding occurrences in y of permutations of x with up to k mismatches, whose number shall be denoted here by $p \leqslant n$, and then determining which of these are actually k-mismatches occurrences of the pattern string. Two algorithms were proposed on this basis. The first requires $O(m)$ space and runs in $O(n + pm)$ time for an alphabet of fixed size, and in $O(n \log |C_x| + pm)$ time for an unbounded one. C_x is the set of distinct symbols in the pattern, and thus $|C_x| \leqslant m$. The second algorithm is more complicated than the first, and involves the construction of a suffix tree. Its space requirement is $O(n)$, and it runs in time $O(n + qk)$ and $O(n \log |C_x| + qk)$ for fixed and arbitrary alphabets, respectively, where $q \leqslant p$ is the number of distinct permutations of x in y with at most k mismatches. Note that in the worst case, the first requires quadratic time and the second $O(kn)$ time. However, empirical evidence suggests that in practice $pm < kn$, and that, on average, $q \ll n$ for $k \leqslant m/2$.

Baeza-Yates and Gonnet (1989, 1992) have shown how their 'shift-add' string-matching algorithm may be extended to handle the k-mismatches problem, and this approach has also been incorporated into the agrep approximate string-matching tool (Wu and Manber, 1991, 1992a, 1992b). The shift-add algorithm is a numerical technique, in which an integer number represents a vector of states holding the results of comparisons between the m prefixes of x and corresponding text substrings for the current pattern/text alignment. The search proceeds by successively reading text symbols and updating the state vector. The latter is done by performing some arithmetic operation on the current state together with another number derived from a preprocessed table indexed by the current text-symbol. The space required is $O(m \, |C|)$ and the preprocessing and searching times are $O(\lceil \frac{mb}{w} \rceil (m + |C|))$ and $O(\lceil \frac{mb}{w} \rceil n)$, respectively, where b is the number of bits per state in the vector and w is the wordsize of the computer. $\lceil \frac{mb}{w} \rceil$ thus represents the time required to perform a constant number of operations on mb-bit integers using a wordsize of w. For the k-mismatches problem, each state acts as a counter to keep track of the numbers of mismatches, and so a value of $\lceil \log_2 k \rceil$ (which is bounded by $\lceil \log_2 m \rceil$) is required for b.

The Boyer-Moore-Horspool string-matching method has been generalised by Tarhio and Ukkonen (1990a, 1990b, 1993). The preprocessing for this may be accomplished in $O(m + (k + 1) \, |C|)$ time, and the working-space requirement is $O((k + 1) \, |C|)$. The actual scan of the text takes $O(mn)$ time in the worst case, but the expected performance is $O(kn(\frac{1}{m-k} + \frac{k}{|C|}))$ for random strings. For small k and large alphabets, then, the search requires sublinear time on average.

Baeza-Yates and Perleberg (1992) have devised an algorithm whose performance is independent of k. The technique uses a circular array of counters associated with the text symbols. The basic idea is to obtain an offset from a preprocessed table indexed by the current text-symbol, and use this to ascertain which, if any, of the counters is to be incremented. The number of mismatches for an occurrence of the pattern at each text position may then be determined from the relevant counter. The space requirement for this method is $O(m + |C|)$. For $|C_x| = m$ (i.e. when all the pattern symbols are distinct), the text scan runs in $O(n)$ time; otherwise its temporal complexity is $O(n + r)$, where r is the total number of ordered pairs of positions at which the two strings match. In the extreme case, $r = mn$, giving a quadratic running time. Assuming the symbols to be equiprobable, the average running time is $O((1 + \frac{m}{|C|})n)$, irrespective of the number of distinct pattern symbols.

Again assuming equiprobable symbols, and for $k \leqslant m/2 \log_{|C|} m$, space and average-case time complexities of $O((m \log^2 m)/ \log \log m)$ and $O((kn \log^2 m)/ (m \log \log m))$, respectively, have been achieved by Quong (1992). However, the method employed for this is probabilistic, and can fail in certain circumstances, e.g. if the pattern is periodic.

Finally, another probabilistic algorithm, which finds with high probability all the k-mismatches pattern occurrences, has been proposed by Atallah, Jacquet and Szpankowski (1992). Here, the number of mismatches is specified as a proportion of the pattern length; the idea being that this ratio is chosen so as to ensure a good degree of selectivity between 'significant' approximate matches and those due only to chance. The algorithm can operate with unbounded alphabets, and its worst case running time is $O(n \log m)$.

Comparative Performance

When the various approaches to the k-mismatches problem are compared, there emerges no clear winner for all cases. When one considers different situations, though, the following observations may be made.

First of all, when k is constant, various algorithms allow the text to be scanned in linear time, such as the early techniques of Landau and Vishkin, and Galil and Giancarlo. However, the first can demand large storage requirements, and in practice the implementation of the second is fairly complex.

Certain alternatives can also perform this task in linear time on average, but not in the worst case. For example, the two algorithms of Grossi and Luccio do so for fixed alphabets. They also have the attraction of being able to cater for unbounded alphabets, for which their expected running times are $O(n \log m)$. Note that in the worst case, these degrade to $O(mn)$ and $O(n(k + \log m))$, and further that the second is mainly of theoretical interest only unless n is very large.

Also for constant k, the text search may be accomplished in time sublinear in n on average. There is, for example, Quong's non-deterministic algorithm. Tarhio and Ukkonen's adaptation of the Boyer-Moore-Horspool algorithm also provides sublinear average performance. This works well for relatively small k, and in common with its antecedent, its performance improves as the pattern length and alphabet size increase. As mentioned above, its worst-case running time is quadratic.

Lastly, the case where k is not constant is considered. k may, for instance, be chosen to be a fixed proportion of the pattern size (i.e. $k = \Theta(m)$), as suggested in the approach of Atallah, Jacquet and Szpankowski. In this situation, those algorithms having a kn term in their complexities become quadratic. On the other hand, however, techniques whose performance is independent of k are well suited to this setting. This is also an important consideration in 'best match' searching, where the requisite value of k is not known in advance.

Atallah, Jacquet and Szpankowski's $O(n \log m)$-time, probabilistic algorithm falls into the above category. Also, for small patterns (i.e. when $m \log_2 m$ is smaller than the computer wordsize) the shift-add algorithm scans the text in linear time, regardless of the value of k. This algorithm is fairly simple to implement and is also very flexible — we shall see later on how it can additionally be applied to the k-differences problem and to cases where the pattern may contain don't-cares and classes of symbols. Another elegant and straightforward-to-implement algorithm is that due to Baeza-Yates and Perleberg. As mentioned earlier, its running time is $O(n)$ when all the pattern symbols are distinct, and can otherwise be quadratic in the worst case. But, its average-case running time is independent of $|C_x|$ and is linear for $m < |C|$. For small alphabets (such as binary, or DNA-nucleotide alphabets), though, m can often be $\gg |C|$, giving rise to a quadratic average running time.

5.1.2   String Matching with k Differences

Sellers (1980) has shown how the dynamic-programming method of computing the distance between two strings may be adapted to solve the k-differences problem. All that is required is a simple modification to the boundary conditions of the $(m + 1) \times (n + 1)$ distance-matrix. On completion of the column by column computation of the table, approximate occurrences (with up to k differences) of the pattern in the text may be located by inspecting the values in the final row. There, each value not exceeding k, $d_{m,j}$, say, indicates that there is at least one substring, s, of y ending at y_j such that $d(x, s) \leqslant k$. The time required for this method is $O(mn)$. Note that in order to find the end positions, the working space may be reduced to $O(m)$. This is because the computation of the elements in any given column of the matrix needs reference only to those already defined in the current column and in that immediately preceding it.

An important property of the dynamic-programming table is its *diagonalwise monotonicity* (Ukkonen, 1985a): the elements on any given diagonal form a non-decreasing sequence, whose increments occur only as unit steps. The positions of the *transitions*, i.e. the points at which a step change in value occurs, along the diagonals of the matrix are thus of much importance. This suggests alternative means of computing and representing the information in the matrix: proceed along the diagonals, and for each one only store the transition locations. This is the approach devised by Ukkonen (1985a) for the $O(md)$-time, dynamic-programming computation of the Levenshtein distance between two strings.

Ukkonen (1985b) also proposed a simple improvement to Sellers' dynamic-programming procedure based on the diagonalwise-monotonicity property. In the resulting 'cut-off' method, the table entries are again calculated column by column, but the computations for the entries along a given diagonal are terminated as soon as the value $k+1$ is obtained. The running time remains quadratic in the worst case, but this straightforward modification leads to an expected running time of $O(kn)$ for random strings (which was recently proven by Chang and Lampe (1992)).

Another approach to the k-differences problem developed by Ukkonen (1985b) comprises separate pattern-preprocessing and text-analysis stages. In the former stage, a deterministic, finite-state automaton that recognises all strings differing from the pattern by a distance of at most k is constructed. This is then used to scan the input text in the latter stage in $O(n)$ time. However, this algorithm is not, in general, practicable owing to its exponential requirements for preprocessing time and space. (For alphabet C, the pattern analysis requires $O(m \mid C \mid \min\{3^m, 2^k \mid C \mid^k m^{k+1}\})$ time and $O((\mid C \mid + m) \min\{3^m, 2^k \mid C \mid^k m^{k+1}\})$ space.)

The diagonalwise-monotonicity property implies that in order to solve the k-differences problem, it suffices to locate the first $k + 1$ transitions on each diagonal of the d matrix. This forms the basis of a number of k-differences algorithms, which essentially differ in the way that the *jumps* from one transition to the next are computed. The sizes of these jumps actually correspond to the lengths of the longest common prefixes of certain pairs of pattern- and text-suffixes.

The jumps may, for example, be calculated by brute force, involving direct comparisons of pattern and text. This is the method employed in a straightforward adaptation of Ukkonen's (1985a) string-distance algorithm (as described, for instance, by Landau and Vishkin (1986b, 1989) or Galil and Park (1989, 1990)). Although this results in a running time of $O(mn)$ in the worst case, it should be noted that Myers (1986b) has shown the expected running time for this technique to be $O(kn)$.

Known information is exploited, in a manner reminiscent of the Knuth-Morris-Pratt string-matching algorithm, to compute the jumps in Landau and Vishkin's (1985, 1988) approach. The pattern is first of all preprocessed in $O(m^2)$ time and space, yielding a *prefix* table, where the value of $prefix(i, j)$ is defined as the length of the longest common prefix of $x(i, m)$ and $x(j, m)$. This table is then used in conjunction with pattern/text comparisons to compute the jumps during a subsequent left-to-right scan of the text. This text-analysis stage tests successive positions for the occurrence — with up to k differences — of the pattern, and is performed in $O(k^2 n)$ time.

In a later version of the algorithm (Landau and Vishkin, 1988), more complicated preprocessing replaces the straightforward *prefix* computation to give a theoretical improvement in the running time. During the text scan, the information that was previously retrieved from the *prefix* table is now obtained by finding the lengths of least common ancestors (LCAs) of pairs of leaves in the suffix tree of the pattern. This is constructed using Weiner's (1973) linear-space algorithm in $O(m)$ time for a fixed-size alphabet, and $O(m \log \mid C_x \mid)$ time otherwise, where C_x is the set of distinct pattern symbols (whose cardinality is $\leqslant m$). The LCA queries are performed using Harel and Tarjan's (1984) algorithm (or Schieber and Vishkin's (1988) simpler algorithm), which, after an initial $O(m)$ time and space preprocessing of the tree, can find an LCA in $O(1)$ time. The overall running time is thus $O(m \log \mid C_x \mid + k^2 n)$ (or $O(m + k^2 n)$ when the alphabet size is fixed), and the working space requirements are $O(m)$.

Landau and Vishkin (1986b, 1989) also discovered a considerably simpler k-differences algorithm as a by-product of developing a parallel procedure. The basis of this method is to compute efficiently the distance matrix in a manner similar to that of Ukkonen's (1985a). However, the determination of the position of each of the first $k + 1$ transitions on each diagonal is achieved in $O(1)$ time. But in order to support the computation of these jumps from one transition to the next in constant time, Harel and Tarjan's algorithm is again applied to find LCAs of pairs of leaves of a previously constructed suffix tree. And this time, it is the suffix tree of the concatenation of both the *text* and the pattern strings that is required. The algorithm uses $O(m+n)$ working space and runs in $O((m + n)\log |C_{xy}| + kn)$ time, where $|C_{xy}| \leqslant m + n$ (and in $O(m + kn)$ time for an alphabet of fixed size).

An alternative preprocessing strategy for this has been developed by Galil and Giancarlo (1988). Although sharing the same asymptotic complexity as the above, their version confines the tree operations to a suffix tree of only the pattern string. The preprocessing also involves scanning the text forwards and then backwards with separate automata. The first of these recognises the pattern, and the second the pattern reversed.

Galil and Giancarlo (1988) also discussed how Masek and Paterson's (1980, 1983) string-distance algorithm may be adapted in order to solve the k-differences problem. This requires the size of the alphabet to be finite, and results in an $O(mn/\log n)$-time computation.

The text-processing time of Landau and Vishkin's (1985, 1988) algorithm has been reduced to $O(kn)$ by Galil and Park (1989, 1990). In this variant, the pattern is still preprocessed in $O(m^2)$ time and space to obtain the *prefix* table, but in an alternative way. As with Landau and Vishkin's method, the preprocessing may be improved in theory by employing a suffix tree and using an LCA algorithm, giving an overall running time of $O(m\log |C_x| + kn)$ for general inputs. (As before, the preprocessing time is reduced to $O(m)$ when the size of the alphabet is fixed.)

Ukkonen and Wood (1990) have developed an algorithm having a structure similar to that of Galil and Park's. The former also uses the *prefix* table and scans the text from left to right in $O(kn)$ time. However, this time the *prefix* table is used together with a finite-state automaton, which scans the text, in order to compute the jump values. At the outset, the automaton — which recognises all of the suffixes of the pattern — is constructed. It is thus a special Aho-Corasick machine having a suffix-trie structure, and may be built in $O(m |C_x| + |C|)$ (which is $O(m^2 + |C|)$) time and space using a modified version of Crochemore's (1986, 1988) suffix-automaton algorithm. The overall running time of the algorithm is therefore $O(m^2 + |C| + kn)$, and its working space is $O(m^2 + |C|)$.

Certain advances in increasing the efficiency of the search have been made recently. For example, several new algorithms employ a two-phase 'scanning and checking' approach. The basic idea behind this is to scan the text rapidly to identify potential approximate occurrences of the pattern, and then to check these more accurately. The aim is thus to minimise the number of text locations at which the slower, dynamic-programming distance computation need be applied.

An example of such an approach is to be found in Chang and Lawler's (1990,

1993) k-differences algorithms. Here, efficient use is made of the suffix tree of the pattern, in which the suffix links play a central rôle. The suffix tree is used in a linear, left-to-right scan of the text to evaluate the *matching statistics*. These statistics give, for each text position j, the length of the longest prefix common to text suffix $y(j, n)$ and any pattern suffix. These, together with LCAs derived from the pattern suffix-tree (using an efficient implementation of Schieber and Vishkin's (1988) algorithm), are sufficient to compute the jumps of Landau and Vishkin's approach. The jump values are then used to discard sections of the text where an approximate match cannot occur, leaving only the statistically rarer, potential match sites to be checked with the Landau-Vishkin dynamic-programming procedure.

Two algorithms have been developed on this basis, both of which require only $O(m)$ extra space and run in $O(kn)$ time in the worst case for fixed, finite alphabets. The first of these two algorithms takes $O(n)$ time on average for a uniform, random text when k is less than a threshold, $k_{th} = m/(\log_{|C|} m + c_1) - c_2$ for certain constants c_1 and c_2. In the second algorithm, the text is partitioned into regions such that any (k-differences approximate) match of the pattern in the text must contain at least one complete region. Jump values are used to ascertain whether or not the regions may contribute to a match. In this way, certain blocks of text symbols may be skipped over, giving a sublinear average running time for random text and $k < k_{th}/2 - 3$. Furthermore, an expected running time of $O(\frac{n}{m} k \log m)$ is obtained for any $k < k_{th}$ by employing a combination of the two algorithms.

Another two-phase approach has been developed by Tarhio and Ukkonen (1990a, 1990b, 1993). In the scanning phase of this algorithm, the appropriate diagonals in the distance matrix for potential approximate pattern occurrences are marked. The $O(kn)$-average-time, cut-off version of the dynamic-programming procedure is then applied in the subsequent verification phase, with the computation restricted to the marked diagonals. Before the scanning phase is embarked upon, two tables, requiring $O(m |C|)$ space, are initially computed in a pattern-preprocessing stage. This takes $O((k + |C|)m)$ time. These tables are then used during the text scan to compute which diagonals to mark and to determine Boyer and Moore-style increments in the text position.

The scanning operation requires $O(mn/k)$ time in the worst case, and

$$O\left(kn \cdot \frac{|C|}{|C| - 2k} \cdot \left[\frac{1}{m} + \frac{k}{|C| + 2k^2} \right] \right)$$

time on average for $k < (|C| - 1)/2$. The dynamic-programming element can contribute $O(mn)$ time at worst, but its maximum expected time of $O(kn)$ is preserved in this method. In practice, though, the actual distance computation is called upon relatively infrequently, giving rise to an overall average running time largely dominated by that for the scanning phase.

The cut-off procedure is also selectively applied to marked diagonals in the checking phase of an adaptation due to Jokinen, Tarhio and Ukkonen (1991) of

Grossi and Luccio's (1989) k-mismatches algorithm. Here, the text is first of all scanned in search of permutations — allowing for k differences — of the pattern; and diagonals are marked for any such potential approximate pattern occurrences found. Again, the worst-case running time is $O(mn)$. But in practice, less dynamic-programming effort is expended than if the $O(kn)$-expected-time procedure were applied over the entire text.

Wu and Manber (1991, 1992a, 1992b) have shown how Baeza-Yates and Gonnet's (1989, 1992) shift-add, string-matching algorithm may be extended to cater for the k-differences[1] problem. This adaptation has been implemented in the agrep[1] approximate-matching package for Unix (see also Manber and Wu (1992)). The algorithm employs k additional state-vectors, one for each value of $l = 1, \ldots, k$. The lth vector keeps track of all the possible matches with up to l differences. In addition to the resources required by the basic shift-add algorithm, this variant also requires $O(km)$ space and $O(\lceil \frac{m}{w} \rceil k)$ initialisation time for the extra state-vectors, where, as before, w is the machine wordsize. The text-scanning time is $O(\lceil \frac{m}{w} \rceil kn)$, giving an $O(kn)$ running time for $m \leqslant w$.

Wu and Manber advocate an alternative, scanning-and-checking, 'partition' approach in order to improve the above performance when k is small in relation to m. This approach involves the division of the pattern into contiguous blocks of length $\lfloor m/(k+1) \rfloor$. At least one of the first $k + 1$ pattern-blocks must appear intact within any k-differences approximate occurrence of the pattern in the text. Undertaking a simultaneous search for all of the first $k + 1$ pattern-blocks, using the multiple-string version of the shift-add algorithm, constitutes the scanning operation of this method. If an exact occurrence of any of these blocks is found, then a direct check for the approximate occurrence of the pattern is then made in the vicinity of the detected block-match.

One further point worth noting here about agrep is its 'best match' searching mode. This is useful in situations where the best approximate match — for which the appropriate value of k is not known in advance — of the pattern in the text is sought. The strategy employed by agrep is to search first of all for an exact match; and then allow 1 difference; and then 3 differences; and so on, successively doubling k and adding 1, until the search is successful. In the worst case, 4 times as many operations are required for this than would have been necessary had the actual value of k been known beforehand.

Baeza-Yates and Perleberg (1992) have suggested combining the above partition approach with the Aho-Corasick multiple-string searching algorithm, and the straightforward dynamic-programming procedure. The scan of the text in search of the pattern blocks is thus performed in linear time. Assuming random strings, the overall process, including checking, also takes $O(n)$ time on average for $k = O(m/\log m)$. The scanning phase may alternatively be implemented us-

---

[1]The authors of this tool have made it available via anonymous ftp from cs.arizona.edu

ing other multiple-string searching techniques, such as Commentz-Walter's or the shift-add algorithm. Improvements were also suggested in order to decrease the dynamic-programming burden by making the scanning phase more selective in its detection of potential approximate matches. This may be achieved, for example, by careful choice of the particular pattern blocks used in the search.

Ukkonen (1992a) has examined the use of two alternative distance functions in the context of the k-differences problem. These two functions were described in Chapter 3. One of them is based on q-grams, and the other is Ehrenfeucht and Haussler's (1988) 'maximal match' distance. Both of these can provide non-trivial lower bounds for the Levenshtein distance. The k-differences problem may therefore be solved in the following way. Compute either of these functions at each position in the scan of the text, and then where the lower bound on the Levenshtein distance is $\leqslant k$, compute its actual value via a dynamic-programming method.

The minimum q-gram distance between the pattern and any substring of the text ending at successive positions j may be computed in $O(n)$ time by scanning the text with a suffix automaton. This is of size $O(m \, |C|)$ and may be constructed from the pattern in $O(m \, |C|)$ time using Crochemore's (1988) method. Although the corresponding task for the maximal-match distance takes $O(m + n \, |C|)$ time, a very good approximation may be obtained in a linear scan of the text. Again, this is performed using a suffix automaton of the pattern.

For either of the above measures, text positions j requiring more accurate examination may therefore be marked in a linear scan of the text. In order to compute up to value $k + 1$ of the d-matrix diagonal ending at $d_{m,j}$, k contiguous diagonals on either side also need to be evaluated. Employing an $O(kn)$-time, dynamic-programming procedure (such as Galil-Park or Ukkonen-Wood) results in a computation time of $O(k^2)$ for the band of $2k + 1$ diagonals for each marked position j. Any diagonals in overlapping bands need be calculated only once, thus preserving the overall $O(kn)$ computation time. Taking into account the $O(m^2)$ preprocessing time for the dynamic programming, both scanning and checking phases may therefore be performed in an overall time of $O(m^2 + m \, |C| + \min\{n + rk^2, kn\})$, where r is the number of text positions marked during the scanning phase.

A recent variation on the dynamic-programming theme due to Chang and Lampe (1992) leads to a very efficient, practical algorithm. This adaptation of the straightforward dynamic-programming procedure is based on a 'column partition' approach, and has a running time that depends on the row averages of the distance matrix. The higher the average, the faster is the algorithm. The basic idea is to divide each column into runs of consecutive integers (i.e. strictly increasing sequences). By using an $O(m \, |C|)$-size table precomputed from the pattern (in $O(m \, |C|)$ time), the end point of each run may be determined in constant time. Also, the computations may be cut short as in the cut-off version of the basic procedure. The worst-case text-processing time for the method is $O((m - \bar{d}_m)n)$, where $\bar{d}_m$ is the average of the final row of the table. The expected time complexity is $O(kn)$, as the procedure is always faster than the simple cut-off method.

As a final note, a variation of the k-differences problem is mentioned here. This is one in which approximate occurrences of many different pattern strings are sought at various times in a single, static text. Here, the text may therefore be preprocessed in order to ease subsequent searches. This type of situation arises, for example, when large biological databases are searched for approximate occurrences of relatively small query sequences.

Myers (1990) has devised an algorithm for this problem that runs in sublinear expected time. The approach requires the alphabet to be fixed, and its general operation is as follows. First of all, an index of the start positions of instances of each of the text's distinct substrings of length $\log_{|C|} n$ is constructed. This takes $O(n)$ time and space. The query pattern is partitioned into regions of length $\log_{|C|} n$, and a set of strings is then generated for each of these pattern blocks. The actual strings in a set are derived from all the possible approximations — as far distant as a given value (which depends on k) — of the associated pattern-block. The members of these sets are then looked up in the text index, and the vicinities of their instances are checked for approximate matches of the complete pattern. This is done by attempting to extend the pattern substring matches by successively doubling the length of the text substring under consideration. The expected search time for this method is $O(kn^{f(k/m)} \log n)$, where the function $f(k/m)$ is increasing and is equal to 0 when $k/m = 0$. Sublinear performance is therefore achieved when $f < 1$. This obtains, for example, for $k/m \leqslant 0.33$ when $|C| = 4$, and for $k/m \leqslant 0.56$ when $|C| = 20$.

Jokinen and Ukkonen (1991) have also addressed this problem. They developed two different approaches — one based on suffix automata, and the other on lists of q-grams. In the former method, a suffix automaton of the text is constructed in $O(n |C|)$ time and space. This automaton together with the pattern string are then used in a dynamic-programming procedure, running in time $O(mn)$ in the worst case and $O(m)$ in the best case.

In the second approach, a q-gram index of the text is constructed. This is then used to locate potential approximate matches in a manner similar to that of Owolabi and McGregor's (1988) algorithm (which is described later in section 5.1.4). These potential matches are then checked using an $O(kn)$-time, dynamic-programming procedure (e.g. Galil-Park or Ukkonen-Wood). The preprocessing time, including that for the checking phase, is $O(m^2 + n + |C|^q)$. And the time complexity of the main processing is $O(m + kn)$ in the worst case and, once again, $O(m)$ in the best case.

Comparative Performance

Various comparisons of the theoretical complexities of the above methods are possible, but a question often of more importance is how they measure up in practice. This section is therefore brought to a conclusion with some observations concerning the practical performance of the k-differences algorithms.

We start off by considering the older approaches to the problem. Firstly, Ukkonen's cut-off method provides a significant reduction from $O(mn)$ to $O(kn)$ in the average-case running time of the dynamic-programming procedure. Next, the improvements in asymptotic running time in Landau and Vishkin's methods are, to a certain extent, offset by their limited practicability owing to the overheads inherent in the suffix-tree construction and processing. In fact, Myers (1986b) has stated that dispensing altogether with the sophisticated, constant-time, jump computation, in favour of a simple, brute-force computation, is likely to be significantly faster in practice. Although quadratic in the worst case, the running time for such an approach (described by Landau and Vishkin (1989) or Galil and Park (1990), for example) is also $O(kn)$ on average.

Also, the approaches that process the text in $O(kn)$ time in the worst case, due to Galil and Park and to Ukkonen and Wood, have been found to be slightly slower in certain conditions than straightforward dynamic-programming (Jokinen, Tarhio and Ukkonen, 1991). This is due to their relatively high overheads, and obtains when m is very small or when k is close to m. When comparing these two $O(kn)$ approaches, Ukkonen and Wood found the text processing of theirs to be slightly faster than that of Galil and Park's.

The scanning-and-checking methods can provide effective means of cutting down the computational effort required. Jokinen, Tarhio and Ukkonen, for instance, have demonstrated this in practice. They found that three such approaches — their adaptation of Grossi and Luccio's algorithm, Ukkonen's (1992) maximal-match method, and Tarhio and Ukkonen's (1990) Boyer-Moore approach — all performed significantly better than the above $O(kn)$-time methods and the plain dynamic-programming procedure. A couple of points worthy of note are that they also discovered the simple cut-off method to be competitive with these scanning-and-checking techniques, and that no clear winner emerged for all settings of the parameters m, k and $|C|$.

However, the empirical evidence did suggest that the cut-off method was the best of the four for binary alphabets or when k was relatively large. Tarhio-Ukkonen came out on top for very small k (i.e. $k = 1$ or 2), and the other two methods vied with each other for superiority in the remaining cases.

The elegance of the shift-add algorithm makes Wu and Manber's approach attractive. This is also an $O(kn)$-time algorithm when m does not exceed the machine wordsize.

Note, however, that, as intimated above, there is little, if any, advantage in using the $O(kn)$ over the $O(mn)$ approaches when $k = \Theta(m)$. But, the value of k may be specified as a fraction of m (up to given logarithmic, bounding functions of m) without affecting performance for the Baeza-Yates–Perleberg linear-expected-time and the Chang-Lawler sublinear-expected-time algorithms.

Finally, Chang and Lampe have observed that current implementations of the latter cannot compete in practice with their $O(kn)$-expected-time, column-partition variant of the dynamic-programming procedure. This they have found to be the fastest dynamic-programming-based technique at present. It is, for example, 10 times faster than the brute-force jump calculation version of Galil-Park for $|C| = 20$.

5.1.3   String Matching with Don't-Cares

A related string-matching problem is that involving don't-care, or wild-card, symbols which match any single symbol, including another don't-care. Note that here the problem is complicated by the fact that the 'match' relation is no longer transitive (e.g. denoting a don't-care by ?: AB matches A? and A? matches AC, but AB does not match AC). This therefore precludes straightforward adaptation of algorithms such as Knuth-Morris-Pratt and Boyer-Moore.

Pinter (1985) has addressed the problem for the case where only the pattern string contains don't-cares. His algorithm is an extension of the Aho-Corasick (1975) string-matching procedure. Recall from Chapter 2 that the latter is a generalisation of the Knuth-Morris-Pratt algorithm, which searches for multiple patterns in the text string in $O(m + n)$ time, where m is the sum of the lengths of the pattern strings. The preprocessing stage of this algorithm constructs in $O(m)$ time a pattern-matching automaton — similar to a deterministic, finite automaton but having two transition functions — from the set of pattern strings. This is then used to scan the text to search simultaneously for occurrences of the pattern strings in $O(n)$ time. The linearity of the method is preserved in Pinter's algorithm provided that the elements of an array of accumulators may be incremented in parallel; otherwise the temporal complexity becomes quadratic.

In a variation of the problem, the pattern may contain a don't-care sequence, variable in length up to some prescribed limit, k. Here, then, patterns sought are of the form $x = uvw$, for particular strings u and w over alphabet C, and any string $v \in \bigcup_{i=0}^{k} C^i$. The problem is thus to find an occurrence of u followed by one of w, with at most k intervening symbols. A direct approach to solving the problem is to search the text for all occurrences of u and w, and then ascertain which pairs satisfy the proximity requirement (e.g. Gonnet, 1987). This method can prove costly, though, when u or v appears frequently in the text.

An alternative technique has, however, been developed by Manber and Baeza-Yates (1991) for situations where the text is static, and thus amenable to being preprocessed. The method involves a 'suffix array' data structure (Manber and Myers, 1990), in which text-suffix starting positions are stored according to the lexicographic order of the respective suffixes. Given the preprocessed text, the number of occurrences of x, r, may be found in $O(\log n)$ time, and the actual positions of these occurrences in $O(n^{1/4} + r)$ time. The space required by the algorithm is $O(n(k + m))$, where m is an upper bound for $|u|$.

The case where both the pattern and text strings may contain don't-care symbols has been examined by Fischer and Paterson (1974). For strings over a finite alphabet, C, they have demonstrated that this problem is equivalent to integer multiplication, and using Schönhage-Strassen (1971; see also Aho, Hopcroft and Ullman, 1974) multiplication have derived an indirect algorithm running in $O(n \log^2 m \log \log m \log |C|)$ time. The constant term of this complexity expression is not, however, inconsiderable, and the algorithm is thus only of practical import for very long strings.

In contrast, the shift-add algorithm (Baeza-Yates and Gonnet, 1989, 1992) provides a practical search technique that can handle don't-cares in both pattern and text. In this method, pattern elements can, in fact, also represent finite classes of symbols and complements of classes. A pattern element may thus be permitted to match: a specific symbol; any symbol in the alphabet; or any symbol in a given subset of the alphabet, which may be specified either directly or as the set of all alphabet symbols not in a particular subset. The preprocessing time for this method is $O(\lceil \frac{m}{w} \rceil (m' + |C|))$, where m' is the size of the pattern description and w is the wordsize in bits of the computer. Recall that the search phase of this algorithm runs in $O(\lceil \frac{m}{w} \rceil n)$ time (for this application, the number of bits per state, b, is equal to 1). For small patterns, then, the search is performed in time linear in the size of the text.

A similar approach for handling patterns comprising elements representing symbol classes and complements of classes was also proposed by Abrahamson (1987). This too requires linear time for patterns smaller than the computer wordsize. He additionally put forward an alternative method running in sub-quadratic time for all sizes of patterns. This is, however, mainly of theoretical interest, as the resulting algorithm, which runs in $O(m + nm^{1/2} \log m \log \log^{1/2} m)$ time, does not provide a very practical solution.

For the case of unbounded alphabets, there is as yet no known algorithm with performance superior to that of the quadratic, brute-force approach to string matching.

5.1.4   Application Areas

Two areas in which approximate string-matching techniques find application are briefly mentioned here. Certain aspects of molecular sequencing in computational biology are mentioned first. The application of approximate-matching techniques in spelling-correction systems is then discussed.

Molecular Sequencing

DNA sequences may be represented as strings over the alphabet {A, C, G, T}. The symbols of this alphabet correspond to occurrences of the nucleotides adenine, cytosine, guanine and thymine, respectively. In order to derive certain statistical results, strands of DNA are sometimes modelled as random sequences whose constituent symbols are independent and identically distributed (i.i.d.). (Similarly, proteins are sometimes modelled as linear i.i.d. sequences of the 20 amino acids (e.g. Sibbald and White, 1987).) The distribution of the length of the longest common substring of two independent, random sequences has, for example, been studied by Arratia by relating it to that of the longest run of heads in a sequence of tosses of a coin. Theoretical results have been obtained for exact matches (Arratia and Waterman, 1985a), and also for the cases where the common substrings may disagree by up to k mismatches or k differences (Arratia and Waterman, 1985b; Arratia, Gordon and Waterman, 1986).

Approximation techniques for the shortest common superstring problem were mentioned in Chapter 3. Recall that these may be employed to estimate a long molecular sequence from many shorter, random segments originating therefrom. In DNA-sequencing procedures, however, symbol insertion, deletion, and substitution errors can often arise in these short fragment sequences (Staden, 1982). Superstrings constructed from inaccurate samples may therefore be significantly longer than those that would be obtained from ideal data.

In an effort to overcome, to a certain extent, this difficulty, Jiang and Li (1991) proposed the shortest k-approximate common superstring problem. Here the objective is to find a good approximation to the shortest string, y, that contains as a substring an occurrence, with up to k differences, of every member of the set of input strings, X. A straightforward extension of Li's (1990) superstring-approximation algorithm leads to a theoretical $O(m^3 n^k)$-time solution, where m is the total length of the input strings (i.e $m = \sum_{x \in X} |x|$) and n is the length of the optimal common superstring.

This type of problem has also been addressed by Kececioglu and Myers (1993) in the context of genetic sequence assembly. They have developed a software package comprising a suite of algorithms to perform the sequence reconstruction. In addition to errors in the sampled fragments, attention has also been directed towards handling the further problems of incomplete coverage of the underlying sequence and unknown orientation of the fragments. Their method proceeds in four stages. A graph of approximate overlaps between pairs of members of the set of input strings is first of all constructed. The orientations of the individual strings are then selected. Next, a set of overlaps is chosen. And, lastly, the selected overlaps are merged, and the actual symbols of the final sequence are determined in a 'voting' operation. The problems involved in the last three stages of the process are all NP-complete[2], and combinations of exact and heuristic approaches are employed according to the actual requirements for the given input. Despite requiring quadratic time, it is the first stage that actually dominates the overall running time of the procedure in practice.

Kececioglu and Myers' method of merging the overlaps into a multiple-string alignment has also been used by Huang (1992) in the Contig Assembly Program (CAP)[3]. This sequence-assembly program uses a quadratic-time, linear-space variation of Smith and Waterman's (1981) dynamic-programming, local-alignment algorithm (Huang, Hardison and Miller, 1990) to find the initial pairwise overlaps. This overlap-detection stage is made more efficient by applying the expensive, dynamic-programming procedure only to those pairs that pass through a filter: Chang and Lawler's (1990) approximate string-matching algorithm is used to exclude pairs of strings that cannot possibly overlap.

Motivated by an application in protein-structure analysis, Fischetti et al. (1992) have examined the problem of determining the optimal local alignment between two strings x^n and y, where, typically, $m \ll n$. The best alignment between some substring of x^n and one of y is thus sought. This particular problem arises when attempting to infer the secondary structure of a protein from its primary structure, i.e. from its sequence of constituent amino acids. A particular form of helical secondary structure is characterised in the primary structure by a repeated pattern of 7 symbols, with the possibility of discontinuities — hence the requirement for finding the optimal alignment between y and the string formed by concatenating n copies of pattern x. A straightforward dynamic-programming approach, with provision for arbitrary edit costs, leads to an $O(mn^2)$-time solution. However, by exploiting the periodic structure of x^n, Fischetti et al. have developed an alternative dynamic-programming method requiring only $O(mn)$ time.

Spelling Correction

The retrieval from a dictionary of words similar to a given pattern string has applications in spelling-correction systems, as used, for example, in word processors to correct misspelt or miskeyed words in a document. This area provides a natural habitat for various approximate-matching techniques.

The process normally involves two stages. As a first step, the spelling of a word is checked. If it is not found to be valid, it is then the objective of the second stage to suggest probable alternatives for manual selection. Note that errors which

---

[2]Various approximation algorithms have been proposed for the problem involved in the final stage, namely that of aligning multiple strings. See, for example, Chan, Wong and Chiu (1992) for a recent review.

[3]The author of this C program (huang@cs.mtu.edu) has made it available via electronic mail for non-commercial purposes.

may have transformed an originally valid word into a different valid word are inherently undetectable in this type of scheme. For these more subtle errors, much more complex checking taking into account the syntax and semantics of the context would be required.

As an alternative to searching a dictionary directly in order to check the validity of a spelling, techniques exploiting the statistical structure of its entries may be used instead. The use of probability distributions of symbol q-grams (which were discussed in Chapter 3) — most commonly digrams and trigrams — has, for example, been studied extensively (e.g. see Peterson, 1980).

The obvious approach to the second stage is to compute the value of some similarity measure, such as the Levenshtein distance or one of the other measures mentioned in Chapter 3, between the dubious word and each entry in the dictionary in turn. Plausible candidates may then be selected by thresholding the results. Such exhaustive techniques are, however, rather costly. The choice of dictionary words used in the comparison can be made more selective, though, by discarding those far distant from the input string. Simple prefiltering processes may involve, for example, thresholds on the acceptable differences in the lengths of, and the numbers of symbols common to, the input and dictionary strings (Okuda, Tanaka and Kasai, 1976).

An alternative approach is to attempt to 'undo' typical forms of errors and then search for valid spellings amongst the set of words generated in this way (e.g. see Peterson, 1980). Hashing techniques, such as the Soundex system (Russell, 1918, 1922), can also be used, with the objective of mapping members of groups of phonetically similar words to identical codes (e.g. Blair, 1960; Davidson, 1962; Bryant and Fenlon, 1976). Finally, the use of q-gram statistics may also be employed in order to lighten the burden of searching for correctly spelt alternatives (e.g. Kohonen and Reuhkala, 1978; and again see Peterson, 1980).

For example, the numbers of occurrences of distinct q-grams in the input string may be compared with those of the dictionary entries. This leads to fairly large storage requirements for the tables of q-gram statistics, though. Knowledge of whether a q-gram is present in or absent from a given string proves just as useful in practice as knowing the actual q-gram frequency (Riseman and Ehrich, 1971). Storage requirements may thus be reduced by employing binary q-gram tables, in which frequencies are quantised to either 0 or 1. Information regarding the positions of the occurrences within a string of the symbols of a q-gram may also be incorporated to aid in error correction (Riseman and Hanson, 1974). This causes the storage requirements to increase again, although Ullmann (1977) has proposed the use of a superimposed-coding technique to help combat the increase.

Further reductions in storage-space requirements have been achieved fairly recently by Owolabi and McGregor (1988) in a hybrid method that combines a q-gram table look-up prefilter with a distance-computation, best-match analysis phase. The method involves a conceptual two-dimensional bit-array with indices corresponding to individual trigrams and to the strings in the dictionary — a bit set (i.e. a 1) at position (i, j) indicates that the jth dictionary string contains trigram i. The saving in space is achieved by employing in practice a much compressed version of the table. Its entries are overloaded, such that each position j actually corresponds not to an individual string but rather to a set of strings in a section of the dictionary. Thus, a bit set at position (i, j) implies that at least one string in the jth section contains trigram i.

The trigram table is used in a coarse, prefiltering stage that yields a superset of the possible candidate replacements for the unrecognised word. The basic idea behind this stage is the fact that the number of q-grams common to two strings may be used as a measure of their similarity (Angell, Freund and Willett, 1983), and its operation is as follows. The trigrams in the unrecognised word are used to index rows in the table. The set bits for each dictionary section in these rows are accumulated, and the sections with totals exceeding a certain threshold are selected for further analysis. Groups of words from the dictionary are thus quickly obtained, and a final selection of candidates made based on the results of a dynamic-programming computation of the distances between these and the unrecognised word.

Division of a sorted dictionary into sections tends to produce clusters of fairly similar words for the fine analysis stage. In practice, an overloading factor of 16 was employed, and the table size was further reduced by overloading it vertically as well. To do this, a hashing function was used to map the 17576 distinct trigrams possible for a 26-symbol alphabet to only 511 distinct values.

Although performing well in practice, no theoretical analysis of the above method was developed. In an effort to overcome this shortcoming, Kim and Shawe-Taylor (1992b) have derived an estimation for the average-case complexity for the look-up phase of an adaptation of the algorithm. In this variant, the q-gram index is constructed in the form of a trie, with each leaf containing a list of those dictionary sections containing its corresponding q-gram. In the look-up phase, the trie is searched for the q-grams in the input string, and the lists at the corresponding leaves are collated. Again, dictionary sections containing more than a given number of the unrecognised word's q-grams are passed to a dynamic-programming stage, in which distances are calculated in order to make the final selection.

Based on certain assumptions about the language to which the dictionary strings belong, it has been estimated that the overall look-up operation requires $O(m \log n)$ time on average, where m is the length of the unrecognised word and n is the total size of the dictionary. It should be noted that to derive this result, the necessary choices of q and the number of sections into which the dictionary is divided are dependent on both the size of the dictionary and the statistical distributions of the q-grams.

A variation of this dictionary look-up problem is one in which the dictionary entries that contain an approximate occurrence of the input word as a substring are sought. This variant has been addressed by Kashyap and Oommen (1983), who proposed a cubic-time solution based on the computation of a generalised Levenshtein distance. Oommen (1987) has also examined the related problem of recognising a word in a dictionary from a corrupted subsequence of one of its entries.

Similar to the problem of retrieving from a dictionary alternatives close to an unknown word is that of retrieving from a database documents containing all or many of the terms given in a query. This is also an area where techniques based on q-gram statistics have been applied. D'Amore and Mah (Kimbrell, 1988) have, for example, implemented a system in which a q-gram 'fingerprint' of the query is compared with those of the documents in the database. In this context, a fingerprint comprises a vector of the numbers of occurrences of selected 2-, 3-, and 4-grams in the corresponding text once commonly occurring words have been removed. In the system, a normalised, cross-correlation similarity measure is used to compare fingerprint vectors, and those documents for which this exceeds a certain threshold are then selected for retrieval.

5.1.5 Dedicated Hardware and Parallel Algorithms

As we have now come to examine approximate-matching techniques in this chapter, and also since the topics of sequence comparison and exact string-matching have been dealt with in previous ones, it might now be appropriate to discuss briefly various hardware approaches that have been developed in these three areas. Mention shall be made of both dedicated hardware designs and certain parallel algorithms intended for implementation on general-purpose parallel architectures. The common feature of these is that, in contrast to the sequential algorithms discussed thus far, multiple symbol comparisons are performed concurrently.

Earlier work in this area tended to concentrate on exact string-matching with extension to handling don't-care symbols. A typical application for this type of hardware is as a 'term comparator' in a text-retrieval system. The rôle of such a device is to perform real-time, keyword searches in large, unformatted document databases as the text stream is read serially from secondary storage.

Latterly, much attention has been focused on the design of hardware systems for the comparison of sequences, with applications predominantly in molecular biology. Such systems compute the distance between strings in order to quantify degrees of similarity between, for example, various genetic sequences.

Hardware Approaches

The major architectures for hardware string-processing machines involve one or more of the following:

- **parallel comparators** (e.g. Stellhorn, 1974; Mead et al., 1976; Lee, Frieder and Mak, 1988; Lee and Mak, 1989)

- **associative memories** (e.g. Bird, Tu and Worthy, 1977; Burkowski, 1982; Lee and Lochovsky, 1985)

- **cellular arrays** (e.g. Copeland, 1978; Mukhopadhyay, 1978, 1979, 1980; Foster and Kung, 1979, 1980; Curry and Mukhopadhyay, 1983; Halaas, 1983; Liu and Fu, 1984; Cheng and Fu, 1987; Lopresti, 1987; Gokhale et al., 1990, 1991; Arnold, Buell and Davis, 1992)

- **finite-state automata** (FSA) (e.g. Roberts, 1977, 1978; Hollaar and Roberts, 1978; Haskin, 1980, 1981; Haskin and Hollaar, 1983)

A parallel comparator comprises a number of comparators, which operate simultaneously. The outputs from the individual comparator units are combined together to give an overall comparison result.

With associative memory, a successful memory access corresponds to a match between the string used to address the memory and the string stored at the accessed location.

A cellular array consists of a network of identical logic cells, with nearest neighbour interconnections. Each cell will typically contain a symbol comparator together with other logic elements. In a linear array, the output generated from one cell is propagated as an input to the next.

Typical FSA architectures involve a current-state register and a state-transition table stored in RAM. In order to enter its next state, the automaton inspects the current input symbol, uses this together with the current state to index the transition table, and then moves to the state indicated by the table by loading the state register.

String Matching with Don't-Cares

The provision of facilities for handling don't-care symbols in hardware is relatively straightforward, and has been incorporated into many designs intended for linear-time string matching. All of the main architectures outlined above have been employed for this task.

In the parallel comparator developed by Mead et al. (1976), for example, a mask register is used to hold the don't-cares. Both this and a register for the pattern string are preloaded in advance of the text search. The text string is then serially shifted through a data register, which thus contains successive text substrings. The symbols of these are compared, in parallel, with their counterparts in the pattern- and mask-registers. The individual symbol-comparison results are effectively connected in a wired AND to provide an overall match signal. This particular LSI device was implemented in pMOS, operates at 2 MHz, and can accommodate patterns of up to 128 bits. Longer patterns may also be handled by connecting several comparators in cascade.

An alternative to using a Serial In Parallel Out (SIPO) data register to obtain substrings for comparison is to broadcast serially each symbol to all the comparators in the device. Parallel comparisons are thus performed between a single symbol from one string and all of those preloaded into the array. A disadvantage of this strategy, however, is the requirement for a high fan-out and long routing distance for the broadcast line. Proposals have been made for a VLSI CMOS device using this approach, in which the pattern symbols are serially broadcast to successive text substrings (Lee, Frieder and Mak, 1988; Lee and Mak, 1989). In this design, the current text-substring is discarded as soon as a broadcast pattern-symbol fails to find a match.

The use of a mask register in a parallel comparator allows fixed-length don't-cares (FLDCs) to be implemented easily. There is, however, no simple way of catering for variable-length don't-cares (VLDCs) in this manner. In general, this is also the case for devices based on associative memories. In such designs, the text may again be shifted through a SIPO register, allowing the symbols of successive substrings to be read in parallel. But this time, these substrings are used to address the associative memory, which may contain multiple pattern strings. A variation on this theme was proposed by Burkowski (1982), who devised a hardware system in which the current text-substring is hashed to select one of the several pattern strings stored in conventional RAM for parallel comparison.

In the cellular array approach, rather than being directly combined as in a parallel comparator, the individual comparator outputs propagate through the linear array from one cell to the next. In both Copeland's and Mukhopadhyay's designs, the pattern string is preloaded into the array and the text is serially broadcast to all the cells. The comparison output from one cell is used as an enable input for the next. A match output from the final cell thus indicates that successive text symbols have matched all the pattern symbols in the array in sequence. Accommodation of FLDCs in this type of architecture is straightforward — a don't-care cell simply acts as a unit delay — and VLDCs can also be implemented. For the latter, all that is required is for a cell continuously to hold its output true once it has been enabled.

Cellular arrays can also be used for string matching in a systolic mode, in which, rather than being broadcast, the input symbols also flow through the array, passing from one cell to the next on each 'beat.' This approach has been adopted by Foster and Kung (1979, 1980), who have produced a cascadable, VLSI string-matching chip, capable of handling 4 million characters/s. With this chip, the text and pattern strings enter the array from opposite ends. Once the latter completes its journey, it is recirculated through the array. Each cell compares two passing symbols and accumulates a temporary result, with the final result stream leaving the array with the text string.

Finally, we have the finite-state-automaton approach, which has, for example, been adopted by the CIA in a text-search system (Roberts, 1977). Both FLDCs and VLDCs may be realised fairly easily in this type of implementation by introducing appropriate states into the automaton. In comparison with on-line hardware solutions, such as cellular-array devices, though, the FSA approach does have certain disadvantages. A relatively large storage space is required for the state-transition tables, the contents of which must be computed during a preprocessing stage. Other hardware overheads are also incurred, for example, in the implementation of an Aho-Corasick machine owing to the requirements for the control of dynamic text-skipping.

Approximate String Matching

A CMOS VLSI device which allows approximate string-matching operations to be performed has been developed fairly recently by the NEC Corporation (Takahashi et al., 1986; Takahashi, Yamada and Hirata, 1987; Hirata et al., 1987, 1988; Yamada et al., 1987a, 1987b). Its architecture combines an associative memory with FSA logic. The 512-character (16 bit) content-addressable memory (CAM), which is preloaded before searching commences, may be variously configured: from a single 512-character pattern up to 64 8-character pattern strings. Serial input data, at a rate of 10 million characters/s, is fed through the CAM, which performs parallel matching and passes match signals to the FSA logic. In addition to exact string-matching, an approximate-matching mode allows occurrences of patterns with up to 1 difference to be found. And finally, the use of both FLDCs — in either the pattern strings or in the input text — and VLDCs is supported by the device.

Sequence Comparison

As discussed earlier, the parallel computation of distance functions to assess the similarity between a pair of sequences has attracted significant attention. Both the problems of computing the string distance only (e.g. Liu and Fu, 1984; Lipton and Lopresti, 1985, 1986; Edmiston and Wagner, 1987; Lopresti, 1987; Lander, Mesirov and Taylor, 1988; Gokhale et al., 1990, 1991), and of additionally finding a least-cost editing sequence that transforms one string into the other (e.g. Cheng and Fu, 1987; Edmiston et al., 1988; Huang, 1989) have been studied.

Two notable hardware designs for computing distances between pairs of strings are the P-NAC chip and the Splash system. The former — the Princeton Nucleic Acid Comparator (Lopresti, 1987) — is a linear, systolic array into which the two strings to be compared enter from opposite ends. The processing elements (PES) of the array effect a parallel computation of the dynamic-programming recurrence relation (which was discussed in Chapter 3) to calculate the distance between the two strings. The basis of the parallelisation of the dynamic-programming method is the fact that all the elements on a given antidiagonal in the distance matrix may be evaluated simultaneously. The initial boundary row and column of the distance matrix enter the array with the strings, and, as they flow through it, are transformed into the final row and column of the matrix. Recall that on a sequential machine, the method runs in $O(mn)$ time. Given a sufficient number of PES, however, the parallel computation requires only linear time. Once the problem size exceeds the limitation imposed by a given array size, the problem must be partitioned and then the running time again scales quadratically.

The editing costs have been hardwired in the chip such that it is the edit distance that is computed, i.e. a cost of 1 is assigned to an insertion or a deletion, and 2 to a substitution. The chip itself comprises 30 PES, and has been fabricated using nMOS VLSI technology. A speed-up over the dynamic-programming method running on a DEC VAX 11/785 by a factor of 125 was reported for a Sun 2 workstation-hosted system using the P-NAC, and it was also remarked that the chip had the potential of operating 10 times faster than its support circuitry was able to drive it.

In an effort to overcome the limited flexibility inherent in fixed architectures such as the P-NAC, the Splash system was designed at the Supercomputer Research Center (Gokhale et al., 1990, 1991). Splash is a Sun-hosted, general-purpose, linear logic array, consisting of a pipeline of 32 Xilinx 3090 field-programmable gate arrays (FPGAs) with distributed memory. The logic function of an FPGA is determined by its configuration data, which, prior to operation of the circuit, are downloaded and stored in on-chip memory. The system therefore offers gate-level programmability, allowing its architecture to be configured to suit varying requirements depending on the particular application.

One of the prime motivations for the design of the Splash system was to implement Lopresti's systolic string-comparison algorithm. For this application, each FPGA is configured as a linear array of PES, with each PE comprising a symbol comparator and a finite-state machine. The rôle of the latter is to compute a new distance value based on the previous one together with the output from the comparator. The overall array comprises a total of 744 PES when configured in this way.

When operating as a sequence comparator, Splash has been reported to have a 45-fold speed advantage over the P-NAC system. Once again, however, the actual performance is limited by the bandwidth of the external interface. A SPARC-hosted system, Splash 2, has therefore been designed as a successor with the aim of increasing the sustainable I/O rate by a factor of 10 (Arnold, Buell and Davis, 1992). The FPGAs for Splash 2 have been upgraded to Xilinx 4010s, which now number 17 per board. The system is expandable by adding duplicate boards, up to an overall total of 16. Also, rather than being hardwired as a pipeline, the FPGA topology is now dynamically reconfigurable using crossbar switching.

Various parallel algorithms have been proposed for the problem of additionally finding optimal editing sequences. Recall from the discussion in Chapter 3 of the Wagner-Fischer approach that this may be performed by tracing a path back through the completed dynamic-programming matrix. Cheng and Fu (1987) have proposed a VLSI architecture to compute optimal edit sequences in this way. Their approach runs in linear time provided that an $m \times n$ array of PEs is available.

Certain other approaches that may be implemented using only up to a linear number of PEs have also been developed. In addition to the running time, the space complexity of such methods is also an important consideration. Edmiston et al. (1988), for example, have devised two techniques — one running on an Intel Hypercube, the other on a Connection Machine. The former consumes $O(mn/p)$ space per processor, where p is the number of PEs. An improvement in the space requirement is obtained for the latter, but linear parallel time and constant space per processor are not guaranteed when a linear number of PEs is available. An algorithm that does fulfil these requirements, however, has been developed by Huang (1989). This is intended for message-passing, parallel architectures such as the above-mentioned Hypercube and Connection Machine, and is implemented on a linear array of processors (of number p, where $p \leqslant \max(m,n)$). The time and space-per-processor complexities of the algorithm are $O((m+n)^2/p)$ and $O((m+n)/p)$, respectively.

5.2   Algorithms in Detail

5.2.1   Landau-Vishkin k-mismatches

In Landau and Vishkin's (1985, 1986a) k-mismatches algorithm, the text string is analysed using a 2-dimensional *pattern-mismatch* table generated during a pattern-preprocessing stage. The calculation of this table, $pm[1 \ldots m-1, 1 \ldots 2k+1]$, shall be considered in due course. Firstly, however, the text-analysis stage shall be examined.

The analysis of the text is performed in a 2-dimensional *text-mismatch* array, $tm[0 \ldots n-m, 1 \ldots k+1]$. On completion of the analysis, row i contains the positions within x of the first $k+1$ mismatches between strings $x(1,m)$ and $y(i+1,i+m)$. Thus, if $tm[i,v] = l$, then $y_{i+l} \neq x_l$ and this is the vth mismatch between $x(1,m)$ and $y(i+1,i+m)$ from left to right. If the number of mismatches, c, say, between x and substring $y(i+1,i+m)$ is less than $k+1$, then the default value $m+1$ appears from location $c+1$ onwards, i.e.

$$tm[i,c+1] = tm[i,c+2] = \ldots = tm[i,k+1] = m+1$$

Note that a value of $m + 1$ for $tm[i, k + 1]$ indicates that text substring $y(i + 1, i + m)$ differs from pattern x by at most k mismatches, and therefore provides a solution to the problem. This is illustrated in the following example. Consider the case where $x = \texttt{tram}$, $y = \texttt{thetrippedtrap}$ and $k = 2$. It may be seen from the following text-mismatch table that occurrences of the pattern with up to 2 mismatches are to be found starting at y_4 and y_{11}, namely substrings $\texttt{trip}$ and $\texttt{trap}$.

	1	2	3
0	2	3	4
1	1	2	3
2	1	2	3
3	3	4	5
4	1	2	3
5	1	2	3
6	1	2	3
7	1	2	3
8	1	2	3
9	1	2	3
10	4	5	5

The text-analysis algorithm is given in Figure 5.1. The pattern is scanned across the text from left to right, one place at a time by the for loop. At iteration i, text substring $y(i + 1, i + m)$ is compared with the pattern. The rightmost position in the text reached by previous iterations is given by j, i.e. it is the maximum value of $r + tm[r, k + 1]$, where $0 \leqslant r < i$. If $i < j$, then procedure $merge$ is called, which finds mismatches between $x(1, j - i)$ and $y(i + 1, j)$ and sets b equal to the number found. If this does not exceed k, then procedure $extend$ is invoked. This scans the text from y_{j+1} onwards, until it either finds $k + 1$ mismatches or it reaches y_{i+m} with at most k mismatches, in which case an approximate pattern occurrence has been found starting at y_{i+1}.

The operation of $extend$ is straightforward, and the procedure is given in Figure 5.2. Pairs of symbols from the substrings $y(j + 1, i + m)$ and $x(j - i + 1, m)$ are compared, and, in the event of a mismatch, b is incremented and the text-mismatch table is updated.

The operation of procedure $merge$ shall now be examined. As noted earlier, this procedure finds mismatches between $x(1, j - i)$ and $y(i + 1, j)$ and sets b equal to the number found. Thus, $merge$ evaluates $tm[i, 1 \ldots b]$ for $b \leqslant k + 1$, and in so doing uses information obtained previously. Firstly, recall that row r of the text-mismatch table gives the mismatches obtained when the start of the pattern is aligned with y_{r+1}, and that $r + tm[r, k + 1]$ is the present rightmost position examined in the text. Mismatches in row r of tm lying to the right of y_i in the text are therefore relevant in the comparison of the pattern with the text starting from y_{i+1}. The appropriate

— initialise
$tm[0 \ldots n - m, 1 \ldots k + 1] = m + 1$
$r = 0$
$j = 0$
— scan text
for $i = 0$ to $n - m$
  $b = 0$
  if $i < j$
    $merge(i, r, j, b)$
  if $b < k + 1$
    $r = i$
    $extend(i, j, b)$

Figure 5.1: Landau-Vishkin k-mismatches string matching

$extend(i, j, b)$
  while $(b < k + 1)$ and $(j - i < m)$
    $j = j + 1$
    if $y_j \neq x_{j-i}$
      $b = b + 1$
    $tm[i, b] = j - i$

Figure 5.2: Procedure $extend$

values from the text-mismatch table are thus $tm[r, q \ldots k + 1]$, where q is the least integer such that $r + tm[r, q] > i$. However, account must be taken of the fact that these mismatches correspond to the start of the pattern being aligned with y_{r+1}, whereas the current pattern position is aligned with y_{i+1} — a difference of $i - r$ places.

The second source of information used by $merge$ is thus the precomputed pattern-mismatch table, pm, which gives the positions of the mismatches between the pattern and itself at various relative shifts. Row i of array $pm[1 \ldots m-1, 1 \ldots 2k+1]$ contains the positions within x of the first $2k + 1$ mismatches between the substrings $x(1, m - i)$ and $x(i + 1, m)$, i.e. the overlapping portions of the two copies of the pattern for a relative shift of i. Thus, if $pm[i, u] = l$, then $x_{i+l} \neq x_l$ and this is the uth mismatch between $x(1, m - i)$ and $x(i + 1, m)$ from left to right. If the number of mismatches, c, say, between these substrings is less than $2k + 1$, then the default value $m + 1$ appears from location $c + 1$ onwards, i.e.

$$pm[i, c + 1] = pm[i, c + 2] = \ldots = pm[i, 2k + 1] = m + 1$$

It is thus row $i - r$ of the pattern-mismatch table which is of interest in $merge$, and the relevant values are $pm[i - r, 1 \ldots t]$, where t is the rightmost mismatch in $pm[i - r, 1 \ldots 2k + 1]$ such that $pm[i - r, t] < j - i + 1$, since only the mismatches in substring $x(1, j - i)$ are required.

In order to see how the information mentioned above may be used in procedure $merge$, consider a text location p within the relevant range, i.e. $i+1 \leqslant p \leqslant j$. Position p may satisfy either, neither, or both of the following conditions.

A: with x_1 aligned with y_{r+1}, text position p corresponds to a previously detected mismatch between pattern and text, i.e. $y_p \neq x_{p-r}$, and this is mismatch number v, for some v such that $q \leqslant v \leqslant k + 1$, i.e. $p - r = tm[r, v]$.

B: with two copies of the pattern, having a relative shift of $i - r$, aligned with the text such that their initial symbols lie above y_{r+1} and y_{i+1}, respectively, text position p corresponds to a mismatch between the two patterns, i.e. $x_{p-r} \neq x_{p-i}$. This will be the uth mismatch for this shift, for some u such that $1 \leqslant u \leqslant t$, i.e. $p - i = pm[i - r, u]$.

Recall that the question of importance at text position p is whether or not the text symbol there matches the corresponding pattern symbol when x_1 is aligned with y_{i+1} — i.e. does $y_p = x_{p-i}$? The bearing on this question of the possible situations with regards to the above two conditions shall now be examined.

Case 1: p satisfies neither Condition A nor Condition B. Thus, $y_p = x_{p-r}$ and $x_{p-r} = x_{p-i}$, so $y_p = x_{p-i}$. No explicit comparison is required between pattern and text as there must therefore be a match at this position.

Case 2: p satisfies only one of the two conditions, i.e. either Condition A or Condition B, but not both. In either case, $y_p \neq x_{p-i}$, which may be shown as follows. If only Condition A is satisfied, then $y_p \neq x_{p-r}$ and $x_{p-r} = x_{p-i}$, so $y_p \neq x_{p-i}$. If, on the other hand, only Condition B holds, then $y_p = x_{p-r}$ and $x_{p-r} \neq x_{p-i}$, so again $y_p \neq x_{p-i}$. Again, no explicit comparison is required since there must be a mismatch at text position p.

Case 3: both Condition A and Condition B hold. No conclusion concerning y_p and x_{p-i} may be drawn, requiring the two symbols to be compared directly.

In Case 2 and if a mismatch is found in Case 3, the mismatch count, b, must be incremented and $tm[i, b]$ updated by procedure *merge*.

We are now in a position to describe procedure *merge*, which is given in Figure 5.3. As noted earlier, the relevant table values for *merge* are $pm[i - r, 1 \ldots t]$ and $tm[r, q \ldots k+1]$. Variables u and v are set initially to index the first elements of these two vectors respectively, and subsequently step through the vector components.

The conditions for terminating the procedure are as follows. Firstly, if $b = k + 1$, then $k + 1$ mismatches have been found for the pattern positioned such that x_1 is aligned with y_{i+1}, and the procedure may therefore be exited. Secondly, recall that the rightmost text position of interest in *merge*, namely j, is equal to $r + tm[r, k+1]$; if $v = k+2$, then $tm[r, k+1]$ will have been used for the previous value of v, namely $v = k + 1$, and position j must therefore have been passed. Hence, the procedure may also be exited in this case. Finally, the procedure may also be terminated if $i + pm[i - r, u] > j$ and $tm[r, v] = m + 1$. If the latter part of this condition holds, then $r + tm[r, v]$ will equal j, as will corresponding sums for subsequent values of v up to $k + 1$. In this case, the procedure may therefore be terminated if the former part of the above condition also holds, as this indicates that text position j has actually been passed.

It now remains to demonstrate that the number of mismatch positions in the pattern-mismatch table is sufficient for *merge* to find all or, if there are more than $k + 1$, the first $k + 1$ mismatches for $y(i + 1, j)$. This may be shown as follows. Condition A holds for at most $k + 1$ text positions in the range $[i + 1, j]$. Condition B holds for some unknown number of positions in the same interval. Row $i - r$ of the pattern mismatch table, $pm[i - r, 1 \ldots 2k + 1]$, contains at most $2k + 1$ mismatch positions between two copies of the pattern with a relative shift of $i - r$. If $pm[i - r, 2k + 1] \geqslant j - i$, then the table contains all the pattern-pattern mismatch positions for which Condition B holds for text positions in the interval $[i + 1, j]$. On the other hand, if $pm[i - r, 2k + 1] < j - i$, then the table can provide $2k + 1$ text positions in the range $[i + 1, j - 1]$ for which Condition B holds. Since $j = r + tm[r, k + 1]$, there are up to k text positions in the range $[i + 1, j - 1]$ for which condition A holds. In the worst case, there could thus be k positions for which Case 3 holds, and which would thus require explicit comparisons. This then leaves at least $k + 1$ positions

---

$merge(i,\ r,\ j,\ b)$

$u = 1$

$v = \min\{q \mid r + tm[r, q] > i\}$

while $(b < k + 1)$ **and** $(v < k + 2)$ **and**

$\qquad (i + pm[i - r, u] \leqslant j$ **or** $tm[r, v] \neq m + 1)$

$\quad$ **if** $i + pm[i - r, u] > r + tm[r, v]$

$\qquad$ — Case 2, Condition A

$\qquad b = b + 1$

$\qquad tm[i, b] = tm[r, v] - (i - r)$

$\qquad v = v + 1$

$\quad$ **else if** $i + pm[i - r, u] < r + tm[r, v]$

$\qquad$ — Case 2, Condition B

$\qquad b = b + 1$

$\qquad tm[i, b] = pm[i - r, u]$

$\qquad u = u + 1$

$\quad$ **else**

$\qquad$ — $i + pm[i - r, u] = r + tm[r, v]$

$\qquad$ — Case 3

$\qquad$ **if** $x_{pm[i-r,u]} \neq y_{i+pm[i-r,u]}$

$\qquad\quad b = b + 1$

$\qquad\quad tm[i, b] = pm[i - r, u]$

$\qquad u = u + 1$

$\qquad v = v + 1$

Figure 5.3: Procedure $merge$

---

satisfying Condition B but not Condition A (Case 2), which is sufficient to establish that there are at least $k + 1$ mismatches between pattern and text for the particular pattern alignment.

The temporal complexity of the text analysis shall now be examined. Excluding calls to procedures $merge$ and $extend$, each of the $n - m + 1$ iterations of the text-analysis loop takes constant time, giving a total of $O(n)$ time. The total number of operations performed by $extend$ during all its calls is $O(n)$, since it inspects each text symbol once at most. On each call, $merge$ operates on the vectors $pm[i-r, 1 \ldots 2k+1]$ and $tm[r, 1 \ldots k+1]$, which have a combined total of $3k+2$ elements. The operations of $merge$ may be accounted for by associating constant-time operations with each of these entries, resulting in a running time for each invocation of $O(k)$. It may thus be seen that the overall running time of the text analysis is $O(kn)$.

— initialise
$$pm[2^{l-1} \ldots 2^l - 1, 1 \ldots \min\{2^{\log_2 m - l}2k + 1, m - 2^l\}] = m + 1$$
$$r = 2^{l-1}$$
$$j = 2^{l-1}$$
— calculate rows of pm in set l
for $i = 2^{l-1}$ **to** $2^l - 1$
    $b = 0$
    if $i < j$
        $merge(i, r, j, b)$
    if $b < \min\{2^{\log_2 m - l}2k + 1, m - 2^l\}$
        $r = i$
        $extend(i, j, b)$

Figure 5.4: Landau-Vishkin pattern preprocessing (at stage l)

All that remains now is to address the computation of the pattern-mismatch table during the pattern-preprocessing stage. Without loss of generality, it may be assumed that m is some power of 2. The preprocessing algorithm uses a partition of the set of the $m - 1$ rows of pm, $\{1, 2, \ldots, m - 1\}$, into the following $\log_2 m$ subsets

$$\{1\}, \{2, 3\}, \{4, 5, 6, 7\}, \ldots, \{m/2, \ldots, m - 1\}$$

and has $\log_2 m$ stages. At stage l, where $1 \leqslant l \leqslant \log_2 m$, the rows of pm in set l are computed, where set l is $\{2^{l-1}, \ldots, 2^l - 1\}$.

The method used to compute the table is based on that used during the text-analysis phase, and the algorithm for stage l is shown in Figure 5.4. At stage l, the inputs to the pattern-analysis algorithm are the pattern substrings $x(1, m - 2^{l-1})$ and $x(2^{l-1} + 1, m)$, which correspond to the pattern and text, respectively, in the text analysis, and the sub-array $pm[1 \ldots 2^{l-1} - 1, 1 \ldots \min\{2^{\log_2 m - l}4k + 1, m - 2^{l-1}\}]$ which contains the outputs from the previous $l - 1$ stages. (The number of elements in the rows of this sub-array shall be explained later.) The outputs of stage l are entered into $pm[2^{l-1} \ldots 2^l - 1, \min\{2^{\log_2 m - l}2k + 1, m - 2^l\}]$. With the exception of stage $\log_2 m$, in which up to $2k + 1$ mismatches are found, it is thus up to $\min\{2^{\log_2 m - l}2k + 1, m - 2^l\}$ mismatches which are to be found for each row of pm at stage l, rather than up to $k + 1$ as in the text-analysis algorithm.

Using arguments similar to those of the previous examination of the correct operation of procedure $merge$, it may be shown that in order to find up to the requisite number of mismatches, $\min\{2^{\log_2 m - l}4k + 1, m - 2^{l-1}\}$ positions for which Condition B holds are required at stage l, and $4k + 1$ such locations for the special case of stage $\log_2 m$.

For each stage, l, of the $\log_2 m$ stages of the pattern analysis, the **for** loop makes 2^{l-1} iterations $(2^{l-1} \leqslant i \leqslant 2^l - 1)$. Excluding calls to $merge$ and $extend$, each iteration takes constant time. For all the iterations of stage l, $extend$ requires $O(m)$ time. It was shown earlier that each call of $merge$ requires time proportional to the number of mismatches searched for. Thus, each call of $merge$ takes $O(\min\{2^{\log_2 m - l} 2k + 1, m - 2^l\})$, which is $O(2k2^{\log_2 m - l})$. The total time for stage l is therefore $O(m + 2^{l-1}(2k2^{\log_2 m - l})) = O(km)$. Summing this for all stages gives a total preprocessing time of $O(\sum_{l=1}^{\log_2 m} km) = O(km \log m)$. The overall time complexity of the pattern preprocessing and the text analysis is thus $O(k(n + m \log m))$.

5.2.2 Shift-Add

Baeza-Yates and Gonnet's (1989, 1992) shift-add algorithm is a very flexible technique that permits real-time searches of unbuffered texts to be performed. The algorithm may be applied to a variety of string-matching problems — principally: exact string matching; k-mismatches searching; matching with patterns involving don't-cares and classes of symbols; matching with multiple patterns; and, as we shall see later in this chapter, the k-differences problem. In this section, the general structure of the algorithm shall first of all be considered from an examination of its application to exact string matching. The ways in which it may be brought to bear on the k-mismatches problem and on the problem of matching with patterns involving classes of symbols shall then be discussed.

The scan of the text proceeds as follows. The text symbols are read in succession, one at a time. For each one, y_i, inspected, each of the m pattern prefixes, $x(1, j)$ for $1 \leqslant j \leqslant m$, is compared with its corresponding text substring ending at y_i, i.e. $y(i - j + 1, i)$. But these comparisons are not performed explicitly. Instead, a vector of states holding the results of these prefix searches is manipulated numerically. The vector is treated as an integer, and is updated as each new text symbol is encountered. Simple arithmetic/logical operations are performed in this updating process, with the vector itself and an another integer — obtained from a preprocessed table indexed by the new text symbol — as the operands.

The operation of the algorithm may be made clearer by examining the particular case of exact string matching. Here, each state, s_j, is used to indicate whether or not there are any mismatches between pattern prefix $x(1, j)$ and text substring $y(i - j + 1, i)$. A single bit suffices for this, and s_j may be defined to be 0 if there are no mismatches, and 1 otherwise. The state vector at stage i in the search, $^i s$, may thus be represented as follows, where $^i s_j$ denotes the value of state j at stage i.

$$
\begin{aligned}
^i s &= {}^i s_m 2^{m-1} + \ldots + {}^i s_2 2^1 + {}^i s_1 2^0 \\
&= \sum_{j=1}^{m} {}^i s_j 2^{j-1}
\end{aligned}
\tag{5.1}
$$

State values are illustrated in the following example for pattern ADAB.

$$
\begin{array}{lccc}
 & & j & {}^i s_j \\
x(1,1) & \text{A} & 1 & 0 \\
x(1,2) & \text{A D} & 2 & 1 \\
x(1,3) & \text{A D A} & 3 & 0 \\
x(1,4) & \text{A D A B} & 4 & 1 \\
\text{text} & \text{A C A E D A D A D A B C} \ldots & & \\
 & \phantom{\text{A C A E D A}}{}_i & &
\end{array}
$$

A zero value for ${}^i s_m$ indicates that there are no mismatches between the complete pattern and the corresponding text substring ending at y_i, i.e. an exact occurrence of the pattern has been found. In terms of the numerical value of the state vector, this means that a match is detected whenever ${}^i s < 2^{m-1}$.

Next to be considered is how the state vector is updated on moving in the text from one position to the next. If there are no mismatches between prefix $x(1, j - 1)$ and substring $y(i - j + 1, i - 1)$ and if $x_j = y_i$, then it follows that are no mismatches between $x(1, j)$ and $y(i - j + 1, i)$. If, on the other hand, there already are mismatches or if $x_j \neq y_i$, then $x(1, j)$ does not match $y(i - j + 1, i)$. This leads to the following recurrence relation for the states, where $\vee$ is the logical OR operator.

$$
{}^i s_j = \begin{cases}
0 & \text{if } j = 0 \\
{}^{i-1} s_{j-1} & \text{if } x_j = y_i \\
{}^{i-1} s_{j-1} \vee 1 & \text{if } x_j \neq y_i
\end{cases} \tag{5.2}
$$

As mentioned earlier, the symbol comparisons are not performed explicitly. Rather, recourse is made to a preprocessed table, T, giving the following recurrence

$$
{}^i s_j = {}^{i-1} s_{j-1} \vee T_j[y_i] \tag{5.3}
$$

again with all ${}^i s_0 = 0$, and where

$$
T_j[a] = \begin{cases}
0 & \text{if } a = x_j \\
1 & \text{if } a \neq x_j
\end{cases} \tag{5.4}
$$

for all a in the alphabet, C.

Just as individual states were combined into an m-bit number, so too may be the individual table elements T_j for symbol a, giving

$$
\begin{aligned}
T[a] &= T_m[a] \cdot 2^{m-1} + \ldots + T_2[a] \cdot 2^1 + T_1[a] \cdot 2^0 \\
&= \sum_{j=1}^{m} T_j[a] \cdot 2^{j-1}
\end{aligned} \tag{5.5}
$$

Returning to the previous example, we can see that the values of T (with the most significant bit, T_m, foremost) for the symbols in alphabet $\{A, B, C, D, E\}$ for pattern ADAB are as follows.

$$T[A] = 1010$$
$$T[B] = 0111$$
$$T[C] = 1111$$
$$T[D] = 1101$$
$$T[E] = 1111$$

From relation (5.3), it may be seen that each bit of the state vector for position i is obtained by ORing the corresponding bit of $T[y_i]$ with the bit in the previous state vector one place to the right. The value beyond the end of the vector, required in the calculation of $^i s_1$, is taken to be 0. The complete state vector may therefore be updated by shifting ^{i-1}s 1 bit to the left and then performing a bitwise OR between it and $T[y_i]$.

The text search thus proceeds as follows. The state vector is initialised to all 1s. Successive text symbols, y_i, are then inspected in turn. For each one, the value of $T[y_i]$ is retrieved from the preprocessed table, and is used to update the state vector as follows:

$$^i s = (^{i-1}s \ll 1) \text{ OR } T[y_i] \tag{5.6}$$

where $\ll$ denotes the left-shift operation. A result less than 2^{m-1} indicates that an occurrence of x has been found in y ending at position i.

Returning once more to the previous example, we may see that for the indicated position, the state is 1010 and the next text symbol to be inspected is D. The next value of s is thus $(1010 \ll 1)$ OR $1101 = 1101$, as demonstrated below.

		j	$^i s_j$
$x(1,1)$	A	1	1
$x(1,2)$	A D	2	0
$x(1,3)$	A D A	3	1
$x(1,4)$	A D A B	4	1
text	A C A E D A D A D A B C . . .		
	i		

And the next value is $(1101 \ll 1)$ OR $T[A] = 1010$, and the next again $(1010 \ll 1)$ OR $T[B] = 0111$. This last value, for $y_i = B$, is less than 2^3, signalling an occurrence of the pattern in the text.

The overall procedure is shown in Figure 5.5, where it is assumed that the size of the pattern is not greater than the computer wordsize, w. In practice, full computer words are used for s and the entries of T. The m-bit values discussed earlier must

— preprocess

$allones = 111 \ldots 11$ — all 1s
— initialise all table entries
for $a = 1$ **to** $|C|$
    $T[a] = allones$
— adjust table entries according to the pattern symbols
$mask = 1$
for $j = 1$ **to** m
    $T[x_j] = T[x_j]$ AND (NOT $mask$)
    $mask = mask \ll 1$

— search text

$s = allones$
for $i = 1$ **to** n
    $s = (s \ll 1)$ OR $T[y_i]$
    if $s_m = 0$
        print $i - m + 1$

Figure 5.5: Shift-add string matching

therefore be left-extended with 1s. As with OR, NOT and AND are bitwise logical operators.

During the preprocessing stage, all the bits of the entries of T are initially set to 1, and the relevant bit positions are subsequently reset to 0 according to the symbols in the pattern. The start positions of all the occurrences of the pattern are then reported as they are detected during the scan of the text. The condition $s_m = 0$ has been shown in the figure as the test for a pattern occurrence. Since the integers are actually left-extended with 1s up to a width of w bits, the previously mentioned equivalent comparison of s with 2^{m-1} would now have to be replaced by one with $\sum_{i=m-1}^{w-1} 2^i$.

A more efficient implementation of the text-search phase is also shown in Figure 5.6. This employs a 'skip loop' (cf. the skip-loop version of the Boyer-Moore algorithm discussed in Chapter 2), which quickly scans through the text until a potential starting position of the pattern is detected, at which point the slower, shift-add loop in entered.

$i = 1$
while $i \leqslant n$
— skip up to possible start of pattern
while $y_i \neq x_1$ — (use sentinel value x_1 for y_{n+1})
$i = i + 1$
$s = allones$
$matching = $ **true**
while $matching$ and $(i \leqslant n)$
$s = (s \ll 1)$ OR $T[y_i]$
if $s_m = 0$
print $i - m + 1$
$i = i + 1$
if $s = allones$
$matching = $ **false**

Figure 5.6: Efficient shift-add text search

Having looked at the operation of the shift-add algorithm for the specific case of exact string matching, we are now in a position to examine how it may be extended. Its application to string matching with mismatches and don't-cares shall, for example, shortly be discussed.

In general, more than a single bit may be required for each state. Denote the actual number of bits used by b; the state vector may now be considered as a base-2^b integer, i.e.

$$
\begin{aligned}
{}^i s &= {}^i s_m 2^{b(m-1)} + \ldots + {}^i s_2 2^{b \cdot 1} + {}^i s_1 2^{b \cdot 0} \\
&= \sum_{j=1}^{m} {}^i s_j 2^{b(j-1)}
\end{aligned}
\tag{5.7}
$$

The entries of T will similarly be base-2^b integers. A shift of b bits is now required to shift the state vector by one state. Also, some generic arithmetic/logical operation will now be involved in the update of the vector. The general form of (5.6) is thus:

$$
{}^i s = ({}^{i-1} s \ll b) \diamond T[y_i]
\tag{5.8}
$$

where $\diamond$ represents the generic operation mentioned above.

In its general form, then, the algorithm requires $bm|C|$ bits of storage space for table T. The time required to set up this table is $O(\lceil \frac{mb}{w} \rceil (m + |C|))$, where the $\lceil \frac{mb}{w} \rceil$ represents the time needed to perform some constant number of operations on mb-bit integers using a wordsize of w. The running time of the text-search phase may be seen to be $O(\lceil\frac{mb}{w}\rceil n)$. When the integers involved may be accommodated within the system wordsize, the text scan thus take linear time. For larger integers, multiple-precision arithmetic operations become necessary in the manipulation of s and T. For constant w and large m, the running time then becomes quadratic.

k-mismatches

We have just seen that for exact string matching, a single bit suffices for each individual state: it indicates whether or not any mismatches have occurred. However, when the shift-add approach is applied to string matching with mismatches, it is necessary to keep track of the actual numbers of mismatches encountered. To do this, the individual states must act as binary counters.

For any position in the text, the maximum number of mismatches between it and the pattern is equal to m. Representing this value in binary requires $\lceil\log_2(m+1)\rceil$ bits. Setting b equal to this allows the general shift-add algorithm to compute the number of mismatches for each position in the text. Addition is then required as the generic operation $\diamond$ of (5.8) so that each state may accumulate its relevant number of mismatches.

When the permitted number of mismatches is limited to k, it suffices to use $b = \lceil\log_2(k+1)\rceil$ bits per mismatch counter. But problems can arise if the number of mismatches counted by a given state exceeds $2^b - 1$, causing a carry bit to propagate into an adjacent state. This problem may be circumvented by using one extra bit per state to register such an overflow. The total number of bits required per state is thus $\lceil\log_2(k+1)\rceil + 1$. Use is made of these extra overflow bits as follows. At each stage of the search, any overflows produced are recorded and then the overflow bits in the state vector are cleared, ready for the next stage. The search procedure is otherwise much the same as before. A value in state s_m (taking into account the status of its overflow) not greater than k indicates that an occurrence of the pattern with at most k mismatches has been found.

The overall algorithm for the k-mismatches search is given in Figure 5.7. As indicated above, the value of b used is dependent on k, and it is assumed that $mb \leqslant w$. The values in table T are computed in the same way as before, only this time the elements $T_j[a]$ are b-bit numbers. All these elements are initially set to equal 1 (i.e. a 1 is placed in only the rightmost of each element's b bits); and they are then selectively reset to 0 according to the symbols in the pattern.

At each position, i, in the search of the text, the new value of the state vector is computed; any resultant overflows are recorded in the overflow vector, ov; and the overflow bits in the state vector are then cleared in anticipation of the next vector computation. Note that during this process, data shifted out from the most significant b bits of the vectors are forced to 'drop off the end' by ANDing the results with $mask$, which contains 0s in the $w - mb$ most significant bit positions of the word.

— preprocess

$b = \lceil \log_2(k+1) \rceil + 1$
— set overflow mask to all 0s except for the overflow bit positions
$ovmask = 0$
$mask = 1 \ll (b-1)$
for $j = 1$ **to** m
    $ovmask = ovmask$ OR $mask$
    $mask = mask \ll b$
— initialise all table entries
$T_{init} = ovmask \gg (b-1)$
for $a = 1$ **to** $|C|$
    $T[a] = T_{init}$
— adjust table entries according to the pattern symbols
$mask = 1$
for $j = 1$ **to** m
    $T[x_j] = T[x_j]$ AND (NOT $mask$)
    $mask = mask \ll b$
— set up mask for use in selecting only the mb least significant
— bits of w-bit words
$mask = 0 \ldots 011 \ldots 111$ — mb 1s

— search text

$s = mask$ AND (NOT $ovmask$)   — mb 1s except for overflow bit positions
$ov = ovmask$
for $i = 1$ **to** n
    — shift-add
    $s = ((s \ll b) + T[y_i])$ AND $mask$
    — record overflows from the addition
    $ov = ((ov \ll b)$ OR $(s$ AND $ovmask))$ AND $mask$
    — clear overflow bits in state vector
    $s = s$ AND (NOT $ovmask$)
    if $(s$ OR $ov) \leqslant k.2^{b(m-1)}$
        — report position and number of mismatches
        print $i - m + 1$, $s \gg b(m-1)$

Figure 5.7: Shift-add k-mismatches string matching

The starting positions and respective numbers of mismatches for all the approximate pattern occurrences having up to k mismatches are reported as they are detected during the scan of the text. And such an occurrence is detected when the most significant mismatch-counter contains a value not exceeding k. The actual value of this counter is obtained by adding the rightmost $b - 1$ bits of s_m to its respective overflow value, ov_m. The test is equivalently shown in the figure as a comparison between s ORed with ov and the value k left-shifted by $b(m - 1)$ bit positions.

Don't-Cares and Symbol Classes

The basic shift-add algorithm may easily be extended to cater for patterns comprising elements representing finite classes of symbols. Each element of such a pattern is permitted to match any symbol in a given subset of the alphabet. These subsets may be specified in various ways. The different types of pattern-element description supported by the algorithm are given below.

- a — an ordinary pattern symbol, matching a single symbol from the alphabet C.
- $[\ldots]$ — a finite class, matching any of its constituent symbols.
- $?$ — a don't-care, matching any symbol. This is equivalent to the class containing all the members of C.
- $\bar{a}$, $\overline{[\ldots]}$ — complements, matching any alphabet symbol not in the specified set.

The text search for this application proceeds just as in the exact string-matching case, the only difference being in the way that table T is precomputed. Since the pattern elements, x_j, now represent sets of symbols, the table definition becomes:

$$T_j[a] = \begin{cases} 0 & \text{if } a \in x_j \\ 1 & \text{if } a \notin x_j \end{cases}$$

$$T[a] = \sum_{j=1}^{m} T_j[a] \cdot 2^{j-1} \tag{5.9}$$

Consider, for example, the pattern $x = ?\overline{[AB]}[AB]E$ over alphabet $\{A, B, C, D, E\}$. The alphabet subsets represented by pattern elements $x_1, \ldots, x_4$ are, respectively: $\{A, B, C, D, E\}$; $\{C, D, E\}$; $\{A, B\}$; and $\{E\}$. The value of T for each symbol of the alphabet is therefore as follows:

$$T[\text{A}] = 1010$$
$$T[\text{B}] = 1010$$
$$T[\text{C}] = 1100$$
$$T[\text{D}] = 1100$$
$$T[\text{E}] = 0100$$

Note in passing that don't-care symbols in the text may readily be catered for by defining $T[?] = 0$.

The requisite preprocessing shall now be considered. First of all, let m' denote the size of the pattern description, i.e. the sum of the numbers of symbols in the description of each of its elements. The size of a don't-care is taken to be 1, and that of a complement class to be the number of symbols used in its description (and not the number of symbols in the set that it actually represents). For example, $m = 4$ and $m' = 6$ for the pattern $x = ?\overline{[\text{AB}]}[\text{AB}]\text{E}$. In the extreme case, $m' = m \, |C|$. A pattern with such a description size serves no useful purpose, though, and in practice m' tends to be considerably smaller than this.

The computation of T may be performed in $O(\lceil\frac{m}{w}\rceil(m' + |C|))$ time, as shown in Figure 5.8. All the bits of the $|C|$ entries of the table are initially set to 1, save for those in positions corresponding to don't-care or complement pattern elements, which are set to 0. This requires $O(\lceil\frac{m}{w}\rceil(m + |C|))$ time. $O(\lceil\frac{m}{w}\rceil m')$ time is then spent updating T for each symbol, a, of the class description for each pattern element, x_j. If the class is specified as a complement, in which case $a \notin x_j$, then bit $T_j[a]$ is reset to a 1 (it will have previously been cleared to 0 in the initialisation); otherwise, the appropriate bit of $T[a]$ is set to 0. On completion, table T is ready for use in a text-search phase identical to that of the exact string-matching procedure (i.e. as in the algorithm given in Figure 5.5).

We conclude this section with some final remarks about the shift-add algorithm. First, it should be pointed out that this approach is amenable to adaptation for searching with multiple patterns. The search time for this is again $O(\lceil\frac{m}{w}\rceil n)$, where this time m denotes the sum of the lengths of the individual patterns.

Second, as has been mentioned previously, the shift-add algorithm forms the basis of the agrep string-matching tool. As we shall see later on, this can perform a variety of types of text search, including k-differences string matching.

Next, the algorithm is competitive with other exact string-matching approaches when the pattern is small. Baeza-Yates and Gonnet (1992) observe, for example, that experiment has shown it to be faster than the Boyer-Moore-Horspool algorithm for patterns smaller than 4–9 symbols, depending on the actual pattern.

And finally, note that an efficient C implementation of the algorithm is to be found in Baeza-Yates and Gonnet (1992).

$T_{init} = 111 \ldots 11$ — all 1s
— set up T_{init} for don't cares and complements
$mask = 1$
for $j = 1$ to m
   if $(x_j = ?)$ or $(x_j$ is specified as a complement)
      $T_{init} = T_{init}$ AND (NOT $mask$)
   $mask = mask \ll 1$
— initialise all table entries
for $a = 1$ to $|C|$
   $T[a] = T_{init}$
— adjust table entries according to the pattern element classes
$mask = 1$
for $j = 1$ to m
   if $x_j \neq ?$
      for all a in the description of x_j
         if x_j is specified as a complement
            $T[a] = T[a]$ OR $mask$
         else
            $T[a] = T[a]$ AND (NOT $mask$)
   $mask = mask \ll 1$

Figure 5.8: Preprocessing for shift-add string matching with classes of symbols

5.2.3 Tarhio-Ukkonen k-mismatches

Tarhio and Ukkonen's (1990a, 1990b, 1993) k-mismatches algorithm is based on the Boyer-Moore-Horspool approach to exact string matching. Before the extension of the latter for approximate matching is discussed, its operation shall first of all briefly be reiterated.

Horspool's variant of the Boyer-Moore approach was discussed in detail in Chapter 2. An implementation of the algorithm in which the first occurrence in text y of pattern x is sought was also given there in Figure 2.8. The basic operation of the algorithm is as follows.

At a given point in the search, x is aligned with some substring of y. Corresponding pattern- and text-symbols are then compared from right to left, i.e. starting with x_m and progressing back towards x_1. If all the comparisons are successful, then an exact occurrence of x in y has been found. Otherwise, as soon as a mismatch is encountered, the pattern is moved forward in the text to some new position and the symbol comparisons are started there anew. The amount by which the pattern is shifted is determined from a preprocessed, 'occurrence-heuristic' table. This $skip$ table is indexed by the text symbol, y_i, say, currently aligned with the final pattern symbol, x_m. The $skip$ values are determined as follows.

If y_i occurs nowhere in x or only as x_m, then on a mismatch the pattern may be shifted all the way past y_i. Otherwise — with the exception of the case where $y_i = x_m$ (and symbol x_m is repeated within the pattern) — the $skip$ value is such that the pattern shift brings the rightmost occurrence in x of y_i into alignment with the latter. And last to be considered is the aforementioned exception. In that case, it is the second-last occurrence of symbol y_i in x that is brought into alignment. The definition of $skip$ for each symbol w in the alphabet, C, may thus be summarised as follows:

$$skip[w] \;=\; \min\{s \mid s = m \text{ or } (1 \leqslant s < m \text{ and } x_{m-s} = w)\} \qquad (5.10)$$

Having reviewed the operation of the algorithm, we may now examine its generalisation for application to the k-mismatches problem. Note firstly that it shall be all, rather than just the first, of the approximate pattern occurrences in the text that are sought. The basic operation of the algorithm remains largely the same as before. But this time, the right-to-left comparisons proceed until either the beginning of the pattern is reached or $k + 1$ mismatches have been encountered. In the former case, the current text substring corresponds to an occurrence of the pattern with up to k mismatches; whereas in the latter, it does not. Also, the calculation of the relevant $skip$ values now becomes more involved, as discussed below.

By definition, a k-mismatches approximate occurrence of x, u, say, is a string of length m whose symbols disagree with those of x in up to k positions. Since there are at most k mismatches, any $k + 1$ contiguous symbols in u must contain at least one symbol that matches its counterpart in x. When the pattern is shifted forward from the current trial position to the next, it is thus necessary to ensure that it is moved the minimum distance that results in at least one match between the pattern and the last $k + 1$ symbols of the current text substring (i.e. $y(i - k, i)$). If no matches occur for any alignment between the current one and that bringing the start of the pattern, $x(1, k + 1)$, into line with $y(i - k, i)$, then the next position to try is one place to the right — aligning x_1 with y_{i-k+1}, and thus x_m with y_{i+m-k}. The maximum $skip$ value is therefore $m - k$.

Observe that whereas before, $skip$ was a function of one symbol, its value now depends on the text substring $y(i - k, i)$, i.e. it is a function of $k + 1$ symbols. Its explicit enumeration would therefore involve $|C|^{k+1}$ values, necessitating rather onerous preprocessing. Fortunately, however, an alternative strategy permits the $skip$ value to be calculated during the scan of the text from the entries of a smaller precomputed table.

The following example serves to illustrate the fact that the required $skip$ value is equal to the minimum of those for the individual symbols of text substring $y(i - k, i)$. For this example, $k = 2$ and $x = $ rebel. The $skip$ values for individual symbols b, e, and r are 2, 1, and 4, respectively, with those for all others being equal to 5. Shifting the pattern by these amounts brings their respective pattern symbols into line with y_i. If, however, the symbol in question is y_{i-l}, say, then a pattern shift of $skip[y_{i-l}] - l$ is required to align the relevant pattern symbol with text symbol y_{i-l}.

    pattern   r e b e l
    text   t e r r i b i l i s e s t l o c u s i s t e
                 i

$k + 1$ mismatches are obtained for $y(i - k, i) = $ rri. The pattern is then moved forward by the minimum distance such that there is at least one match between it and rri, i.e. $x_1 = $ r is aligned with y_{i-2}.

    pattern   r e b e l
    text   t e r r i b i l i s e s t l o c u s i s t e
                 i

$k + 1$ mismatches are obtained for $y(i - k, i) = $ ibi. The pattern is then moved forward by the minimum distance such that there is at least one match between it and ibi, i.e. $x_3 = $ b is aligned with y_{i-1}.

```
pattern        r e b e l
text       t e r r i b i l i s e s t l o c u s i s t e
                       i
```

An occurrence of rebel with 2 mismatches is found ending at position i in the text.

At the first step, a shift of 2 positions is the minimum such that there is at least one match between the pattern and $y(i - k, i)$. This is equal to $\min\{skip[\text{i}] - 0, skip[\text{r}] - 1, skip[\text{r}] - 2\} = \min\{5, 3, 2\}$. Similarly, at the second step, the required shift of 1 position is equal to $\min\{skip[\text{i}] - 0, skip[\text{b}] - 1, skip[\text{i}] - 2\}$.

The values over which the minimisation to determine the required pattern skip is performed may thus be seen to depend on both the actual symbols themselves and their positions within the current substring $y(i - k, i)$. The relevant information may therefore be stored in a $(k + 1) \times |C|$ table, $skip_k$. Combining (5.10) with the above-mentioned amendment for symbols offset from the end of the current text substring leads to the following definition of $skip_k$ for $m - k \leqslant j \leqslant m$ and for each $w \in C$.

$$skip_k[j, w] = \min\{s \mid s = m - k \text{ or } (1 \leqslant s < m - k \text{ and } x_{j-s} = w)\} \qquad (5.11)$$

Each of the $k + 1$ rows of $skip_k$ could be computed on a separate scan through the pattern, as for the evaluation of the original $skip$ table. However, the task may be performed more efficiently on a single right-to-left pass through the pattern, as shown in Figure 5.9.[4]

The operation of the preprocessing stage is as follows. All of the entries of $skip_k$ are initially set to the maximum skip value of $m - k$. Each of the pattern symbols, x_j, from the second last down to the first is then inspected in turn. For each of these, its offset from each pattern position $\max\{j + 1, m - k\} \leqslant i \leqslant ready[x_j] - 1$ is entered into $skip_k[i, x_j]$, where $ready[x_j]$ gives the lowest current index i for which $skip_k[i, x_j]$ has already been correctly defined. At the outset, the values of $ready[w]$ for all $w \in C$ are therefore initially set to $m + 1$. After all the relevant $skip_k$ entries for x_j have been updated, the value of $ready[x_j]$ is then set to the lowest pattern position for which this was done, namely $\max\{j + 1, m - k\}$.

Note that the values produced by the preprocessing algorithm can, in certain circumstances, depart slightly from definition 5.11 in so far as values greater than $m - k$, but less than m, can sometimes result. Such cases are, however, implicitly taken care of in the text-scanning phase, where the actual pattern shift may never exceed $m - k$.

Taking account of the tables $ready$ and $skip_k$, the working-space requirement for the preprocessing may be seen to be $O((k + 1) |C|)$. The time taken to initialise

---

[4]This is slightly different from the procedure given in Tarhio and Ukkonen (1990a, 1990b, 1993), as the latter can erroneously enter values of 0 into the $skip_k$ table.

---

for $w = 1$ **to** $|C|$
   — initialise $ready$
   $ready[w] = m + 1$
   — initialise $skip_k$
   for $j = m - k$ **to** m
     $skip_k[j, w] = m - k$
— right-to-left scan of the pattern
for $j = m - 1$ **downto** 1
   for $i = ready[x_j] - 1$ **downto** $\max\{j + 1, m - k\}$
     $skip_k[i, x_j] = i - j$
   $ready[x_j] = \max\{j + 1, m - k\}$

Figure 5.9: Tarhio-Ukkonen k-mismatches preprocessing

---

these tables is thus also $O((k + 1)\,|C|)$. Table $ready$ is subsequently updated $m - 1$ times, and at most $(k + 1)\,|C_x|$ entries of $skip_k$ are rewritten once, where C_x is the set of distinct pattern symbols (whose cardinality is bounded by $\min\{m, |C|\}$). (Note that in the straightforward computation of $skip_k$, involving $k + 1$ left-to-right scans of the pattern, table entries for symbols repeated in the pattern may be rewritten several times before the final value is obtained.) The overall preprocessing time is therefore $O(m + (k + 1)(|C| + |C_x|))$, which is $O(m + (k + 1)\,|C|)$.

As an example, table $skip_2$ (i.e. for $k = 2$) for pattern ABAACD and alphabet {A, B, C, D, E} is shown below.

	A	B	C	D	E
4	1	2	4	4	4
5	1	3	4	4	4
6	2	4	1	4	4

The algorithm for the text-search phase is shown in Figure 5.10. Index i corresponds to the position in the text of the final pattern symbol, x_m, for the current alignment. At this alignment, corresponding pattern- and text-symbols are compared from right to left in the inner **while** loop. The minimisation over the individual skip values for the symbols of text substring $y(i - k, i)$ is also performed in this loop as the respective symbols are met with. If the start of the pattern is reached without encountering more than k mismatches, then the start position in the text and the number of mismatches for the detected approximate occurrence of the pattern are reported. The pattern is then moved forward by incrementing index i by the appropriate skip value, and the whole process is repeated until the end of the text is reached.

$i = m$
while $i \leqslant n$
  $h = i$ — initialise text index
  $j = m$ — initialise pattern index
  $mismatches = 0$
  $skip = m - k$
  while $(j > 0)$ **and** $(mismatches \leqslant k)$
    — minimise over the $k + 1$ skip values for the symbols in $y(i - k, i)$
    if $j \geqslant m - k$
      $skip = \min\{skip,\ skip_k[j, y_h]\}$
    if $y_h \neq x_j$
      — a mismatch
      $mismatches = mismatches + 1$
    $h = h - 1$
    $j = j - 1$
  if $mismatches \leqslant k$
    — a pattern occurrence with up to k mismatches
    print $h + 1, mismatches$
  $i = i + skip$

Figure 5.10: Tarhio-Ukkonen k-mismatches string matching

As with the Boyer-Moore-Horspool algorithm, the worst-case running time for the scan of the text is quadratic. This situation obtains for pathological cases such as that where $x = A^m$ and $y = A^n$. However, Tarhio and Ukkonen have theoretically examined the running time in the average case. Their analysis assumes random strings, whose symbols are independent and occur with equal probabilities. The lengths of different pattern shifts are also assumed to be mutually independent. Under these conditions, the expected running time was found to be

$$O\left(kn\left(\frac{1}{m-k} + \frac{k}{|C|}\right)\right)$$

The method therefore performs well on average for small k, and large patterns and alphabets.

5.2.4   Baeza-Yates–Perleberg k-mismatches

Baeza-Yates and Perleberg's (1992) k-mismatches algorithm provides a very practical and straightforward solution to this approximate-matching problem. Its operation shall first of all be described here for the case where all the pattern symbols are distinct. The more general case, where the pattern string may contain repeated symbols, shall then subsequently be examined.

Associated with each text symbol, y_i, is a counter, c_i, initially cleared to zero. The basic idea of the algorithm is to examine each y_i in turn, and if this symbol also occurs in the pattern as x_j, say, to increment the counter for the text symbol corresponding to the start of the pattern when x_j and y_i are in alignment. For a pattern with no repeated symbols, x_j is unique, and it is counter c_{i-j+1} that is incremented. Once all the symbols of text substring $y(i, i + m - 1)$ have been processed, c_i may be examined. A counter value of m indicates that the sequence of symbols in the text substring corresponds exactly to that of the pattern, and an exact occurrence of x has therefore been found. Similarly, a count of $l < m$ indicates that $y(i, i + m - 1)$ is an instance of x with l matches, or, equivalently, $m - l$ mismatches. Occurrences in the text of the pattern with up to k mismatches may therefore readily be found from inspection of the contents of the counters. The situation is illustrated below for the case of $x = \texttt{tram}$ and $y = \texttt{thetrippedtrap}$.

x	t	r	a	m										
i	1	2	3	4	5	6	7	8	9	10	11	12	13	14
y_i	t	h	e	t	r	i	p	p	e	d	t	r	a	p
c_i	1	0	0	2	0	0	0	0	0	0	3	0	0	0
$m - c_i$	3	4	4	2	4	4	4	4	4	4	1	4	4	4

In practice, the counters may initially be set to m and then decremented, so that the number of mismatches is given directly by their contents. Also, since only m counters are required at any given time, a circular array of that size may be employed, rather than having an individual counter for each of the text symbols.

When text symbol y_i is read, the offset to the relevant counter is found by consulting a preprocessed table. This is an array having an entry for each symbol of the alphabet, C: if a symbol occurs in the pattern, then its table entry gives the appropriate offset; otherwise, some special indicator value, such as a negative integer, is stored instead.

Having outlined the basic operation of the procedure, we may now turn our attention to the modification necessary for the more general case, in which symbols in x may be repeated. This time, the offset for a given text symbol is not necessarily uniquely defined. If, for example, text symbol y_i occurs within the pattern f times, then f different counters must be updated for that symbol. The offsets necessary to do this may be retrieved from the preprocessed table if its entries are now defined to be linked lists of offsets. The operation of the search process remains similar to before: text symbol y_i is used to address the table, and the offsets in the retrieved list are used to determine the appropriate counters to update.

The complete algorithm is given in Figure 5.11. Array *offsets* contains the heads of the $|C|$ linked lists of offset values. The elements of this array are pairs (*offset*, *pointer*), where *offset* is an offset value and *pointer* points to another such pair. Two procedures are employed in connection with the lists: *insert*(L, v) creates a node containing offset value v, and inserts it into the list having node L as its head; *next*(p) returns the list node pointed at by p.

In practice, the mismatch counts are accumulated at positions corresponding to the final symbol of the pattern rather than the first. This avoids problems involving positions before the start of the text, and means that the offsets involved are positive. The counter array c is accessed in a circular fashion, and its m elements are initially set to some large value, BIG ($\geqslant 2m$), so that false results cannot be obtained when the first $m - 1$ text symbols are being inspected.

The operation is otherwise basically as described earlier. At each text position, the possibly-empty linked list of offsets corresponding to the current text symbol is used to determine which counters to decrement. (Note that the inner **while** loop that traverses the linked lists is superfluous in the case where all the pattern symbols are distinct.) The counter corresponding to the current text position is then compared with the specified limit on the number of mismatches, k. If this limit is not exceeded, then the position in the text and the number of mismatches for the detected pattern occurrence are reported. Finally, the value of the counter for the current text position is reset to m, for use in the next cycle through the counter array.

Note that Baeza-Yates and Perleberg provide an implementation in C of the algorithm in which various optimisations have been effected. For example, the strings are accessed via pointers rather than array indices. A fixed size of 256 is also used for the counter array, so that instead of using the mod operation, a fast, bitwise AND with the value 255 may be employed to address it circularly.

It now remains to examine the space and time requirements of the algorithm. The former shall be considered here first of all. There are m elements in the counter array, and $|C|$ in array *offsets*. When all the pattern symbols are distinct, no further linked-list nodes are required; when repeated pattern symbols are involved, at most $m - 1$ become necessary. The required storage space (over and above that for the input strings x and y) is thus $O(m + |C|)$.

During the preprocessing stage, the $|C|$ entries of *offsets* are initialised, the offsets for the m pattern symbols are then stored, and the m counters initialised. The running time for this phase is therefore $O(m + |C|)$.

For each symbol inspected during the scan of the text, an offset value is retrieved,

— preprocess

— initialise all offsets
for $w = 1$ **to** $|C|$
    $offsets[w] = (-1, \text{null})$
— set offsets for the pattern symbols
for $i = 1$ **to** m
    $c[i] = \text{BIG}$
    if $offsets[x_i] = (-1, \text{null})$
        $offsets[x_i] = (m - i, \text{null})$
    else
        $insert(offsets[x_i], m - i)$

— search text

for $i = 0$ **to** $n - 1$
    $(offset, pointer) = offsets[y_{i+1}]$
    if $offset \geqslant 0$
        — y_{i+1} occurs in x; update the relevant counters
        $c[(i + offset) \bmod m + 1] = c[(i + offset) \bmod m + 1] - 1$
        — traverse linked list
        while $pointer \neq \text{null}$
            $(offset, pointer) = next(pointer)$
            $c[(i + offset) \bmod m + 1] = c[(i + offset) \bmod m + 1] - 1$
    if $c[i \bmod m + 1] \leqslant k$
        — a pattern occurrence with up to k mismatches
        print $i - m + 2$, $c[i \bmod m + 1]$
    $c[i \bmod m + 1] = m$

Figure 5.11: Baeza-Yates–Perleberg k-mismatches string matching

zero or more counters are decremented, and one counter is reset to value m. The total number of counter decrements, r, is equal to the number of ordered pairs of positions at which x and y match. The text search therefore runs in $O(n + r)$ time. When all the pattern symbols are distinct, $r \leqslant n$ and hence the worst-case running time is $O(n)$. And for the case where repeated symbols occur in the pattern, $r \leqslant mn$, resulting in a quadratic worst-case running time.

Assuming a uniform symbol probability distribution, the expected running time for the text scan is $O((1 + \frac{m}{|C|})n)$. The average running time is thus linear for patterns smaller than the alphabet size.

5.2.5 Dynamic Programming k-differences

The dynamic-programming computation of the Levenshtein distance between two strings, as discussed in Chapter 3, provides a very straightforward method for solving the k-differences problem. This is described here together with the simple cut-off variation of the technique.

Sellers

Recall that the element $d_{i,j}$ (defined by (3.5)) of the distance matrix gives the distance between prefixes of the strings x and y, of lengths i and j, respectively. In order to solve the k-differences problem, the distance matrix may be adapted such that $d_{i,j}$ represents the minimum distance between $x(1, i)$ and any substring of y ending at y_j (Sellers, 1980). This change may be accommodated simply by altering the boundary conditions (given by (3.8)) such that

$$d_{0,j} = 0 \quad \text{for } 0 \leqslant j \leqslant n \tag{5.12}$$

since the minimum distance between ϵ and any substring of y is 0.

The rest of the matrix is then computed as before using the Levenshtein-distance edit costs, (3.6), and the recurrence relation for $d_{i,j}$, (3.7). On completion, any value not exceeding k in the final row indicates a position in the text where a substring having at most k differences from the pattern ends. This is illustrated in the example given below, which depicts the distance matrix for the case of $x =$ ABCDE and $y =$ ACEABPCQDEABCR. For the case of $k = 2$, it may be seen from row 5 of the matrix that occurrences of the pattern, with up to 2 differences, end at text positions 3, 10, 13 and 14. The corresponding text substrings for these positions are ACE, ABPCQDE, ABC and ABCR.

— initialise array borders
for $i = 0$ to m
   $d_{i,0} = i$
for $j = 1$ to n
   $d_{0,j} = 0$
— calculate $d_{i,j}$
for $j = 1$ to n
  for $i = 1$ to m
    if $x_i = y_j$
      $d = d_{i-1,j-1}$
    else
      $d = d_{i-1,j-1} + 1$
    $d_{i,j} = \min\{d_{i-1,j} + 1,\ d_{i,j-1} + 1,\ d\}$
    if $d_{m,j} \leqslant k$
      print $j,\ d_{m,j}$

Figure 5.12: Dynamic-programming k-differences string matching

j		0	1	2	3	4	5	6	7	8	9	10	11	12	13	14
i			A	C	E	A	B	P	C	Q	D	E	A	B	C	R
0		0	0	0	0	0	0	0	0	0	0	0	0	0	0	0
1	A	1	0	1	1	0	1	1	1	1	1	1	0	1	1	1
2	B	2	1	1	2	1	0	1	2	2	2	2	1	0	1	2
3	C	3	2	1	2	2	1	1	1	2	3	3	2	1	0	1
4	D	4	3	2	2	3	2	2	2	2	2	3	3	2	1	1
5	E	5	4	3	2	3	3	3	3	3	3	2	3	3	2	2

The process may be performed as shown in Figure 5.12. After setting up the boundary conditions of the $(m + 1) \times (n + 1)$ table, the algorithm computes the table entries column by column. For each text symbol encountered in a left-to-right scan, a column of the table is computed, which involves comparisons between the current text symbol and every pattern symbol. Once the final value in a column has been evaluated, it is compared with k. If, and only if, it does not exceed k, then there ends at the current text position at least one approximate occurrence of the pattern with no more than k differences. In this case, the end position and the minimum number of differences for such an occurrence are reported. It is clear that this approach requires quadratic time and space in all cases.

Cut-off

Ukkonen's (1985b) simple improvement to the above procedure is based on the diagonalwise monotonicity (Ukkonen, 1985a) of the Levenshtein distance table. Recall that this property may be stated as follows. The sequence of values on any given diagonal is non-decreasing, and changes in value in that sequence occur only in unit steps (i.e. $d_{i-1,j-1} \leqslant d_{i,j} \leqslant d_{i-1,j-1} + 1$ for $i = 1, \ldots, m$ and $j = 1, \ldots, n$). A derivation of this property is given below, which is then followed by a description of the cut-off method itself.

To prove the property, we shall first of all show that adjacent entries along a row or down a column differ by at most 1. Starting with the entries of a column, it is thus necessary to show that:

$$-1 \leqslant d_{i,j} - d_{i-1,j} \leqslant 1 \qquad (5.13)$$

since the d values are integers. The minimisation in the $d_{i,j}$ computation may be stated as follows:

$$d_{i,j} = \min\{d_{i-1,j} + 1, d_{i,j-1} + 1, d_{i-1,j-1} + w(x_i, y_j)\} \qquad (5.14)$$

$$w(x_i, y_j) = \begin{cases} 0 & \text{if } x_i = y_j \\ 1 & \text{if } x_i \neq y_j \end{cases}$$

from which we have:

$$d_{i,j} \geqslant \min\{d_{i-1,j} + 1, d_{i,j-1} + 1, d_{i-1,j-1}\} \qquad (5.15)$$

We also have the following from (5.14).

$$d_{i-1,j} + 1 \geqslant d_{i,j}$$
$$\Rightarrow d_{i,j} - d_{i-1,j} \leqslant 1 \qquad (5.16)$$
$$d_{i,j-1} + 1 \geqslant d_{i,j}$$
$$\Rightarrow d_{i,j} - d_{i,j-1} \leqslant 1 \qquad (5.17)$$

Inequality (5.16) goes part of the way to proving (5.13). To complete its derivation it remains to show that:

$$d_{i,j} - d_{i-1,j} \geqslant -1 \qquad (5.18)$$

This is done by induction. Inequality (5.18) may be seen to hold for $j = 0$, given the boundary values for the zeroth column. Assume it also holds for value $j - 1$, giving:

$$d_{i,j-1} + 1 \geqslant d_{i-1,j-1} \qquad (5.19)$$

From (5.17), we also have that:

$$d_{i-1,j-1} \geqslant d_{i-1,j} - 1 \qquad (5.20)$$

Substituting (5.19) and (5.20) into (5.15) gives the following:

$$d_{i,j} \;\geqslant\; \min\{d_{i-1,j} + 1,\, d_{i-1,j} - 1,\, d_{i-1,j} - 1\}$$
$$\Rightarrow d_{i,j} \;\geqslant\; d_{i-1,j} - 1 \tag{5.21}$$

which is equivalent to (5.18). Since the inequality holds for $j = 0$ and the inequality for j is implied by that for $j - 1$, it may be seen to be valid for all values of j. Combining (5.18) and (5.16) gives the desired result (5.13).

A similar proof by induction over i, the details of which are omitted here, shows that $d_{i,j} - d_{i,j-1} \geqslant -1$. When taken together with (5.17), this gives:

$$-1 \;\leqslant\; d_{i,j} - d_{i,j-1} \;\leqslant\; 1 \tag{5.22}$$

which confirms that adjacent entries along a row also differ by at most 1.

It is now a fairly straightforward matter to prove the diagonalwise-monotonicity property itself. For the sequence of values along a diagonal to be non-decreasing, we must have:

$$d_{i,j} \;\geqslant\; d_{i-1,j-1} \tag{5.23}$$

From (5.14), the following must in turn be valid in order for (5.23) to hold.

$$d_{i-1,j} + 1 \;\geqslant\; d_{i-1,j-1} \tag{5.24}$$
$$d_{i,j-1} + 1 \;\geqslant\; d_{i-1,j-1} \tag{5.25}$$

These indeed follow immediately from (5.22) and (5.13), respectively, thereby proving (5.23). The final remaining task is to consider the maximum increment in the sequence of values along a diagonal. Inspection of (5.14) provides the desired information:

$$d_{i,j} \;\leqslant\; d_{i-1,j-1} + 1 \tag{5.26}$$

Putting together (5.23) and (5.26) then gives the final result:

$$d_{i-1,j-1} \;\leqslant\; d_{i,j} \;\leqslant\; d_{i-1,j-1} + 1 \tag{5.27}$$

The monotonicity of the table's diagonals is exploited in the cut-off method as follows. The table is still computed in a columnwise fashion, but when a distance value of $k + 1$ is computed, no further entries on the same diagonal are evaluated, as these too will all be greater than k. This is achieved by keeping track of the maximum position in each column for which the distance is $\leqslant k$. Let this position for column j be p. Then only entries $0, \ldots, p + 1$ need be calculated in column $j + 1$.

Consider an example, similar to the previous one, where $x = $ ABCDE and $y = $ ACEABPCQDEABCD. The table below shows only the entries that would actually be computed in this way were we to search for occurrences of x with $k = 1$.

$p = k + 1$
— initialise column 0
for $i = 0$ to m
  $c_i = i$
— calculate columns j
for $j = 1$ to n
  $d = 0$
  for $i = 1$ to p
    if $x_i = y_j$
      $e = d$
    else
      $e = \min\{c_{i-1}, c_i, d\} + 1$
    $d = c_i$
    $c_i = e$
  — find maximum position in c with value $\leqslant k$
  while $c_p > k$
    $p = p - 1$
  if $p = m$
    print j, c_m
  else
    $p = p + 1$

Figure 5.13: Cut-off dynamic-programming k-differences string matching

j		0	1	2	3	4	5	6	7	8	9	10	11	12	13	14
i			A	C	E	A	B	P	C	Q	D	E	A	B	C	D
0		0	0	0	0	0	0	0	0	0	0	0	0	0	0	0
1	A	1	0	1	1	0	1	1	1	1	1	1	0	1	1	1
2	B	2	1	1	2	1	0	1	2	2	2	2	1	0	1	2
3	C	3		1	2		1	1	1	2				1	0	1
4	D	4		2				2	2	2				1	0	
5	E	5														1

An implementation of the cut-off method is given in Figure 5.13 (which is based on the 'Enhanced Dynamic Programming' algorithm presented in Jokinen, Tarhio and Ukkonen (1991)). The working-space requirement is only $O(m)$ rather than $O(mn)$, since only one column, c, is stored at any one time. This is possible since access is required to only the neighbouring column to the left of any given column in the table whilst the latter is being computed.

The zeroth column is initialised as before. But for subsequent values of j, the column is computed only as far as entry c_p, where p is one greater than the maximum position for which the value in the previous column was $\leqslant k$ (unless this position was m, in which case p is also equal to m). Variable d is used to store the value of $d_{i-1,j-1}$ while that of $d_{i,j}$ is being evaluated. (The value of $d_{i,j}$ is held in c_i on the jth iteration of the outer loop.) After completion of the current column, the value of p is set ready for the next column. And if the computations have reached the mth entry of the current column, then, as before, the end position and corresponding minimum number of differences are reported if the latter does not exceed k.

Ukkonen (1985b) stated that the expected value of p is $O(k)$ for random strings, leading to an $O(kn)$ average-case running time. This bound for the expected performance has since been proven theoretically by Chang and Lampe (1992).

5.2.6 Landau-Vishkin k-differences

Landau and Vishkin's (1986b, 1989) k-differences algorithm is based on an approach similar to Ukkonen's (1985a) dynamic-programming Levenshtein-distance procedure. The basic idea is to compute the locations of the first $k + 1$ transitions in value along each diagonal of the distance matrix. A method in which the jump from one transition to the next is computed by brute force is described here first of all. (A similar approach is to be found in 'algorithm MN2' in Galil and Park (1990).) The modification of the method necessary to support constant-time jump computations is then discussed. This leads to an asymptotically faster, but less practical, version of the algorithm.

As we saw in Ukkonen's string-distance algorithm in Chapter 3, the matrix diagonals may be numbered with integers, $p \in [-m, n]$, such that diagonal p consists of elements (i, j) for which $j - i = p$. The transitions on the diagonals shall be represented as follows. Let $r_{p,q}$ represent the largest row i such that $d_{i,j} = q$ and (i, j) is on diagonal p. Thus, q is the minimal number of differences between $x(1, r_{p,q})$ and any text substring ending at $y_{p+r_{p,q}}$, and furthermore $x_{r_{p,q}+1} \neq y_{p+r_{p,q}+1}$, since $r_{p,q} + 1$ would otherwise be a row larger than $r_{p,q}$ satisfying the required conditions.

Returning to a previous example, diagonal 9 of the distance matrix for $x =$ ABCDE and $y =$ ACEABPCQDEABCR is shown below. It may be seen that the $r_{p,q}$ values for this are as follows: $r_{9,0} = 0$, $r_{9,1} = 4$ and $r_{9,2} = 5$.

	j	0	1	2	3	4	5	6	7	8	9	10	11	12	13	14
i			A	C	E	A	B	P	C	Q	D	E	A	B	C	R
0									0							
1	A									1						
2	B										1					
3	C											1				
4	D												1			
5	E													2		

An $r_{p,q}$ value of m, for $q \leqslant k$, indicates that there is at least one occurrence of the pattern, with up to k differences, in the text ending at y_{p+m}. In order to solve the k-differences problem, it is thus sufficient to calculate for each diagonal p the $r_{p,q}$ values for which $q \leqslant k$, i.e. $r_{p,0}$ to $r_{p,k}$.

To see how the $r_{p,q}$ values may be computed, consider the evaluation of the $d_{i,j}$ entries in the dynamic-programming matrix. If $d_{i,j} = q$, and this entry is on diagonal p, and i is the largest row satisfying these requirements, then by definition $r_{p,q} = i$. The value of $d_{i,j}$ will have been derived from one of the adjacent previous values in the matrix according to (5.14). It will thus have been obtained from one or more of the following possibilities.

1. $d_{i-1,j-1} = q$ and $x_i = y_j$

2. $d_{i-1,j-1} = q - 1$ and $x_i \neq y_j$

3. $d_{i,j-1} = q - 1$

4. $d_{i-1,j} = q - 1$

If the last occurrence of value $q - 1$ in diagonal p, i.e. row $r_{p,q-1}$, has previously been found, the last occurrence on the diagonal of value q may then be found by stepping through subsequent elements on the diagonal while $x_i = y_j$.

Note that the first possible k-differences pattern occurrence ends at position $j = m - k$ in the text. This position in row m lies on diagonal $-k$, and thus diagonals $p < -k$ are of no interest in the computation. The last possible occurrence ends at position $j = n$, which for row m lies on diagonal $n - m$. In order to determine correctly whether entries on diagonal $p = n - m$ exceed k, at most $k + 1$ diagonals above this need to be considered. Only diagonals $-(k + 1)$ to $n - m + k + 1$ need therefore be involved in the computations.

The algorithm given in Figure 5.14 may be used to compute the $r_{p,q}$ values. An initial value for row r is obtained from previous values $r_{p,q-1}$, $r_{p-1,q-1}$ and $r_{p+1,q-1}$, and is then incremented successively by one at a time until the correct value of $r_{p,q}$ is reached. Previous values outside the valid range, i.e. those for $q = -1$, are taken to be -1 so that the values for $q = 0$ are computed correctly.

   — initialise

for $p = -(k + 1)$ **to** -1

   $r_{p,|p|-1} = |p| - 1$

   $r_{p,|p|-2} = |p| - 2$

for $p = 0$ **to** $n - m + k + 1$

   $r_{p,-1} = -1$

   — calculate $r_{p,q}$ values

for $q = 0$ **to** k

   for $p = -q$ **to** $n - m + k - q$

      $r = \max\{r_{p,q-1} + 1, r_{p-1,q-1}, r_{p+1,q-1} + 1\}$

      $r = \min\{r, m\}$

      while $(r < m)$ **and** $(p + r < n)$ **and** $(x_{r+1} = y_{p+r+1})$

         $r = r + 1$

      $r_{p,q} = r$

      if $(r_{p,q} = m)$ **and** $(p + m \leqslant n)$

         print $p + m$, q

Figure 5.14: Landau-Vishkin (brute-force) k-differences string matching

---

Recall that in the initialisation of the d matrix, $d_{i,0} = i$. The first value on each diagonal $p = -i$, for $i = 1, \ldots, m$, is thus equal to i. So for a given value of q, only diagonals down to $p = -q$ need be considered, as the distance on diagonals $p < -q$ is always greater than q.

Two antidiagonals in the $r_{p,q}$ table are also filled in during the initialisation so that the necessary previous values are available when it comes time to compute entries $r_{-q,q}$. The two particular $r_{p,q}$ antidiagonals are defined by $p + q = -1$ and $p + q = -2$, for negative p. These antidiagonals therefore comprise entries $r_{p,|p|-1}$ and $r_{p,|p|-2}$ with $p < 0$. The corresponding values of $|p| - 1$ and $|p| - 2$ are obtained by imagining extensions for $j < 0$ of the negative diagonals p in the d matrix.

In order that the last $r_{p,q}$ of interest, namely $r_{n-m,k}$, be computed correctly, the entries for $q = k - 1$ must be computed as far as $p = n - m + 1$. For this to be the case, those for $q = k - 2$ must in turn be completed as far as $p = n - m + 2$, and so on back to the initial column $q = -1$, which must go as far as $p = n - m + k + 1$. In general, then, the entries in column q must be computed as far as $p = n - m + k - q$. (Note that in the algorithm presented in Landau and Vishkin (1989), the $r_{p,q}$ table — known there as $L_{d,e}$ — is computed up to $p = n$ for all values of q.)

Partial $r_{p,q}$-tables for the example strings $x = $ ABCDE and $y = $ ACEABPCQDEABCR with $k = 2$ are shown below. Only the initialised values are given in the first, whereas the second also contains the computed entries.

		q		
	-1	0	1	2
-3			1	2
-2		0	1	
-1	-1	0		
0	-1			
p 1	-1			
2	-1			
3	-1			
4	-1			
5	-1			
⋮	⋮			

		q		
	-1	0	1	2
-3			1	2
-2		0	1	5
-1	-1	0	3	4
0	-1	1	2	3
p 1	-1	0	1	4
2	-1	0	3	4
3	-1	2	3	4
4	-1	0	3	4
5	-1	0	1	5
⋮	⋮	⋮	⋮	⋮

The algorithm may be shown to calculate correctly the $r_{p,q}$ values by induction on q as follows. Consider first of all the case where $q = 0$ and the initial values $r_{p,0}$ ($p \geqslant 0$) are being calculated. From the boundary conditions, r is initialised to 0. The while loop then finds that $x(1, r_{p,0}) = y(p + 1, p + r_{p,0})$ and $x_{r_{p,0}+1} \neq y_{p+r_{p,0}+1}$, thus setting $r_{p,0}$ to the correct value. Now consider the computation at subsequent values of q. Assume that all $r_{p,q-1}$ values are correct. In the calculation of $r_{p,q}$ ($p \geqslant -q$), variable r is set to the largest row on diagonal p such that $d_{r,p+r}$ can become value q by possibilities 2, 3 or 4 described earlier. The while loop then steps through successive positions on the diagonal where the pattern- and text-symbols match to arrive at the correct value for $r_{p,q}$.

The algorithm computes the $r_{p,q}$ values on $n - m + 2k + 1$ diagonals. Row variable r may be assigned at most m different values for each diagonal, leading to an $O(mn)$ worst-case computation time. However, Myers (1986b) has shown that this type of approach runs in $O(kn)$ time on average, and provides a fairly fast, practical method of solving the problem.

It shall now be shown how the framework of the above method has been employed to develop a theoretically improved, though somewhat less practical, algorithm. This involves altering the way in which the $r_{p,q}$ values are calculated. In the above, brute-force method, variable r is incremented successively in unit steps until it reaches the correct value of $r_{p,q}$. However, by virtue of appropriate preprocessing of both the pattern *and* the text, the value of $r_{p,q}$ may alternatively be found in constant time. The manner in which this may be done shall be described in due course, but first we turn our attention to the requisite preprocessing.

In the preprocessing stage, the suffix tree of the string $y\#x\$$, where $\#$ and $\$$ are symbols not in the alphabet over which x and y are strings, is constructed using Weiner's (1973) algorithm (which was mentioned together with alternative construction techniques in Chapter 4). Building this tree requires linear space and, for a fixed-size alphabet, linear time. For arbitrary alphabets, the algorithm may be adapted to run in $O((m+n)\log|C_{xy}|)$ time, where $|C_{xy}|$ is the number of distinct symbols in the combined input string. The preprocessing stage thus requires $O(m+n)$ and $O((m+n)\log|C_{xy}|)$ time for the cases of fixed and arbitrary alphabets, respectively. In order to provide information necessary in the later use of the tree, each of its nodes is augmented with the length of the substring represented by the given node.

The algorithm of Figure 5.14 may now be modified to take advantage of the above preprocessing. Just before the **while** loop for diagonal p, r has been assigned a value such that $x(1,r)$ has been matched, up to q differences, with some text substring ending at y_{p+r}. The function of the **while** loop is then to find the largest jump, h, say, for which $x(r+1,r+h) = y(p+r+1,p+r+h)$. This is equivalent to finding the length of the longest common prefix of the suffixes $x(r+1,m)\$$ and $y(p+r+1,n)\#x\$$ of the preprocessed concatenated string. The rôle of the symbol # is to prevent the situation arising whereby an erroneous prefix consisting of symbols from both y and x might be considered. The desired value of h may be found by retrieving from the suffix tree the length associated with the least common ancestor (LCA) of the pair of leaves defined by the above suffixes. The LCA algorithm of Harel and Tarjan (1984) or of Schieber and Vishkin (1988) may therefore be used in the k-differences algorithm as an alternative means of deriving the lengths of the requisite matching substrings.

The suffix tree has $O(n)$ nodes. A transformation, in linear time, of the tree is required by the LCA algorithms in order to support the determination of an LCA in $O(1)$ time. As noted before, $r_{p,q}$ values are calculated on $O(n)$ diagonals. Furthermore, $k+1$ such values are required for each diagonal, leading to a total of $O(kn)$ LCA queries. This $O(kn)$-time computation is the most significant element in the overall calculation of the $r_{p,q}$ values. The total running time for this k-differences algorithm is therefore $O(m+kn)$ for a fixed-size alphabet and $O((m+n)\log|C_{xy}| + kn)$ otherwise.

5.2.7 Chang-Lawler k-differences

Chang and Lawler (1990, 1993) devised two k-differences algorithms involving the use of the suffix tree of the pattern string. Least common ancestors in the tree are used together with *matching statistics* to compute the jumps of Landau and Vishkin's method (see section 5.2.6). The matching-statistics data structure shall be described below first of all. We shall then see how this is used in the approximate-matching algorithms.

Matching Statistics

The matching statistics of text y for pattern x comprise two vectors: M and M'. The first is a vector of integer values, such that $M_j = |u|$, where u is the longest substring of x to occur exactly in y starting from position j. In other words, M_j is the length of the longest common prefix of $y(j, n)$ and any suffix of the pattern. And M' is a vector of pointers to nodes in the pattern's suffix tree, X, such that M'_j points to the extended locus of string u, i.e. the node representing the shortest extension of u that is defined in the tree.

Vectors M and M' may be computed in $O(m + n)$ time as follows. The suffix tree X is first of all built in $O(m)$ time (assuming a fixed alphabet), as discussed in Chapter 4. This is then used in a left-to-right scan of the text. At the first text symbol that also occurs in the pattern, the longest match is found by following edges in X downwards from the root. The longest matches at subsequent positions are then determined by traversing suffix links and judiciously following edges down the tree.

But before this text-scanning process is described in detail, it might be helpful to give a few reminders about the suffix tree of $x\$$ (where $\$$ is a special terminator symbol occurring nowhere in either x or y). First, recall that the edges of suffix tree X are labelled with pairs of indices, (h, l), representing substrings $x\$(h, l)$. The second reminder concerns the relationship between the strings represented by pairs of connected nodes in X. If the loci of strings u and v are, respectively, r and s (i.e. nodes r and s represent strings u and v), and if s is a child of r, connected to it by an edge labelled (h, l), then string v is obtained by appending $x\$(h, l)$ to string u. Finally, the initial symbols of the strings corresponding to the outgoing edges from any given node in the tree are all distinct.

Given a parent node r and a child s, connected in X by edge (h, l), where $x\$_h = a$, the functions $child$, $first$, and len may now be defined as follows.

$$child(r, a) \;=\; s \qquad\qquad (5.28)$$

$$first(r, a) \;=\; h \qquad\qquad (5.29)$$

$$len(r, a) \;=\; l - h + 1 \qquad\qquad (5.30)$$

Thus, $child$ returns the node arrived at by following the edge from r corresponding to a string starting with symbol a; $first$ gives the left-hand index of this string; and len returns its length.

These three functions are used in the computation of M and M', as shown in Figure 5.15. Vector elements M_j and M'_j are computed at step j of the outer loop. The rightmost text symbol to have been read at any time is y_l, and text position h lies somewhere between j and l.

The algorithm starts off by trying to match successive text symbols against those belonging to the strings on a downward sequence of edges in the suffix tree, starting from the root. While the text symbols do not match any pattern symbol, indices h and l keep pace with j, and r stays at the root.

As soon as the first text symbol occurring in x is encountered, at position $j = j'$, say, the second **while** loop is entered. This follows a sequence of edges down from

---

$r = root$ — the root of suffix tree, X, of $x\$$
$h = 1$
$l = 1$
for $j = 1$ to n
    while $(h < l)$ and $(h + len(r, y_h) \leqslant l)$
        $oldr = r$
        $r = child(r, y_h)$
        $h = h + len(oldr, y_h)$
    if $h = l$
        while $(child(r, y_h) \neq$ null$)$ and $(y_l = x\$_{first(r,y_h)+l-h})$
            $l = l + 1$
            if $h + len(r, y_h) = l$
                $r = child(r, y_h)$
                $h = l$
    $M_j = l - j$
    if $h = l$
        $M'_j = r$
    else
        $M'_j = child(r, y_h)$
    if $r = root$
        if $h = l$
            $h = h + 1$
            $l = l + 1$
        else if $h < l$
            $h = h + 1$
    else
        $r =$ node pointed to by suffix link from r

Figure 5.15: Chang-Lawler matching-statistics computation

the root, until it can proceed no further: h indexes the text symbol corresponding to the start of a string associated with an edge; l then steps through successive text positions from h onwards, and symbols y_l are compared with those of the current edge's string. When l reaches the end of this string, a new node r is reached, h skips forward, and the above process is repeated. This continues until there is no match for y_l. On completion, then, both $y(j', h - 1)$ and $y(j', l - 1)$ are substrings of x, but $y(j', l)$ is not. Furthermore, $y(j', h - 1)$ corresponds to the explicit node r, and this is the contracted locus of $y(j', l - 1)$. In other words, $y(j', h - 1)$ is the longest prefix of $y(j', l - 1)$ to be represented by a node in X, and $y(h, l - 1)$ is a possibly-empty prefix of a string on an outgoing edge from r. Also, $y(j', l - 1)$ is the longest substring of x occurring in y starting from position j'.

During the next iteration ($j = j' + 1$), it will be required to try to extend the match of $y(j' + 1, l - 1)$. If r is still at the root at the end of iteration j', then $h = j'$ and h is incremented ready for the next iteration. On the other hand, if r has ventured further than the root, then its suffix link is traversed, with r ending up at the locus of $y(j' + 1, h - 1)$.

There are now two cases to consider. Firstly, if $h = l$ at the start of iteration $j' + 1$, then r is the locus of $y(j' + 1, l - 1)$, and the second **while** loop attempts to extend the match from y_l onwards. Otherwise, in the second case, $h < l$ and the first **while** loop ensures that r becomes the contracted locus of $y(j' + 1, l - 1)$. As a result, the value of h may then become equal to l. If so, the situation is now the same as the above, and the second **while** loop tries to extend the match. However, if h is still less than l, then the path in the tree down from the root corresponding to $y(j' + 1, l - 1)$ must end part way through the string on an edge. The same must also have been true for $y(j', l - 1)$. Since neither ends at a node, both corresponding pattern substrings can only be extended by the same single symbol. Recall that $y(j', l)$ was not a pattern substring: y_l is thus not the required symbol, and the match $y(j' + 1, l - 1)$ can therefore be extended no further.

Node r is then again set ready for the coming iteration, or, if it is currently at the root, the appropriate indices are incremented. The whole process is repeated in this way until the end of the text is reached. Note that the values of h and l can become equal to at most $n + 1$: a fictitious sentinel value ($\notin C \cup \{\$\}$) should therefore be set beforehand for y_{n+1} to ensure that a symbol comparison fails in such a case.

The value of j is clearly bounded by n. At least one of the three indices j, h and l is incremented for each constant amount of work done in the algorithm, and they are never decremented. The running time is thus $O(n)$. Taking into account the initial construction of the suffix tree, the overall computation time for the matching statistics is $O(m + n)$.

As an example, consider the computation of the matching statistics for pattern $x = \texttt{ABBCAAA}$ and text $y = \texttt{DEAABBCAD}$. The pattern's suffix tree is shown in Figure

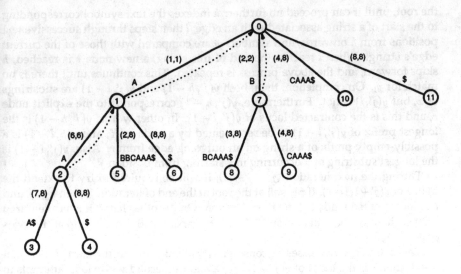

Figure 5.16: Suffix tree for string ABBCAAA$

5.16. For convenience, each edge is labelled with its respective substring in addition to the corresponding pair of indices. Suffix links are indicated by the broken arrows, and the node numbering scheme serves only to identify individual nodes: the actual numbers bear no other significance. The operation of the algorithm is outlined briefly below for a scan of the text, evaluating M_1 up to M_8.

$j = 1, 2$: h and l remain equal to j, $child(root, y_h)$ does not exist, and r stays at the root. The longest match at these two positions is ϵ.

$j = 3$: initially, $h = l = 3$. The second **while** loop takes r down from the root to node 2, at which point $h = l = 5$. Matching can then proceed no further, as $child(2, B)$ does not exist. So, the longest match is $y(3, 4) = $ AA. r moves along the suffix link from node 2 to node 1.

$j = 4$: initially, $h = l = 5$. Starting from node 1, BBCA is matched in the second **while** loop against the string on the edge leading to node 5. A mismatch is then obtained for $l = 9$. h remains equal to 5. The longest match is $y(4, 8) = $ ABBCA. Traversing the suffix link from node 1 brings r back to node 0, the root.

$j = 5$: initially, $h = 5$; $l = 9$. The first **while** loop takes r down to node 7 and sets $h = 6$. As for $j = 4$, $h \neq l$: the previous longest match ABBCA could not be extended by y_9, so neither can $y(5,8) = $ BBCA. Following node 7's suffix link returns r to the root.

$j = 6$: initially, $h = 6$; $l = 9$. Again, the first **while** loop shifts r down to node 7, this time setting $h = 7$. As for $j = 5$, $h \neq l$; y_9 therefore cannot extend the match $y(6,8) = $ BCA. The suffix link traversal takes r back to node 0.

$j = 7$: initially, $h = 7$; $l = 9$. This time, r remains at the root. As in the previous iteration, $h \neq l$; thus y_9 cannot extend the match $y(7,8) = $ CA. The value of h is incremented by one so that the matching on the next iteration starts from y_8.

$j = 8$: initially, $h = 8$; $l = 9$. The first **while** loop takes r down to node 1 and sets $h = 9$. The match cannot be extended any further, as $child(1, D)$ does not exist. The longest match is thus $y(8,8) = $ A. Once more, r is returned to the root via the suffix link from node 1.

The above algorithm incidentally provides an on-line solution to the exact string-matching problem: if $M_j = m$, then $y(j, j + m - 1) = x$, i.e. an exact occurrence of the pattern is to be found as a substring of the text starting from position j. The matching statistics need not be stored for this; so the working-space requirement is $O(m)$. And the preprocessing time, spent building the pattern's suffix tree, is also $O(m)$.

We are now in a position to see how the matching statistics may be used to solve the k-differences problem.

k-differences String Matching

Chang and Lawler use matching statistics in an efficient implementation of Landau and Vishkin's algorithm. This is then employed in two versions of a scanning-and-checking technique to improve the average performance. For the time being, however, attention shall be focused here on their implementation of the Landau-Vishkin method.

That algorithm was described in detail in section 5.2.6. Recall that in order to run in $O(kn)$ time in the worst case, it relies on being able to compute in constant time the jump from one transition to the next along a diagonal of the distance matrix. The size of such a jump corresponds to the length of the longest common prefix of a pattern- and a text-suffix. We may thus define the jump function, $J(i,j)$, as the length of the longest prefix common to both $x(i, m)$ and $y(j, n)$. In Landau and Vishkin's algorithm, the value of $J(i,j)$ is determined in constant time by finding the LCA of these two strings in the suffix tree of a combined text-pattern string (which requires the text as well as the pattern to be preprocessed).

In contrast, Chang and Lawler's implementation requires preprocessing (in $O(m)$ time) of only the pattern. The matching statistics, computed from the pattern's suffix tree, are exploited as follows in order to evaluate in constant time each required $J(i, j)$:

$$J(i, j) = \min\{M_j, |u|\} \qquad (5.31)$$

where u is the string represented by the LCA of node M'_j and the leaf corresponding to suffix $x(i, m)\$$.

Recall that M'_j is the extended locus of the longest matching prefix between $y(j, n)$ and any pattern suffix. If it so happens that M'_j coincides with $x(i, m)\$$'s leaf or is an ancestor thereof (in which case, the longest match — $y(j, j + M_j - 1)$ — is a prefix of $x(i, m)$), then the LCA is node M'_j itself. The string corresponding to the LCA can thus be longer than the actual match: hence the minimisation in (5.31).

As an example, consider once more the case where x = ABBCAAA and y = DEAABBCAD. In particular, consider the situation for text position 5. The longest match with the pattern there is BBCA; M_5 is thus equal to 4 and, referring to Figure 5.16, M'_5 gives the extended locus of BBCA, namely node 8. For $i = 2$, M'_5 and the leaf for $x(2, 7)\$$ are, in fact, one and the same. Node 8 is therefore the required LCA, with a corresponding string of length 7. The correct value of $J(2, 5)$, i.e. 4, is thus given by M_5 in this case. For $i = 3$, however, the LCA of M'_5 and the leaf for $x(3, 7)\$$ (node 9) turns out to be node 7, whose corresponding string has a length of 1: the correct value of $J(3, 5)$.

The LCA queries required by (5.31) are performed using a fast version of Schieber and Vishkin's (1988) algorithm. This has been efficiently implemented using only simple machine instructions (Chang, 1990).

Recall that in the Landau-Vishkin algorithm, table $r_{p,q}$ — where $r_{p,q}$ represents the largest row i such that $d_{i,j} = q$ and (i, j) lies on diagonal p of the dynamic-programming distance matrix — is computed rather than the distance matrix itself. Here, however, an alternative, but equivalent, $(k+1) \times (n+1)$ table, L, is computed. This is defined such that $L_{q,s}$ is the largest row i for which $d = q$ on diagonal $p = s - q$ of the distance matrix.

To see how to compute the values of $L_{q,s}$, we must consider the entries, $d_{i,j}$, in the distance table. The final occurrence of value $q - 1$ on not only diagonal $p = s - q$, but also on the one below and the one above should be taken into account.

First of all, on the diagonal below (i.e. $p = s - q - 1$), the largest row at which $d = q - 1$ is $L_{q-1, s-2}$. The entry on the same row in diagonal $s - q$ can therefore become equal to q (corresponding to the insertion of $y_{s-q+L_{q-1, s-2}}$ after $x_{L_{q-1, s-2}}$). Secondly, on the same diagonal (i.e. $p = s - q$), the largest row at which $d = q - 1$ is $L_{q-1, s-1}$. The entry on this diagonal in the next row (i.e. $L_{q-1, s-1} + 1$) is thus equal to q (corresponding to the substitution of $y_{s-q+L_{q-1, s-1}+1}$ for $x_{L_{q-1, s-1}+1}$). And finally, on the diagonal above (i.e. $p = s - q + 1$), the largest row at which $d = q - 1$ is $L_{q-1, s}$. The entry on the next row (i.e. $L_{q-1, s} + 1$) in diagonal $s - q$ can therefore become equal to q (corresponding to the deletion of $x_{L_{q-1,s}+1}$).

To arrive at the correct value of $L_{q,s}$, we may start at the largest of the rows from the above three possibilities, and thence slide down diagonal $s - q$ as long as the corresponding pattern- and text-symbols match. In other words, letting $r = \max\{L_{q-1,s-2}, L_{q-1,s-1} + 1, L_{q-1,s} + 1\}$ (if the result of this maximisation is greater than m, then r is taken to be equal to m), then $L_{q,s} = r + J(r+1, r+1+s-q)$.

Note that $L_{q-1,s-1} + 1$ always provides a valid starting point for the computation of $L_{q,s}$, i.e. the value on diagonal $s - q$ at row $L_{q-1,s-1} + 1$ is always equal to q. But, although it was stated above that the other two entries mentioned *can* become equal to q, if either occurs on a row greater than $L_{q-1,s-1} + 1$, then, owing to the diagonal's monotonicity, it *does* become equal to q.

The $L_{q,s}$ table may thus be computed column by column using the above recurrence. The entire table need not be stored though, as values in only the current and the two previous columns are required to compute those in any given current column. The initial value in column s, $L_{0,s}$, gives the largest row whose intersection with diagonal s in the distance matrix has value $d = 0$. $L_{0,s}$ is thus equal to the length of the longest prefix common to x and $y(s + 1, n)$, i.e. $L_{0,s} = J(1, s + 1)$. Two further sets of boundary values are also required to evaluate the table: columns $L_{q,-1}$ and $L_{q,-2}$. In the distance table, the first element of a negative diagonal, $-p$, say, is entry $d_{p,0} = p$. All the distance values on this diagonal are thus $\geqslant p$. So, we can see that all the entries on diagonal $-(q + 1)$ are greater than q. The values of $L_{q,-1}$ may therefore be taken to be $-\infty$ (in practice, values of -1 suffice), and so too for $L_{q,-2}$.

In summary, the computation of $L_{q,s}$, for $0 \leqslant q \leqslant k$ and $-2 \leqslant s \leqslant n$, is as follows:

$$L_{q,s} = \begin{cases} -\infty & \text{if } s = -1 \text{ or } s = -2 \\ J(1, s + 1) & \text{if } q = 0 \text{ and } s \geqslant 0 \\ r + J(r + 1, r + 1 + s - q) & \text{otherwise} \end{cases} \qquad (5.32)$$

where $r = \min\{m, \max\{L_{q-1,s-2}, L_{q-1,s-1} + 1, L_{q-1,s} + 1\}\}$. If $L_{q,s} = m$, then an occurrence of the pattern with up to q differences ends at position $s - q + m$ in the text.

Table L may be evaluated as the matching statistics are computed during a scan of the text. Not all of the statistics need be kept to do this: it suffices to store only the m most recent ones at any given stage, since at most $M_{s+1}, \ldots, M_{s+m}$ are required in the calculation of column s of L.

Thus, for a fixed, finite alphabet, the Chang-Lawler implementation of the Landau-Vishkin method requires $O(m)$ working space and runs in $O(m + kn)$ time in the worst case. When the alphabet size is not fixed, the pattern's suffix tree requires $O(m |C|)$ space when implemented using direct indexing for offspring nodes.

Scanning and Checking

The above implementation of the Landau-Vishkin method is selectively applied to parts of the text in the two scanning-and-checking approaches. This significantly reduces the average amount of work required; and at worst, the technique is equivalent to computing all of the above-mentioned L table. The two approaches are described below. Under certain assumed conditions, the average text-processing time for the first one is linear, and that for the second sublinear in n.

Linear-Expected-Time Algorithm

In this version of the algorithm, a succession of text start positions, s_j, is computed, and L is evaluated only for certain substrings of y dictated by the values of s_j. The sequence starts with $s_1 = 1$, and subsequent values are obtained from the recurrence:

$$s_{j+1} = s_j + M_{s_j} + 1 \qquad (5.33)$$

Start position s_{j+1} is thus reached by taking the maximum possible jump from s_j, and thence moving one position forward. Table L is then computed for text substrings $y(s_j, s_{j+k+2} - 1)$ only if $s_{j+k+2} - s_j \geqslant m - k$.

The operation of the above scheme may be shown to be correct as follows. Let an approximate occurrence of the pattern, with up to k differences and of length l ($m - k \leqslant l \leqslant m + k$), start at position t in the text, i.e. $y(t, t + l - 1)$ approximately matches x. This match may be represented as:

$$y(t, t + l - 1) = u_1 v_1 u_2 v_2 \ldots u_{k+1} v_{k+1} \qquad (5.34)$$

where, for $1 \leqslant h \leqslant k + 1$, u_h is a substring of x, and $v_h \in C \cup \{\epsilon\}$ (at least one v_h is empty). Further, let t be bracketed by two successive start positions:

$$s_j \leqslant t \leqslant s_{j+1} \qquad (5.35)$$

The first difference from the pattern (a symbol deletion, insertion or substitution) is given by v_1. If this occurs to the left of or at position s_{j+1}, then:

$$s_{j+1} + 1 \geqslant t + |u_1 v_1| \qquad (5.36)$$

If, on the other hand, v_1 occurs to the right of s_{j+1}, then the portion of $u_1 v_1$ to the right of s_{j+1} has a length no greater than $M_{s_{j+1}}$, giving:

$$s_{j+1} + M_{s_{j+1}} \geqslant t + |u_1 v_1| - 1 \qquad (5.37)$$

which subsumes the previous case (5.36). Combining the above with (5.33) produces:

$$s_{j+2} \geqslant t + |u_1 v_1| \qquad (5.38)$$

Since we also have that $s_{j+1} \geqslant t$ (from (5.35)), the following result for $0 \leqslant h \leqslant k+1$ may be obtained by induction.

$$s_{j+h+1} \geqslant t + |u_1 v_1 \ldots u_h v_h| \qquad (5.39)$$

Setting $h = k + 1$ in (5.39) gives: $s_{j+k+2} \geqslant t + l$. Since $t \geqslant s_j$ (from (5.35)), we then have that $s_{j+k+2} - s_j \geqslant l$, or, taking the lowest possible value for l:

$$s_{j+k+2} - s_j \geqslant m - k \qquad (5.40)$$

Table L will therefore be computed for $y(s_j, s_{j+k+2} - 1)$, and hence the approximate match ending at y_{t+l-1} will be detected.

Duplication of effort is avoided by keeping track of the rightmost column of L computed so far. When successive text substrings overlap, evaluation of the table may thus be resumed from where it was last left off. This ensures that the running time in the worst case is the same as that for the computation of the entire table.

Chang and Lawler have shown that the average effort involved in checking potential matches is $O(n)$ provided: the alphabet C is finite; y is a uniformly random string; and k is less that a certain threshold k_{th}, given by:

$$k_{th} = \frac{m}{\log_{|C|} m + c_1} - c_2 \qquad (5.41)$$

for suitably chosen constants c_1 and c_2. Experimental evidence suggests that for $|C| \geqslant 4$, a value as low as 2 suffices for c_1. Practical threshold values for fairly large patterns (with lengths measured in hundreds of symbols) of 7, 15, 25, and 35% of m for alphabet sizes of 2, 4, 16, and 64, respectively, have been reported.

Sublinear-Expected-Time Algorithm

In this version of the algorithm, the text is partitioned into contiguous substrings, and these are tested for possible inclusion in approximate matches of the pattern. Sections of the text containing potential matches are again closely checked by computing the appropriate parts of the L table; whereas those partitions that cannot possibly contribute to a match are skipped over.

The length of each of the adjoining regions into which the text is divided is $(m - k)/2$. As the minimum length of an approximate occurrence of x is $m - k$, any text substring approximately matching the pattern must contain at least one complete region. A coarse filter is applied to each region to decide whether it may be discarded or whether closer inspection is called for. The filtering operation is as follows.

Starting from the first symbol in a region, $k+1$ maximum jumps are taken, as per (5.33), ultimately arriving at text position t, say. If t lies within the current region, then the latter cannot possibly be completely contained within an approximate match; the remainder of the region may then be ignored. If, on the other hand, the jumps have sent t further than the end of the region, extra work is then required to check for an approximate match involving this region. Since such a match could end at the last symbol of the region, and as the maximum length of an approximate match is $m + k$, $(m + 3k)/2$ symbols to the immediate left of the current region must also be taken into account. Table L is therefore computed for the text from that leftmost point up to position t.

Chang and Lawler have shown that the average number of text symbols examined in the above procedure is $\frac{2n}{m-k}(k + 1)(\log_{|C|} m + O(1))$ for $k < k_{th}/2 - 3$. By combining the previous, linear-expected-time procedure (for $k \geqslant k_{th}/2 - 3$) with the current method (for $k < k_{th}/2 - 3$), an overall, average-case, text-processing time of $O(\frac{n}{m} k \log m)$ is obtained for $k < k_{th}$. This then provides true sublinear running time when $k \prec m/\log_{|C|} m$.

5.2.8 Chang-Lampe k-differences

Chang and Lampe's (1992) k-differences algorithm efficiently computes values in the dynamic-programming distance matrix. Instead of laboriously evaluating every entry in the matrix, it only computes the ends of runs of consecutive integers down each column. In the following description, these runs are defined first of all. The way that the end points of the runs in one column may be found from those in the previous column is then examined. Finally, it is shown how these end-point recurrences may be implemented to compute the distance matrix.

Each column of the distance table may be partitioned into runs of consecutive integers. Element $d_{i,j}$ belongs to run r only if

$$r = i - d_{i,j} \tag{5.42}$$

The values of r going down a column j form a non-decreasing sequence starting from 0. As an example, consider the table for $x =$ ABCDE and $y =$ ACEABPCQDEABCR, shown below.

j		0	1	2	3	4	5	6	7	8	9	10	11	12	13	14
i			A	C	E	A	B	P	C	Q	D	E	A	B	C	R
0		0	0	0	0	0	0	0	0	0	0	0	0	0	0	0
1	A	1	0	1	1	0	1	1	1	1	1	1	0	1	1	1
2	B	2	1	1	2	1	0	1	2	2	2	2	1	0	1	2
3	C	3	2	1	2	2	1	1	1	2	3	3	2	1	0	1
4	D	4	3	2	2	3	2	2	2	2	2	3	3	2	1	1
5	E	5	4	3	2	3	3	3	3	3	3	2	3	3	2	2

In column 5, $d_{0,5}$ and $d_{1,5}$ belong to run 0, and $d_{2,5}, \ldots, d_{5,5}$ belong to run 2. Notice that no element in this column belongs to run 1; in such a case, it is said that the run in question has a length of zero.

Run r in column j ends at position i if i is the minimum value such that the next element, i.e. $d_{i+1,j}$, belongs to a run greater than r. From the above, run 0 in column 5 ends at $i = 1$. The zero-length run 1 in the same column also ends at $i = 1$.

By definition, element $d_{i,j}$ belongs to run $r = i - d_{i,j}$. Let the next element down column j belong to run r', where $r' = i + 1 - d_{i+1,j}$. Remembering that the difference between adjacent entries in a column is restricted to the values -1, 0, or 1 (see (5.13)), we can see that the maximum value of r' is $r + 2$. This implies that at most one run may fail to have any members between any two adjacent column entries. In other words, no two consecutive runs, r and $r + 1$, may both have lengths of zero.

The relation between the positions of the ends of the runs in one column and those in the next is now considered. The case of a zero-length run is examined first of all. Assume that in column j, run r has a length of zero and ends at position i. Run $r - 1$ in the same column is thus of length greater than zero and also ends at position i, giving:

$$r - 1 = i - d_{i,j}$$
$$\Rightarrow r = i + 1 - d_{i,j} \tag{5.43}$$

Since run r ends at i:

$$i + 1 - d_{i+1,j} > r \tag{5.44}$$

Combining this with (5.43) gives:

$$d_{i+1,j} < d_{i,j} \tag{5.45}$$

Together with the diagonalwise-monotonicity property, (5.27), and the fact that adjacent row entries may not differ by more than 1, (5.22), this implies that:

$$d_{i+1,j+1} = d_{i,j} \tag{5.46}$$

The entry at position $i + 1$ in column $j + 1$ thus belongs to run $i + 1 - d_{i,j} = r$. Now consider the next position down this column, $i + 2$. Also from (5.45) and (5.27), we have:

$$d_{i+2,j+1} \leqslant d_{i,j} \tag{5.47}$$

showing that $d_{i+2,j+1}$ belongs to run $i + 2 - d_{i+2,j+1} > r$. It therefore follows that in column $j + 1$, run r ends at position $i + 1$.

Non-zero-length runs are considered next. Assume this time that in column j, run r ends at position i and is of length $l \geqslant 1$. Run r therefore starts at $i - l + 1$, and run $r - 1$ ends at $i - l$, implying that:

$$i - l + 1 - d_{i-l+1,j} > i - l - d_{i-l,j}$$

$$\Rightarrow d_{i-l+1,j} < d_{i-l,j} + 1$$

$$\Rightarrow d_{i-l+1,j} \leqslant d_{i-l,j} \tag{5.48}$$

since adjacent column entries may differ by only -1, 0, or 1.
Combining (5.48) and (5.27) gives the following.

$$d_{i-l+1,j+1} \geqslant d_{i-l+1,j} \tag{5.49}$$

If the equality holds, i.e. if $d_{i-l+1,j+1} = d_{i-l+1,j}$, then the entry at position $i - l + 1$ in column $j + 1$ belongs to run r. Otherwise, if $d_{i-l+1,j+1} > d_{i-l+1,j}$, the start of run r in column $j + 1$ has not yet been reached by position $i - l + 1$. Hence, $i - l + 1$ is the minimum position at which run r can end in column $j + 1$.

The maximum position at which run r can end in column $j+1$ is the next point to examine. From the diagonalwise-monotonicity property, $d_{i+1,j+1}$ can equal $d_{i,j} + 1$, in which case $d_{i+1,j+1}$ belongs to run r. But is this also possible for the next element, $d_{i+2,j+1}$? The answer to this is no, which may be seen as follows. From (5.27), $d_{i+2,j+1} \leqslant d_{i+1,j} + 1$. Since run r ends at i in column j, $i - d_{i,j} < i + 1 - d_{i+1,j}$, giving $d_{i+1,j} \leqslant d_{i,j}$. Combining these provides the result:

$$d_{i+2,j+1} \leqslant d_{i,j} + 1 \tag{5.50}$$

So, $d_{i+2,j+1}$ is less than $d_{i,j} + 2$, and thus cannot belong to run r.

The end point of run r in column $j + 1$ must therefore lie somewhere in the range $[i - l + 1, i + 1]$. To find out exactly where, consider pattern index s such that $x_s = y_{j+1}$. From the diagonalwise-monotonicity property and the dynamic-programming minimisation (5.14), $d_{s,j+1} = d_{s-1,j}$. If $i - l + 2 \leqslant s \leqslant i + 1$, then $d_{s-1,j}$ belongs to run r, i.e. $s - 1 - d_{s-1,j} = r$. Element $d_{s,j+1}$ then belongs to run $s - d_{s,j+1} = r + 1$. Thus, run r ends in column $j + 1$ at position $s - 1$, where s is the lowest index such that $x_s = y_{j+1}$ and $i - l + 2 \leqslant s \leqslant i + 1$.

If there is no such s, then run r continues in column $j + 1$ up to the maximum possible position, namely $i + 1$, unless the length of run $r + 1$ in column j is zero. In such a case, $d_{i+1,j} < d_{i,j}$ and thus $d_{i+1,j+1} = d_{i,j}$. This means that $d_{i+1,j+1}$ belongs to run $r + 1$, and therefore in this situation run r ends at position i in column $j + 1$.

The above recurrences, together with a preprocessed table of pattern indices, allow the end of a run to be computed in constant time. Column j of the distance matrix may therefore be processed in $O(m - d_{m,j})$ time, since the final run in that column is $r = m - d_{m,j}$. The time taken to compute all n columns is thus $O((m - \overline{d}_m)n)$, where $\overline{d}_m$ is the average value of the entries in the mth row of the matrix.

---

for $a = 1$ **to** $|C|$
$\quad loc_{m+1}[a] = m + 2$ — default value
$\quad loc_{m+2}[a] = m + 2$
for $s = m$ **downto** 1
$\quad$ **if** $x_s = a$
$\qquad loc_s[a] = s$
$\quad$ **else**
$\qquad loc_s[a] = loc_{s+1}[a]$

Figure 5.17: Chang-Lampe k-differences preprocessing

The precomputed table is of size $O(m \ |C|)$, and is defined below. It may be built in $O(m \ |C|)$ time, as shown in Figure 5.17.

$$loc_i[a] = \min\{s \mid s = m + 2 \text{ or } (i \leqslant s \leqslant m \text{ and } x_s = a)\} \tag{5.51}$$

An implementation of the $O((m - \bar{d}_m)n)$-time text search, in which the end points (end_r) and lengths (l_r) of the runs are computed, is given in Figure 5.18. As may be seen from (5.51), the default values in table loc (for occasions where there is no pattern position satisfying the match criterion) are equal to $m + 2$. This ensures that the test $s \leqslant end_r + 1$ fails when there is no appropriate match. The maximum possible index value used for $loc[a]$ (i.e. the maximum value of $end_r - l_r + 2$) is $m + 2$. Default values are therefore placed in the fictitious entries loc_{m+1} and loc_{m+2} during preprocessing.

During the processing of the text, variable t keeps track of the highest valid run in each column. Recall that adjacent entries along a row in the distance matrix can differ in value by at most 1 (see (5.22)). So, if the first run in column j to end at position m is t, then the highest possible run to do the same in column $j + 1$ is $t + 1$. Thus, if the current run r is greater than t, then it must end at position m. Otherwise, the run end-points are computed according to the recurrences discussed earlier, until the bottom of the column is encountered.

The lengths of the new runs are computed next. If an approximate match of the pattern with up to k differences ends in the text at the current position, then this is reported together with the corresponding minimum distance value. The whole process is then repeated until the end of the text is reached.

We have already seen how the performance of the straightforward dynamic-programming procedure can be improved by cutting off unnecessary computation. Chang and Lampe's column-partition algorithm similarly benefits from such a strategy. When this technique is applied, the text-processing time of the algorithm in the average case is $O(kn)$, as it is always faster than the simple cut-off method.

```
— initialise run 0 in column 0
end_0 = m
l_0 = m + 1
— highest valid run
t = 0
— process text
for j = 1 to n
   r = 0
   running = true
   while running
      if r > t
         end_r = m
      else
         if l_r = 0
            — zero-length run
            end_r = end_r + 1
         else
            — non-zero-length run
            s = loc_{end_r - l_r + 2}[y_j]
            if s ⩽ end_r + 1
               end_r = s - 1
            else
               if (r + 1 ⩽ t) and (l_{r+1} ≠ 0)
                  end_r = end_r + 1
      if end_r ⩾ m
         running = false
         end_r = m
      r = r + 1
   t = r - 1
   — calculate run lengths
   l_0 = end_0 + 1
   for r = 1 to t
      l_r = end_r - end_{r-1}
   if t ⩾ m - k
      — report approximate match
      print j, m - t
```

Figure 5.18: Chang-Lampe k-differences string matching

$end_0 = k + 1$; $l_0 = k + 2$ — run 0 in column 0
$t = 0$ — highest valid run
$p = k + 1$ — cut-off position
— process text
for $j = 1$ **to** n
  $r = 0$; $cutoff$ = **false**
  while not $cutoff$
    if $r > t$ **then** $end_r = p + 1$
    else
      if $l_r = 0$
        — zero-length run
        $end_r = end_r + 1$
      else
        — non-zero-length run
        $s = loc_{end_r - l_r + 2}[y_j]$
        if $s \leqslant end_r + 1$ **then** $end_r = s - 1$
        else
          if $(r + 1 \leqslant t)$ **and** $(l_{r+1} \neq 0)$ **then** $end_r = end_r + 1$
    if $end_r \geqslant p$
    $cutoff$ = **true**
    if $end_r > m$ **then** $end_r = m$
    $r = r + 1$
  $t = r - 1$
  — calculate run lengths
  $l_0 = end_0 + 1$
  for $r = 1$ **to** t
    $l_r = end_r - end_{r-1}$
  — calculate new cut-off value
  $r = t$; $d = k + 1$
  while $(r \geqslant 0)$ **and** $(d > k)$
    $l = 0$
    while $(l < l_r)$ **and** $(d > k)$
      $p = end_r - l$; $d = p - r$; $l = l + 1$
    $r = r - 1$
  if $p = m$
    print j, $m - t$ — report approximate match
  else $p = p + 1$

Figure 5.19: Chang-Lampe k-differences string matching (cut-off version)

The cut-off version of the algorithm is illustrated in Figure 5.19[5] (cf. the straightforward cut-off method, Figure 5.13). The preprocessed table, loc, is computed in exactly the same way as before. This time, variable p keeps track of the maximum position that need be visited down each column. During computation of the runs, if the current one, r, is greater than the maximum one defined in the previous column (t), then the end of r is set to $p+1$; for this is the maximum possible position of the cut-off point in the next column. The end positions and lengths of the runs in each column are otherwise computed as before, but only until position p is reached. Once the runs in a column have been evaluated, the new value of p is found by scanning the column entries up from the bottom until the distance value is less than or equal to k.

5.2.9   Wu-Manber k-differences

The shift-add algorithm, which was covered earlier in this chapter in Section 5.2.2, has been adapted by Wu and Manber (1991, 1992a, 1992b) for string matching with k differences. This is one of the algorithms that they incorporated into the flexible, Unix string-matching utility, agrep. Their shift-add extension is described here together with their alternative 'partition' approach. Baeza-Yates and Perleberg's (1992) subsequent adaptation of the partition method is then also briefly mentioned.

Alternative Shift-Add String Matching

Wu and Manber employ an alternative implementation of the shift-add algorithm, which differs from the original as follows. Firstly, a bitwise logical AND is employed as the generic operator $\diamond$ of (5.8), which necessitates the use of the complements of the previously defined values $T[a]$ (see (5.4) and (5.5)). Whereas a 0 previously indicated a symbol match, this is now represented by a 1. Another difference is the significance of the bit positions in the vectors — the convention opposite to that described earlier is adopted. This results in the state vector being shifted to the right rather than to the left. Furthermore, it is assumed that 1s enter the left-hand end of the vector on these shifts. This may be realised in practice with an extra OR operation using an appropriate bit mask.

Before the k-differences algorithm itself is discussed, a brief description shall first of all be given of the exact string-matching form of this version of the shift-add algorithm.

As before, ^{i}s denotes the state vector after inspection of text symbol y_i. This time, however, individual state s_1, rather than s_m, is associated with the most significant (left-hand) end of the vector (cf. (5.1)). (Again, it is assumed that m is not greater

---

[5] An optimised C implementation of the cut-off column-partition method has been written by Chang (1993).

than the wordsize, w, of the computer, and full-width vectors are actually used in practice.) Also, s is initially set to all zeros, as opposed to all ones, i.e. $^0s_j = 0$ for $j = 1, \ldots, m$. Subsequent values of the state vector are given by the following (cf. (5.2)):

$$^is_j = \begin{cases} 1 & \text{if } j = 0 \\ 1 & \text{if } ^{i-1}s_{j-1} = 1 \text{ and } x_j = y_i \\ 0 & \text{otherwise} \end{cases} \tag{5.52}$$

This leads to the following recurrence involving the preprocessed table T:

$$^is_j = {}^{i-1}s_{j-1} \wedge T_j[y_i] \tag{5.53}$$

where $\wedge$ is the logical AND operator (cf. (5.3)). Table T is now defined as follows (cf. (5.4)):

$$T_j[a] = \begin{cases} 0 & \text{if } a \neq x_j \\ 1 & \text{if } a = x_j \end{cases} \tag{5.54}$$

And the basic working of the algorithm centres on the following operation (cf. (5.6)):

$$^is = (({}^{i-1}s \gg 1) \text{ OR } 2^{w-1}) \text{ AND } T[y_i] \tag{5.55}$$

where $\gg$ denotes the right-shift operation and the OR effectively shifts a 1 into s_1 from the fictitious s_0. A value of $^is_m = 1$ indicates that a complete match of the pattern ends at position i in the text, and hence starts at position $i - m + 1$.

The above variation of the shift-add algorithm is given in Figure 5.20[6] (cf. Figure 5.5).

k-differences Shift-Add

We are now in a position to see how the above method may be generalised for string matching with k differences. In addition to the original state vector, which shall henceforth be denoted by s^0, k extra state vectors, s^1 to s^k, are also required for this. The purpose of vector s^l, $1 \leqslant l \leqslant k$, is to record all the pattern-prefix matches with up to l differences.

During the scan of the text, s^0 is computed as before. However, we now also require recurrence relations for the k additional vectors so that their values at stage i, $^is^l$, may be computed from the previous values. Initially, $^0s^l_j = 1$ if there is a match, with up to l differences, between $x(1,j)$ and $y(1,0)$ (i.e. ϵ). All prefixes of x up to length l satisfy this condition, as up to l deletions are sufficient to transform them into the empty string. At the outset, then, vectors $^0s^l$ have l 1s in the leftmost bit positions and 0s elsewhere.

---

[6]An implementation in C of the algorithm is presented by Manber and Wu (1992), in which table T is computed in $O(m\,|C|)$ time. The alternative preprocessing given in Figure 5.20 performs this task in $O(m + |C|)$ time.

— preprocess

$msb = 1 \ll (w - 1)$ — 2^{w-1}, i.e. a 1 in only the leftmost bit position
— initialise all table entries
for $a = 1$ **to** $|C|$
    $T[a] = 0$
— adjust table entries according to the pattern symbols
$mask = msb$
for $j = 1$ **to** m
    $T[x_j] = T[x_j]$ OR $mask$
    $mask = mask \gg 1$

— search text

$s = 0$
for $i = 1$ **to** n
    $s = ((s \gg 1)$ OR $msb)$ AND $T[y_i]$
    if $s_m = 1$
        print $i - m + 1$

Figure 5.20: Alternative shift-add string matching

To obtain the required recurrence relations, the ways in which a match with up to l differences between pattern prefix $x(1, j)$ and the text ending at position i may be obtained must be analysed. There are four possibilities:

1. $x(1, j-1)$ occurs with up to l differences in the text ending at y_{i-1}, and $x_j = y_i$

2. $x(1, j-1)$ occurs with up to $l-1$ differences in the text ending at y_{i-1}

3. $x(1, j-1)$ occurs with up to $l-1$ differences in the text ending at y_i

4. $x(1, j)$ occurs with up to $l-1$ differences in the text ending at y_{i-1}

Case 1 corresponds to the extension of an existing l-differences occurrence of $x(1, j-1)$. In this situation, an l-differences occurrence of $x(1, j)$ ends at y_i (i.e. ${}^i s_j^l = 1$) if ${}^{i-1} s_{j-1}^l = 1$ and $x_j = y_i$. The appropriate values in ${}^i s^l$ may thus be obtained by shifting ${}^{i-1} s^l$ one place to the right and then ANDing with $T[y_i]$.

Case 2 corresponds to an l-differences occurrence of $x(1, j)$ in which y_i has been substituted. If an $(l-1)$-differences occurrence of $x(1, j-1)$ ends at y_{i-1}, then

---

— initialise state vectors
$s^0 = 0$
$olds^0 = 0$
for $l = 1$ to k
$\quad olds^l = (olds^{l-1} \gg 1)$ OR msb

— search text
for $i = 1$ to n
$\quad$ — exact match vector
$\quad s^0 = ((s^0 \gg 1)$ OR $msb)$ AND $T[y_i]$
$\quad$ — l-differences match vectors
$\quad$ for $l = 1$ to k
$\quad\quad s^l = ((olds^l \gg 1)$ AND $T[y_i])$ OR $((olds^{l-1}$ OR $s^{l-1}) \gg 1)$ OR
$\quad\quad olds^{l-1}$ OR msb
$\quad$ — save state vectors for next iteration
$\quad$ for $l = 0$ to k
$\quad\quad olds^l = s^l$
$\quad$ if $s^k_m = 1$
$\quad\quad$ print i

Figure 5.21: k-differences shift-add string matching

$^{i-1}s^{l-1}_{j-1} = 1$. The appropriate values in $^i s^l$ may therefore be obtained by shifting $^{i-1}s^{l-1}$ one place to the right.

Case 3 corresponds to an l-differences occurrence of $x(1, j)$ in which x_j has been deleted. When an $(l - 1)$-differences occurrence of $x(1, j - 1)$ ends at y_i, $^i s^{l-1}_{j-1} = 1$. Shifting $^i s^{l-1}$ one place to the right thus produces the appropriate values for $^i s^l$.

Finally, case 4 corresponds to an l-differences occurrence of $x(1, j)$ in which y_i has been inserted. If an $(l - 1)$-differences occurrence of $x(1, j)$ ends at y_{i-1}, then $^{i-1}s^{l-1}_j = 1$. The appropriate values in $^i s^l$ are thus given by the corresponding values in $^{i-1}s^{l-1}$.

Putting together these four cases gives the following relation for $^i s^l$, $1 \leqslant l \leqslant k$, where the right-shift operation $\gg_1$ shifts in a 1 at the left-hand end of its operand.

$$^i s^l = ((^{i-1}s^l \gg_1 1) \text{ AND } T[y_i]) \text{ OR } (^{i-1}s^{l-1} \gg_1 1) \text{ OR } (^i s^{l-1} \gg_1 1) \text{ OR } {}^{i-1}s^{l-1}$$
$$= ((^{i-1}s^l \gg_1 1) \text{ AND } T[y_i]) \text{ OR } ((^{i-1}s^{l-1} \text{ OR } {}^i s^{l-1}) \gg_1 1) \text{ OR } {}^{i-1}s^{l-1} \qquad (5.56)$$

The search procedure incorporating the above recurrence is shown in Figure 5.21. The computation of the bit mask msb and table T are the same as before (see Figure 5.20). The $olds$ vectors are used to store the previous vector values so that $^{i-1}s^{l-1}$ may be used in the computation of $^{i}s^{l}$. An occurrence, with up to l differences, of the pattern in the text ending at y_i is indicated by a value of $^{i}s^{l}_m = 1$. Any k-differences pattern matches in the text are therefore signalled by the condition $^{i}s^{k}_m = 1$. Note that this time it is the end positions of such occurrences that are reported. The minimum number of differences for an approximate match ending at position i may also easily be determined from inspection of the state vectors. The desired value is the minimum l such that $^{i}s^{l}_m = 1$.

It has been assumed here that $m \leqslant w$, in which case a constant number of operations are performed on the $k + 1$ w-bit state-vectors for each text symbol, leading to an $O(kn)$ search time. In general, $\lceil\frac{m}{w}\rceil$ steps are required for each such operation, giving an $O(\lceil\frac{m}{w}\rceil kn)$ search time. The overall preprocessing and initialisation takes $O(\lceil\frac{m}{w}\rceil(k + m + |C|))$ time, and the working-space requirements are $O(m(k + |C|))$.

Pattern-Partition Approach

Wu and Manber suggest an alternative approximate-matching strategy for cases where k is small relative m. This is based on a pattern-partition approach, and involves separate scanning and checking operations. Regions containing potential approximate matches with the pattern are located during a scan of the text. And once found, these are directly checked for actual k-differences occurrences of the pattern.

The basis of the scanning operation is a simultaneous search for exact occurrences in the text of any of a number of certain substrings of the pattern. This is performed in $O(\lceil\frac{m}{w}\rceil n)$ time using the multiple-string version of the shift-add algorithm. The actual choice of pattern substrings employed in this process shall now be examined.

Consider the longest possible pattern substring to appear exactly in a k-differences approximate occurrence of the pattern. At best, this is of length m. In this case, the substring is the pattern itself, and the approximate match comprises the pattern together with a total of k insertions immediately before and/or after it.

At worst, however, there can be k substitutions or deletions distributed uniformly throughout the pattern. This cuts x into $k + 1$ regions. Rounding down, these are of length $r = \lfloor m/(k + 1)\rfloor$. Note that in this situation, the number of original pattern symbols in each of k of these blocks is one less than this, owing to the associated substitution or deletion error. This means that at least one of the first $k + 1$ contiguous blocks of length r in the pattern must appear intact in the approximate occurrence. The exact appearance in the text of any one of these $k + 1$ substrings therefore signals the possibility of a k-differences occurrence of the pattern.

The multiple-string version of the shift-add algorithm is thus used to scan the text in search of any one of the pattern substrings $x(1, r)$, $x(r + 1, 2r)$, ..., $x(kr + 1, (k + 1)r)$. The operation of the multiple-string version is similar to the basic exact-matching shift-add procedure. For the former, however, a state vector corresponding to a composite pattern formed by interleaving the $k + 1$ blocks is used, and the shifts are performed $k + 1$ bit positions at a time.

If an exact occurrence of one of the blocks is found starting at symbol y_i, then text substring $y(i + r - m - k, i + m + k - 1)$ must be searched for a match, with up to k differences, of the full pattern. As r increases (i.e. as k decreases relative to m), the probability of any of the $k + 1$ blocks appearing in random text decreases. And the average number of locations found by the scanning phase, and hence requiring closer examination, therefore also decreases.

Baeza-Yates and Perleberg (1992) have suggested using a traditional multiple-string algorithm, such as Aho-Corasick, to search for occurrences of the $k+1$ pattern substrings. The scan of the text may thus be accomplished in linear time in the worst case. Each potential approximate match in the text may be checked in $O(m^2)$ time when straightforward dynamic programming is employed. However, Baeza-Yates and Perleberg have shown that, assuming random strings, the scanning and checking phases may be performed in overall time $O(n)$ on average for $k = O(m / \log m)$.

5.3 Further Reading

An overview of approximate string-matching algorithms is presented by Galil and Giancarlo (1988), and a comparison of the complexities of certain algorithms is also provided by Gonnet and Baeza-Yates (1991). Also, some of the more recent approaches have been compared empirically by Jokinen, Tarhio and Ukkonen (1991) and Chang and Lampe (1992).

A review of techniques applicable in the automatic detection and correction of spelling errors is given by Peterson (1980). Matching techniques suited to approximate dictionary look-up applications are also covered in a survey by Hall and Dowling (1980).

Finally, Hollaar (1979) presents an early survey of the major parallel hardware architectures employed in string-matching systems intended for information retrieval.

6

Repeated Substrings

Experience isn't interesting till it begins to repeat itself — in fact, till it does that, it hardly is experience.
— Elizabeth Bowen (1899–1973), *Death of the Heart*, 1938.

6.1 Overview

The detection of repeated patterns in strings is an important activity which crops up in a variety of different situations. The elimination of unnecessary duplications in a sequence of data, and the efficient encoding of the data can, for example, rely on just such a process. Two variations of the problem are considered here, both of which involve repeated substrings, x, in an input string, y. First of all, the problem where the repeated substring instances occur consecutively in the input string is briefly considered. The more general problem in which the instances need not necessarily occur contiguously is then examined in greater detail.

6.1.1 Repetitions

In order to discuss the first variation, some relevant terminology will first of all be introduced. A string contains a *repetition* if there occur therein two or more consecutive instances of one of its substrings. A string is said to be *primitive* if it cannot be expressed as the concatenation of two or more instances of any other non-empty string, i.e. string x is primitive if $x \neq u^k$ for any non-empty string u and integer $k \geqslant 2$. Thus, string y contains a repetition at position i, $1 \leqslant i \leqslant |y| = n$, if $y(i, i + mk - 1) = x^k$, where x is primitive and $m = |x|$ is the *period*. Furthermore, a

191

repetition x^k is *maximal* if there occurs within y neither an instance of x immediately to the left nor to the right of the repetition. A repetition is thus maximal only if it is not itself part of a longer repetition.

To determine whether or not a given string contains any repetitions, it suffices to search for the first occurrence of a square substring. Note that for alphabets comprising 3 or more symbols, there exist arbitrarily long strings containing no repetitions at all (Thue, 1912). The required search may be accomplished in $O(n^2)$ time using a straightforward approach to scanning y for repetitions. More efficient methods, running in time $O(n \log n)$, have, however, been devised (e.g. Main and Lorentz, 1979). Rabin (1985) has developed an algorithm which involves the use of substring *fingerprints*, based on representative polynomials, in the execution of substring comparisons. But its expected-case running time is $O(n \log^2 n)$ (the proportionality constant implied by this O expression varies inversely with the log size of the alphabet).

The extended problem of finding all the repetitions in the input string may also be solved in $O(n \log n)$ time. Note that, a fortiori, this also solves the above problem. Such a bound on the running time is, in fact, optimal, as the number of distinct occurrences of squares in a string can be $\Theta(n \log n)$, which is the case for Fibonacci strings (Crochemore, 1981). A method based on the use of an improvement of a partitioning technique (Aho, Hopcroft and Ullman, 1974) to compute sequences of equivalence relations was developed by Crochemore (1981). The relations in question comprise equivalence classes of positions within the string; the substrings of length k, say, starting from all the positions belonging to a given class of the k-equivalence being identical. (The initial computation of the 1-equivalence relation actually adds $O(|C| \, n)$ time, for alphabet C, to the overall execution time.) Alternative approaches based on suffix trees have also been devised (Apostolico and Preparata, 1983; Main and Lorentz, 1984). Apostolico and Preparata's algorithm is based on the fact that if y has as a substring starting at position i the primitive string x squared, then in its suffix tree, suffixes $y(i, n)$ and $y(i + |x|, n)$ will be represented by consecutive leaves in the subtree rooted at the extended locus of x.

As noted in Chapter 4, Apostolico and Szpankowski (1992) have observed that the brute-force suffix-tree construction may be modified in a straightforward manner in order to solve this problem; whereas rather elaborate postprocessing of the tree becomes necessary to preserve the optimal $O(n \log n)$ performance if a linear-time suffix-tree construction is adopted. Also, recall that the average-case running time of the brute-force construction is itself $O(n \log n)$.

6.1.2   Longest Repeated Substrings

Relaxing the above stipulation for the consecutiveness of repeated substrings results in a related problem. In this context, a repeated substring is one having at least two matching occurrences at distinct positions within the string, with the possibility that such occurrences may overlap. A repeated substring may be said to be maximal if the match of a pair of its instances can be extended no further in either direction. The problem of finding the *Longest Repeated Substring* may then be stated as follows:

Given string y, with $|y| = n$, where $n > 0$, identify and locate the longest substring, x, occurring at two or more distinct, possibly overlapping, positions in y.

The above may be illustrated by way of a couple of examples. Firstly, consider the string PABCQRABCSABTU. Substrings A, B, C, AB, BC and ABC are all repeated in the original string. Strings AB and ABC are maximal repeated substrings, and ABC is thus the longest repeated substring. Secondly, the longest repeated substring of ABABABA is ABABA, which has two overlapping occurrences: one starting at position 1, and the other at position 3.

A straightforward, brute-force approach to the problem, requiring quadratic time, involves a conceptual, $n \times n$ match-matrix, M. This is defined such that $M_{i,j} = 1$ if $y_i = y_j$, otherwise $M_{i,j} = 0$. With the exception of the main diagonal, groups of contiguous 1s on the diagonals in the matrix represent maximal recurring substrings, the longest of which being the longest repeated substring. Note that the matrix is symmetrical about the main diagonal, and thus only the upper half, say, (i.e. elements $M_{1...n-1,i+1...n}$) need be utilised.

An $O(n \log n)$-time solution to the problem has been proposed by Karp, Miller and Rosenberg (1972). In common with Crochemore's later repetition algorithm, their approach is based on the successive computation of k-equivalence relations of substring positions.

But, more efficiently yet, longest repeated substrings may be found by making avail of Weiner's (1973) substring index (or of its equivalents). In fact, the index constructions of Pratt (1973) and Slisenko (1983) are based on a search for repeated substrings. The suffix-tree data structure examined in Chapter 4 may therefore be employed in this situation, yielding a linear-time solution. Recall that internal nodes of a suffix tree represent longest common prefixes of suffixes of the input string. It is thus evident that the longest substring represented by an internal node in the tree is the longest repeated substring of the input.

A variation of the problem involves finding all the maximal repeated substrings of a given string. Again, the quadratic-time, brute-force approach may be brought to bear on this problem. The use of suffix trees in solving this variation has, however, been investigated by Baker (1992). She has developed a software-visualisation tool for finding occurrences of duplicated or related sections of code in large software systems. Hash codes of program lines, excluding comments and white space, are taken to be the component string symbols, and a threshold on the minimum length of repeated substrings may be set in order to filter out trivial duplications. The method is based on McCreight's (1976) suffix-tree construction, and the overall algorithm runs in $O(n+r)$ time, where r is the number of pairs of maximal repeated substrings found (which can be quadratic in the worst case, but is normally small in comparison with n).

Finally, it is sometimes desirable to rule out those repeated substrings whose occurrences overlap. In such a situation, it is possible to determine in $O(|x|)$ time the maximum number of distinct, non-overlapping occurrences in y of a substring x by querying an augmented suffix-tree for y (Apostolico, 1985; Apostolico and Preparata, 1985). In the creation of such an index, any substring loci that are implicit in the suffix tree and whose extended loci would not give the correct number of instances must be made explicit by splitting the appropriate edges and inserting unary nodes. If the tree has first been constructed using a linear-time algorithm, then the requisite postprocessing is rather complicated and may be performed in $O(n \log^2 n)$ time. Alternatively, however, if the brute-force construction is employed, then the augmentation may be carried out fairly readily as the tree is being built (Apostolico and Szpankowski, 1992).

6.2   Algorithms in Detail

6.2.1   Brute Force

A brute-force approach to the Longest Repeated Substring problem for the text string y involves an $n \times n$ match-matrix, M. The elements of this matrix are defined as follows:

$$M_{i,j} = \begin{cases} 1 & \text{if } y_i = y_j \\ 0 & \text{otherwise} \end{cases} \tag{6.1}$$

The matrix for the example string PABCQRABCSABTU is given in Figure 6.1, showing the symmetry about the main diagonal (for clarity, only the non-zero elements are explicitly shown). It is thus only elements above, or only those below, the main diagonal that need be considered. Groups of diagonally contiguous 1s in the matrix, with the exception of those on the main diagonal, represent maximal recurring substrings within y. From the foregoing, it may be seen that, in this example, ABC — with occurrences $y(2,4)$ and $y(7,9)$ — and AB — with occurrences $y(2,3)$, $y(7,8)$, and $y(11,12)$ — are maximal recurring substrings. The longer of the two, namely ABC, is thus the longest repeated substring.

Detection of the maximal repeated substrings may be performed by scanning the diagonals of the match matrix. As mentioned earlier, only elements above the main diagonal, i.e. $M_{1...n-1,i+1...n}$, need be considered — a total of $n(n-1)/2$. As the operations required at each location may be performed in constant time, the overall

	j	1	2	3	4	5	6	7	8	9	10	11	12	13	14
i		P	A	B	C	Q	R	A	B	C	S	A	B	T	U
1	P	1													
2	A		1					1				1			
3	B			1					1				1		
4	C				1					1					
5	Q					1									
6	R						1								
7	A		1					1				1			
8	B			1					1				1		
9	C				1					1					
10	S										1				
11	A		1					1				1			
12	B			1					1				1		
13	T													1	
14	U														1

Figure 6.1: Match matrix for string PABCQRABCSABTU

process thus takes $O(n^2)$ time. Note also that matrix M need not actually be stored, since each of its elements is required at most once only. The space requirement is therefore linear in n.

A procedure to perform the scan of the diagonals just mentioned is shown in Figure 6.2. The scan commences at the top right-hand corner of the matrix, $M_{1,n}$, and works back to the diagonal immediately above the main one. The number of elements in the current diagonal is given by the value of d. Elements $M_{i,j}$ are evaluated as the scan proceeds, and when the start of a pair of maximal repeated substrings is detected, k and l are set to their respective starting positions. The length of the current match is stored as m. The procedure outputs the start positions and length of each such pair. The longest repeated substring may be found, then, simply by keeping a running tally on the maximum length of the repeated substrings so detected. Note also that it is a simple matter to determine whether or not each pair occurs in y as a square — it suffices to test whether or not $k + m = l$.

```
for d = 1 to n − 1
    j = n − d + 1
    k = 0          — initialise first substring-instance start position
    l = 0          — initialise second substring-instance start position
    m = 0          — initialise substring length
    for i = 1 to d
        if yᵢ = yⱼ
            m = m + 1
            if k = 0
                — the start of a maximal repeated substring
                k = i
                l = j
        else
            if k ≠ 0
                — the end of a maximal repeated substring
                — y(k, k + m − 1) = y(l, l + m − 1), k ≠ l
                print (k, l, m)
                k = 0
                l = 0
                m = 0
        j = j + 1
    if k ≠ 0
    — the end of a maximal repeated substring
    — y(k, k + m − 1) = y(l, l + m − 1), k ≠ l
    print (k, l, m)
```

Figure 6.2: Brute-Force detection of repeated substrings

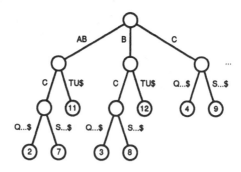

Figure 6.3: Partial suffix-tree for string PABCQRABCSABTU$

6.2.2 Suffix Trees

Longest Repeated Substring

A more efficient solution to the longest repeated substring problem involves the construction of a suffix tree of the text string. A detailed description of this data structure was presented in Chapter 4. The way in which it may be utilised in the solution of this problem shall now be examined.

It is, as we have observed earlier, apparent that the longest substring represented by an internal node in the suffix tree Y is the longest repeated substring of the input string y. It therefore suffices to keep track of the maximum length of the internal-node substrings as the tree is being built, which, as we have seen, may be accomplished in linear time.

A partial suffix-tree for the previous example string of $y = $ PABCQRABCSABTU$ is shown in Figure 6.3. Leaf nodes have been labelled with the relevant value of i for their respective suffixes $y(i, 15)$. Also, for convenience, all leaves having the root as their parent have been omitted from the diagram. In viewing the tree, attention may be restricted exclusively to those internal nodes that are parents of only leaves: for any internal node having as a child another internal node represents a string shorter than that of the latter, and hence may be ruled out as a possible candidate locus. From the figure, it may be seen that ABC is the longest substring represented by an internal node, and is thus the longest repeated substring of y.

We have just noted that the maximum length of the internal-node substrings may be determined as the suffix tree is being built. It could, however, alternatively be found after construction of the tree by performing a walk of the structure. In fact, such a walk is required in many suffix-tree applications, and may be accomplished in $O(n)$ time by recursing over the tree. A suffix tree can be implemented in the

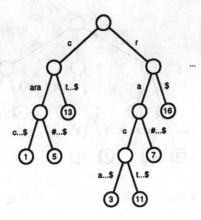

Figure 6.4: Partial suffix-tree for string `caracara#tractor$`

'left-child, right-sibling' form discussed in Chapter 4, or, if the alphabet is bounded and small enough, in a form employing direct indexing of child pointers. In the latter case, for example, one recursive call to the walk procedure would be made for each symbol in the alphabet at each node in the suffix tree. As the number of the latter is $O(n)$, the walk may thus be completed in linear time.

Longest Common Substring

It may be noted in passing that the longest common substring of two strings, x and y, may also be determined in a similar fashion in $O(m + n)$ time for a fixed alphabet. In this case, the suffix tree for the string $x\#y\$$, where symbols # and \$ are not members of the alphabet over which x and y are strings, is constructed. The presence of the # symbol ensures that no string formed by the concatenation of a suffix of x and a prefix of y is wrongly taken into consideration.

Figure 6.4 shows the relevant part of the suffix tree for the example of the pair of strings `caracara` and `tractor`. This serves to illustrate the further restriction that in the subtree rooted at the node representing the longest common substring, there must be at least one leaf representing a suffix starting from either side of #. (This time, the locus of the longest common substring need not necessarily beget only leaves.) Inspection of the tree reveals that the longest substring represented by an internal node is `cara`, but that both its instances (i.e. at $i = 1, 5$) occur only in one of the two strings. On the other hand, however, `rac` is the longest substring whose locus has descendent leaves representing positions in both input strings. It is, consequently, the longest substring common to both `caracara` and `tractor`.

Maximal Repeated Substrings

Baker's (1992) approach to the problem of finding all the maximal repeated substrings, longer than some predetermined threshold value, of an input string involves postprocessing the suffix tree of the string. The substring x, say, represented by the least common ancestor of two leaves in Y is the longest common prefix of the two suffixes represented by those leaves. It is thus a substring occurring at two distinct positions with differing right contexts in the input string. To determine whether x is a maximal repeated substring, it remains to establish whether the left contexts of its two occurrences in y also differ. If they do not, then x is merely a suffix of some longer recurring substring.

Pairs of maximal repeated substrings are found by recursing over the tree. For each internal node, lists of the positions of the suffixes represented by the leaves in the subtree rooted at the given node, and sharing identical left-contexts, are created. Pairs of maximal repeated substrings are then identified by enumerating, at each subtree, all pairings of positions from pairs of lists with distinct left-contexts (i.e. members of the cartesian products of pairs of lists). For instance, consider the suffix tree for the previous example string PABCQRABCSABTU$ (Figure 6.3). Looking for maximal repeated substrings of length 2 or greater, we find that AB is a maximal repeated substring (the left context of $y(11, 15)$ is S, and those of $y(2, 15)$ and $y(7, 15)$ are P and R, respectively); whereas BC is not (the left contexts of $y(3, 15)$ and $y(8, 15)$ are both A). By restricting the above activity to only those internal nodes representing substrings longer than the preset threshold, the overall process may be performed in $O(n + r)$ time, where r is the number of pairs of maximal repeated substrings found.

Baker has also extended the above approach in order to find parameterised matches — useful, for example, for identifying similar sections of code in large computer programs.

Non-overlapping Repeated Substrings

The task of determining the maximum number of distinct, non-overlapping occurrences in string y of any of its substrings, x, say, may be accomplished in $O(|x|)$ time by locating the extended locus of x in a precomputed, augmented suffix-tree for y.

Consider, for example, the string ABABABA. It was noted before that when overlaps are permitted, the longest repeated substring of this is ABABA. When overlaps are forbidden, however, its longest repeated substring is ABA, with occurrences $y(1, 3)$ and $y(5, 7)$. Figure 6.5 shows the suffix tree for y. Next to each node there appears a value giving the maximum number of non-overlapping occurrences within y of the substrings for which the node is an extended locus — well, almost each node: an exception shall be considered in due course. These values are stored

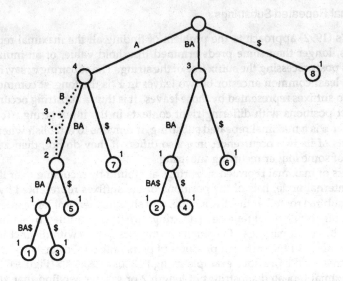

Figure 6.5: Augmented suffix-tree for string ABABABA$

in the nodes of the augmented structure. Incidentally, the values associated with the leaves are, necessarily, all equal to 1, since any substring containing $ can occur only once in the string.

To break the suspense, the exception mentioned above shall now be examined. Notice that substring AB has 3 distinct, non-overlapping occurrences in y, but that the corresponding number for the string represented by its extended locus, i.e. ABA, is only 2. In cases such as this, a supplementary, unary node must be inserted into the incoming edge of the extended locus in the augmented tree. This then provides an explicit locus so that the particular substring's non-overlapping frequency may accurately be recorded. The extra node and the new edges are shown using dotted lines in the figure. In the augmented suffix-tree, these replace the edge labelled BA entering the locus of ABA.

The actual number of supplementary nodes required in the augmented suffix-tree is dependent on the number of squares of primitive strings occurring in y. The following property obtains for such supplementary nodes (Apostolico and Preparata, 1985). If a substring is represented by a supplementary node, then it will be expressible as u^k, for some substring u of y and some integer $k \geqslant 1$. Moreover, y will also have some other substring, v, say, equal to $u^l w$, where $l \geqslant 2k$ and w is a prefix of u. The minimum number of supplementary nodes required is thus bounded from above by $\Theta(n \log n)$, as this is the maximum number of distinct instances of squares that may occur in string y. In the previous example, then, the supplementary node represents AB, giving $u = $ AB and $k = 1$. Possibilities for v are ABABA and ABABABA, for which l is equal to 2 and 3 respectively (which are both $\geqslant 2k$), and $w = $ A.

Finally, note that Apostolico and Szpankowski (1992) have made the following observation concerning the complexity of augmenting the suffix tree. Whereas an elaborate, $O(n \log^2 n)$-time postprocessing operation (Apostolico and Preparata, 1985) is required to insert the supplementary nodes and evaluate the substring frequencies in a suffix tree built in linear time, the brute-force construction may be modified to produce the augmented tree directly. If the latter strategy is adopted, redundant nodes introduced during the construction may be removed afterwards to obtain a minimal augmented tree, with an overall processing time of $O(n \log n)$ on average and $O(n^2)$ in the worst case.

A

Asymptotic Notation

In working with algorithmic complexities, it is often useful to classify certain functions of n in terms of the relative speed with which they approach infinity for increasing values of n. This appendix describes some of the asymptotic notation commonly used in this regard.

The relational operator $\prec$, introduced by Paul du Bois-Reymond (1871), may be used to order asymptotic growth rates. The operator is defined below.

$$f(n) \prec g(n) \quad \Leftrightarrow \quad \lim_{n \to \infty} \frac{f(n)}{g(n)} = 0 \qquad \text{(A.1)}$$

The use of this operator is demonstrated in the following asymptotic hierarchy.

$$1 \prec \log n \prec n^a \prec n^b \prec b^n \prec n^n$$

where a and b are arbitrary constants such that $0 < a < 1 < b$.

The relation $f(n) \prec g(n)$ may equivalently be written as $g(n) \succ f(n)$, where the operator $\succ$ is defined in a similar manner. Certain extensions to this notation were made by Hardy (1910), who for example defined $\sim$ as follows.

$$f(n) \sim g(n) \quad \Leftrightarrow \quad \lim_{n \to \infty} \frac{f(n)}{g(n)} = 1 \qquad \text{(A.2)}$$

An alternative, and when it comes to complexity results perhaps more familiar, notation involves oh (omicron), omega, and theta. Big Oh, introduced by Paul Bachman (1894), provides a convenient means of expressing upper bounds and is defined as follows.

$$f(n) = O(g(n)) \quad \Leftrightarrow \quad |f(n)| \leqslant c\,|g(n)| \quad \text{for all } n \geqslant n_0 \qquad \text{(A.3)}$$

for some positive constants n_0 and c

Note that it has become customary to use the '=' sign in the above type of expression. It does not, however, stand for equality and should be read as 'is' (unidirectional) rather than 'equals' (symmetrical). Following the suggestion by Ron Rivest, Knuth (1976) proposed that $O(g(n))$ should not be considered merely as an arbitrary function, but rather as the set of all functions $f(n)$ satisfying the inequality of (A.3). In this case '=' thus stands for the set inclusion operator $\subseteq$.

Less common than Big Oh is the little oh notation introduced by Landau (1909), which may be defined as follows.

$$f(n) = o(g(n)) \quad \Leftrightarrow \quad f(n) \prec g(n) \tag{A.4}$$

When lower bounds are involved, Big Omega may be used. This was originally defined by Hardy and Littlewood (1914), but Knuth (1976), to the chagrin of some number theorists, proposed the following variation of their definition. (The original definition was not for *all* large n, but rather only infinitely many n in a sequence going off to infinity.)

$$f(n) = \Omega(g(n)) \quad \Leftrightarrow \quad |f(n)| \geqslant c\,|g(n)| \quad \text{for all } n \geqslant n_0 \tag{A.5}$$
$$\text{for some positive constants } n_0 \text{ and } c$$

If $g(n)$ is a lower bound for $f(n)$, then $f(n)$ must be an upper bound for $g(n)$, i.e.

$$f(n) = \Omega(g(n)) \quad \Leftrightarrow \quad g(n) = O(f(n)) \tag{A.6}$$

Lastly, we come to Big Theta, which is used to indicate an exact order of growth. This was proposed by Knuth (1976) following independent suggestions by Michael Paterson and Robert Tarjan, and is defined as follows.

$$f(n) = \Theta(g(n)) \quad \Leftrightarrow \quad f(n) = O(g(n)) \text{ and } f(n) = \Omega(g(n)) \tag{A.7}$$

B

String Symbology

x	string of symbols $x_1 x_2 \ldots x_m$ of length m
$\lvert x \rvert$	the length of string x
x_i	the ith component symbol of string x
$x(i,j)$	the substring of x, $x_i x_{i+1} \ldots x_j$ (for $i,j \leqslant \lvert x \rvert$ and $j \geqslant i$)
$x_R(i,j)$	the reversed substring of x, $x_i x_{i-1} \ldots x_j$ (for $i,j \leqslant \lvert x \rvert$ and $i > j$)
ϵ	the empty string
C	the symbol alphabet
C_x	the set comprising the distinct symbols of string x
$x \lhd y$	string x is a subsequence of string y
$x \rhd y$	string x is a supersequence of string y
$d(x,y)$	the distance between strings x and y
$\text{hcs}(x,y)$	a heaviest common subsequence of strings x and y
his	a heaviest increasing subsequence
$\text{lcs}(x,y)$	a longest common subsequence of strings x and y
lis	a longest increasing subsequence
$N\text{-lcs}(X)$	an lcs of a set of N strings, X
$N\text{-scs}(X)$	a shortest common supersequence of a set of N strings, X
$w(a,b)$	the cost of transforming symbol a into symbol b

C

Glossary

Alphabet — any set of symbols; also known as a *character class*.

Concatenation — the concatenation of two strings x and y, xy, is the string obtained by appending y to x. The concatenation of two languages A and B, AB, is defined as:

$$AB = \{xy \mid x \text{ is in } A, y \text{ is in } B\}$$

i.e. the set of all strings formed by concatenating any string from A with any one from B.

Edit distance — a distance metric between two strings, possibly of unequal lengths, given by the minimum number of symbol insertions and deletions required to transform one string into the other, e.g. the edit distance between zeitgeist and preterit is 7.

Empty string, ϵ — the string with zero length.

Exponentiation — following on from an analogy between string concatenation and multiplication, exponentiation is defined as follows:

$$x^0 = \epsilon, \quad x^i = x^{i-1}x \text{ for integer } i > 0$$

Thus, $x^1 = \epsilon x = x$, $x^2 = xx$, $x^3 = xxx$ ...

Extension of a string x — a superstring y, say, of x such that x is a prefix of y.

Fibonacci string — a string defined by $f_1 = \text{B}$; $f_2 = \text{A}$; $f_n = f_{n-1}f_{n-2}$ for $n > 2$; e.g. $f_5 = \text{ABAAB}$.

Hamming distance — a distance metric between two strings of equal length, equal to the number of symbol positions at which the two strings differ, e.g. the Hamming distance between master and pastes is 2.

Indel — the generic term for a symbol insertion or deletion.

Kleene closure of a language A, A^* — the language formed by the union of zero and more concatenations of A, i.e.

$$A^* = \bigcup_{i=0}^{\infty} A^i$$

Language — a set of strings over a given alphabet.

Least common ancestor of a set of nodes in a tree — the node that is an ancestor of each member of the set and that is furthest from the root of the tree.

Length of a string x, $|x|$ — the number of instances of symbols in x.

Levenshtein distance — a distance metric between two strings, not necessarily of the same length, given by the minimum number of symbol insertions, deletions and substitutions required to transform one string into the other, e.g. the Levenshtein distance between zeitgeist and preterit is 6.

Locus of a string u — the node representing u in a given suffix tree (of string x, say, where u is a substring of x). The *extended locus* of u is the locus of the shortest extension of u that is represented in the given suffix tree. Also, the *contracted locus* of u is the locus of the longest prefix of u that is represented in the tree.

Period — the period of a repetition x^k, where x is primitive, is equal to the length of the primitive base, i.e. $|x|$.

Positive closure of a language A, A^+ — the language formed by the union of one and more concatenations of A, i.e.

$$A^+ = \bigcup_{i=1}^{\infty} A^i$$

Prefix of a string x — a string obtained by deleting zero or more symbols from the end of x, e.g. jorm is a prefix of jormungand. A *proper* prefix of x is a non-empty prefix of x not equal to x itself.

Primitive string — a string, x, say, that cannot be expressed as the exponentiation, with a power greater than 1, of any non-empty string, i.e. x is primitive only if $x \neq u^k$ for any non-empty u and integer $k \geqslant 2$. The term *strongly primitive* is sometimes applied to a string if it contains no repetitions, i.e. if it is *square-free*.

Repetition — a string has a repetition if it contains two or more consecutive instances of one of its substrings, e.g. haha is a repetition in brouhaha. A repetition, x^k, in string y is said to be *maximal* if y contains an instance of x neither immediately to the left nor to the right of the given repetition.

Square — a string whose first half equals its second half, i.e. one of the form x^2, e.g. caracara.

String over a given alphabet — a sequence of symbols drawn from the alphabet. The terms *sentence* and *word* are sometimes used synonymously with *string*. Note that both ϵ and x are prefixes, suffixes, substrings and subsequences of string x.

Subsequence of a string x — a string obtained by deleting zero or more symbols, which need not be contiguous, from x, e.g. nnnaa is a subsequence of ginnungagap. A *proper* subsequence of x is a non-empty subsequence not equal to x itself.

Substring of a string x — a string obtained by deleting zero or more symbols from the beginning and end of x (i.e. by deleting a prefix and a suffix), e.g. gna is a substring of ragnarok. A *proper* substring of x is a non-empty substring not equal to x itself.

Suffix of a string x — a string obtained by deleting zero or more symbols from the beginning of x, e.g. asill is a suffix of yggdrasill. A *proper* suffix of x is a non-empty suffix not equal to x itself.

Suffix tree of a string x (where $m = |x|$ and symbol x_m is unique within x) — a tree with m terminal nodes, each representing a different suffix of x, $x(i, m)$, for $1 \leqslant i \leqslant m$. All its internal nodes have degree $\geqslant 2$, and represent longest common prefixes of suffixes of x. Two nodes representing substrings b and a, where $b = ac$ for some non-empty string c, are connected by an edge only if a is the longest prefix of b represented by a node in the tree.

Supersequence of a string x — any string y such that x is a subsequence of y, e.g. facetious is a supersequence of aeiou.

Superstring of a string x — any string y such that x is a substring of y, i.e. $y = uxv$ for some strings u and v; e.g. illumination is a superstring of mina.

Trie — a digital search tree representing a set of keyword strings. Each of its internal nodes has at most one outgoing edge for each symbol of the alphabet in use. Each keyword is spelt out by the sequence of edges on the path from the root to the unique node representing the keyword in question.

Union of languages A and B, $A \cup B$ — the language containing all the strings of both A and B, i.e.

$$A \cup B = \{x \mid x \text{ is in } A \text{ or } x \text{ is in } B\}$$

Vocabulary of a string x — the set of all distinct, non-empty substrings of x.

D

Bibliography

Abrahamson, K. (1987) "Generalized string matching," *SIAM Journal on Computing*, Vol. 16, No. 6, p. 1039–51, December 1987.

Aho, A.V., Hopcroft, J.E., Ullman, J.D. (1974) *The Design and Analysis of Computer Algorithms*, Addison-Wesley, Reading, MA.

Aho, A.V., Corasick, M.J. (1975) "Efficient string matching: an aid to bibliographic search," *Communications of the ACM*, Vol. 18, No. 6, p. 333–40, June 1975.

Aho, A.V., Hirschberg, D.S., Ullman, J.D. (1976) "Bounds on the complexity of the longest common subsequence problem," *Journal of the ACM*, Vol. 23, No. 1, p. 1–12, January 1976.

Aho, A.V. (1980) "Pattern matching in strings," in Book, R.V. (ed.) *Formal Language Theory*, p. 325–47, Academic Press, New York.

Aho, A.V. (1990) "Algorithms for finding patterns in strings," in Leeuwen, J. van (ed.) *Handbook of Theoretical Computer Science*, Chapter 5, p. 255–300, Elsevier Science Publishers, Amsterdam.

Alberga, C.N. (1967) "String similarity and misspellings," *Communications of the ACM*, Vol. 10, No. 5, p. 302–13, May 1967.

Allison, L., Dix, T.I. (1986) "A bit-string longest-common-subsequence algorithm," *Information Processing Letters*, Vol. 23, p. 305–10, December 1986.

Altschul, S.F., Gish, W., Miller, W., Myers, E.W., Lipman, D.J. (1990) "Basic local alignment search tool," *Journal of Molecular Biology*, Vol. 215, p. 403–10.

Angell, R.C., Freund, G.E., Willett, P. (1983) "Automatic spelling correction using a trigram similarity measure," *Information Processing and Management*, Vol. 19, p. 255–61.

Aoe, J. (1989) "An efficient implementation of static string pattern matching machines," *IEEE Transactions on Software Engineering*, Vol. 15, No. 8, p. 1010–6, August 1989.

Apostolico, A., Preparata, F.P. (1983) "Optimal off-line detection of repetitions in a string," *Theoretical Computer Science*, Vol. 22, p. 297–315.

Apostolico, A. (1985) "The myriad virtues of subword trees," in Apostolico, A., Galil, Z. (eds.) *Combinatorial Algorithms on Words*, NATO ASI Series, Vol. F12, p. 85–96, Springer-Verlag, Berlin.

Apostolico, A., Guerra, C. (1985) "A fast linear-space algorithm for computing longest common subsequences," *Proceedings of the 23rd Allerton Conference on Communication, Control and Computing*, p. 76–84, University of Illinois, Urbana-Champaign, IL.

Apostolico, A., Preparata, F.P. (1985) "Structural properties of the string statistics problem," *Journal of Computer and Systems Sciences*, Vol. 31, No. 2, p. 394–411.

Apostolico, A. (1986) "Improving the worst-case performance of the Hunt-Szymanski strategy for the longest common subsequence of two strings," *Information Processing Letters*, Vol. 23, p. 63–9, August 1986.

Apostolico, A., Giancarlo, R. (1986) "The Boyer-Moore-Galil string searching strategies revisited," *SIAM Journal on Computing*, Vol. 15, No. 1, p. 98–105, February 1986.

Apostolico, A., Guerra, C. (1987) "The longest common subsequence problem revisited," *Algorithmica*, Vol. 2, p. 315–36.

Apostolico, A., Browne, S., Guerra, C. (1992) "Fast linear-space computations of longest common subsequences," *Theoretical Computer Science*, Vol. 92, p. 3–17.

Apostolico, A., Szpankowski, W. (1992) "Self-alignments in words and their applications," *Journal of Algorithms*, Vol. 13, p. 446–67.

Arlazarov, V.L., Dinic, E.A., Kronod, M.A., Faradzev, I.A. (1970) "On economic construction of the transitive closure of a directed graph," (Russian) *Doklady Akademii nauk SSSR*, Vol. 194, p. 487–8 (translated in *Soviet Mathematics — Doklady*, Vol. 11, p. 1209–10, 1975).

Arnold, J.M., Buell, D.A., Davis, E.G. (1992) "Splash 2," *SPAA 92*, Proceedings of the 4th Annual ACM Symposium on Parallel Algorithms and Architectures, p. 316–24, ACM Press, New York.

Arratia, R., Waterman, M.S. (1985a) "Critical phenomena in sequence matching," *The Annals of Probability*, Vol. 13, No. 4, p. 1236–49.

Arratia, R., Waterman, M.S. (1985b) "An Erdős-Rényi law with shifts," *Advances in Mathematics*, Vol. 55, p. 13–23.

Arratia, R., Gordon, L., Waterman, M. (1986) "An extreme value theory for sequence matching," *The Annals of Statistics*, Vol. 14, No. 3, p. 971–93.

Atallah, M.J., Jacquet, P., Szpankowski, W. (1992) "Pattern matching with mismatches: a probabilistic analysis and a randomized algorithm," in Apostolico, A., Crochemore, M., Galil, Z., Manber, U. (eds.) *Combinatorial Pattern Matching*, Lecture Notes in Computer Science, Vol. 644, p. 27–40, Springer-Verlag, Berlin.

Bachman, P. (1894) *Die Analytische Zahlentheorie*, Teubner, Leipzig.

Baeza-Yates, R.A. (1989a) "Improved string matching," *Software — Practice and Experience*, Vol. 19, No. 3, p. 257–71, March 1989.

Baeza-Yates, R.A. (1989b) "String searching algorithms revisited," in Dehne, F., Sack, J.R., Santoro, N. (eds.) *Algorithms and Data Structures*, Proceedings of the 1989 Workshop, Lecture Notes in Computer Science, Vol. 382, p. 75–96, Springer-Verlag, Berlin.

Baeza-Yates, R.A. (1989c) "Algorithms for string searching: a survey," *SIGIR Forum*, Vol. 23, No. 3/4, p. 34–58, ACM Special Interest Group on Information Retrieval.

Baeza-Yates, R.A., Gonnet, G.H. (1989) "A new approach to text searching," in Belkin, N.J., Rijsbergen, C.J. van (eds.) *SIGIR 89*, Proceedings of the 12th Annual International ACM SIGIR Conference on Research and Development in Information Retrieval, p. 168–75, ACM, New York (published as a special issue of *SIGIR Forum*, Vol. 23, No. 1–2, Fall 88/Winter 89).

Baeza-Yates, R.A. (1990) "Fast algorithms for two dimensional and multiple pattern matching," in Gilbert, J.R., Karlsson, R. (eds.) *SWAT 90*, Proceedings of the 2nd Scandinavian Workshop on Algorithm Theory, Lecture Notes in Computer Science, Vol. 447, p. 332–47, Springer-Verlag, Berlin.

Baeza-Yates, R.A. (1991) "Searching subsequences," *Theoretical Computer Science*, Vol. 78, No. 2, p. 363–76.

Baeza-Yates, R.A., Gonnet, G.H. (1992) "A new approach to text searching," *Communications of the ACM*, Vol. 35, No. 10, p. 74–82, October 1992.

Baeza-Yates, R.A., Perleberg, C.H. (1992) "Fast and practical approximate string matching," in Apostolico, A., Crochemore, M., Galil, Z., Manber, U. (eds.) *Combinatorial Pattern Matching*, Lecture Notes in Computer Science, Vol. 644, p. 185–92, Springer-Verlag, Berlin.

Baeza-Yates, R.A., Régnier, M. (1992) "Average running time of the Boyer-Moore-Horspool algorithm," *Theoretical Computer Science*, Vol. 92, No. 1, p. 19–31, January 1992.

Baker, B.S. (1992) "A program for identifying duplicated code," *Proceedings of the 24th Symposium on the Interface: Computer Science and Statistics*, College Station, Texas, 18–21 March 1992.

Bellman, R., Dreyfus, S. (1962) *Applied Dynamic Programming*, Princeton University Press, Princeton, NJ.

Bickel, M.A. (1987) "Automatic correction to misspelled names: a fourth-generation language approach," *Communications of the ACM*, Vol. 30, No. 3, p. 224–8, March 1987.

Bird, R.M., Tu, J.C., Worthy, R.M. (1977) "Associative/parallel processors for searching very large textual data bases," in McGill, M.J. (ed.) *Proceedings of the 3rd Workshop on Computer Architecture for Non-numeric Processing*, p. 8–16, ACM, New York (published as a special issue of *SIGIR Forum*, Vol. 12, No. 1).

Blair, C.R. (1960) "A program for correcting spelling errors," *Information and Control*, Vol. 3, p. 60–7.

Blum, A., Jiang, T., Li, M., Tromp, J., Yannakakis, M. (1991) "Linear approximation of shortest superstrings," *Proceedings of the 23rd ACM Symposium on Theory of Computing*, p. 328–36.

Blumer, A., Blumer, J., Ehrenfeucht, A., Haussler, D., McConnel, R. (1984a) "Building a complete inverted file for a set of text files in linear time," *Proceedings of the 16th ACM Symposium on Theory of Computing*, p. 349–58.

Blumer, A., Blumer, J., Ehrenfeucht, A., Haussler, D., McConnel, R. (1984b) "Building the minimal DFA for the set of all subwords of a word on-line in linear time," in Paredaens, J. (ed.) *Automata, Languages and Programming*, Proceedings of the 11th International Colloquium, Lecture Notes in Computer Science, Vol. 172, p. 109–18, Springer-Verlag, Berlin.

Blumer, A., Blumer, J., Ehrenfeucht, A., Haussler, D., Chen, M.T., Seiferas, J. (1985) "The smallest automaton recognizing the subwords of a word," *Theoretical Computer Science*, Vol. 40, No. 1, p. 31–56.

Blumer, A., Blumer, J., Haussler, D., McConnel, R., Ehrenfeucht, A. (1987) "Complete inverted files for efficient text retrieval and analysis," *Journal of the ACM*, Vol. 34, No. 3, p. 578–95.

Bois-Reymond, P. du (1871) "Sur la grandeur relative des infinis des fonctions," *Annali di Matematica Pura e Applicata*, series 2, Vol. 4, p. 338–53.

Boyer, R.S., Moore, J.S. (1977) "A fast string searching algorithm," *Communications of the ACM*, Vol. 20, No. 10, p. 762–72, October 1977.

Bradford, J.H., Jenkyns, T.A. (1991) "On the inadequacy of tournament algorithms for the *N*-SCS problem," *Information Processing Letters*, Vol. 38, p. 169–71, May 1991.

Briandais, R. de la (1959) "File searching using variable length keys," *Proceedings of the Western Joint Computer Conference*, p. 295–8.

Brown, M.R., Tarjan, R.E. (1978) "A representation of linear lists with movable fingers," *Proceedings of the 10th Annual ACM Symposium on Theory of Computing*, p. 19–29.

Brown, M.R., Tarjan, R.E. (1979) "A fast merging algorithm," *Journal of the ACM*, Vol. 26, p. 211–26.

Bryant, J.R., Fenlon, S.M. (1976) "The design and implementation of an on-line index," *Database Technology*.

Burkowski, F.J. (1982) "A hardware hashing scheme in the design of a multiterm string comparator," *IEEE Transactions on Computers*, Vol. C-31, No. 9, p. 825–34, September 1982.

Chan, S.C., Wong, A.K.C., Chiu, D.K.Y. (1992) "A survey of multiple sequence comparison methods," *Bulletin of Mathematical Biology*, Vol. 54, No. 4, p. 563–98, July 1992.

Chang, W.I. (1990) Fast Implementation of the Schieber-Vishkin Lowest Common Ancestor Algorithm (computer program), Computer Science Division, University of California, Berkeley.

Chang, W.I., Lawler, E.L. (1990) "Approximate string matching in sublinear expected time," *Proceedings of the 31st Annual IEEE Symposium on Foundations of Computer Science*, Vol. 1, p. 116–24.

Chang, W.I., Lampe, J. (1992) "Theoretical and empirical comparisons of approximate string matching algorithms," in Apostolico, A., Crochemore, M., Galil, Z., Manber, U. (eds.) *Combinatorial Pattern Matching*, Lecture Notes in Computer Science, Vol. 644, p. 175–84, Springer-Verlag, Berlin.

Chang, W.I. (1993) *clp.c*, C program implementing Chang and Lampe's (1992) approximate string-matching algorithm, Cold Spring Harbor Laboratory, Cold Spring Harbor, NY, 29 January 1993.

Chang, W.I., Lawler, E.L. (1993) "Sublinear approximate string matching and biological applications," *Algorithmica* (in press).

Chen, M.T., Seiferas, J. (1985) "Efficient and elegant subword-tree construction," in Apostolico, A., Galil, Z. (eds.) *Combinatorial Algorithms on Words*, NATO ASI Series, Vol. F12, p. 97–107, Springer-Verlag, Berlin.

Cheng, H.D., Fu, K.S. (1987) "VLSI architectures for string matching and pattern matching," *Pattern Recognition*, Vol. 20, No. 1, p. 125–41.

Chin, F.Y.L., Poon, C.K. (1990) "A fast algorithm for computing longest common subsequences of small alphabet size," *Journal of Information Processing*, Vol. 13, No. 4, p. 463–9, Information Processing Society of Japan.

Colussi, L., Galil, Z., Giancarlo, R. (1990) "On the exact complexity of string matching," *Proceedings of the 31st Annual IEEE Symposium on Foundations of Computer Science*, Vol. 1, p. 135–44.

Commentz-Walter, B. (1979) "A string matching algorithm fast on the average," in Maurer, H.A. (ed.) *Automata, Languages and Programming*, Lecture Notes in Computer Science, Vol. 71, p. 118–32, Springer-Verlag, Berlin.

Cook, S.A. (1972) "Linear time simulation of deterministic two-way pushdown automata," *Information Processing*, Vol. 71, p. 75–80.

Copeland, G.P. (1978) "String storage and searching for database applications: implementation on the INDY backend kernel," *Proceedings of the 4th Workshop on Computer Architecture for Non-numeric Processing*, p. 8–17, ACM, New York.

Crochemore, M. (1981) "An optimal algorithm for computing the repetitions in a word," *Information Processing Letters*, Vol. 12, No. 5, p. 244–50, 13 October 1981.

Crochemore, M. (1986) "Transducers and repetitions," *Theoretical Computer Science*, Vol. 45, p. 63–86.

Crochemore, M. (1988) "String matching with constraints," in Chytil, M.P., Janiga, L., Koubek, V. (eds.) *Proceedings of the 13th International Symposium on Mathematical Foundations of Computer Science*, Lecture Notes in Computer Science, Vol. 324, p. 44–58, Springer-Verlag, Berlin.

Crochemore, M., Perrin, D. (1989) *Two Way Pattern Matching*, Technical Report 89-8, LITP, Université Paris 7.

Crochemore, M. (1992) "String-matching on ordered alphabets," *Theoretical Computer Science*, Vol. 92, No. 1, p. 33–47, January 1992.

Curry, T., Mukhopadhyay, A. (1983) "Realization of efficient non-numeric operations through VLSI," in Anceau, F., Aas, E.J. (eds.) *VLSI 83: VLSI Design of Digital Systems*, Proceedings of the IFIP International Conference on Very Large Scale Integration, North-Holland, Amsterdam.

Davidson, L. (1962) "Retrieval of misspelled names in an airlines passenger record system," *Communications of the ACM*, Vol. 5, No. 3, p. 169–71, March 1962.

Davies, G., Bowsher, S. (1986) "Algorithms for pattern matching," *Software — Practice and Experience*, Vol. 16, No. 6, p. 575–601, June 1986.

Edmiston, E.W., Wagner, R.A. (1987) "Parallelization of the dynamic programming algorithm for comparison of sequences," in Sahni, S.K. (ed.) *Proceedings of the 1987 International Conference on Parallel Processing*, p. 78–80, Pennsylvania State University Press, PA.

Edmiston, E.W., Core, N.G., Saltz, J.H., Smith, R.M. (1988) "Parallel processing of biological sequence comparison algorithms," *International Journal of Parallel Programming*, Vol. 17, No. 3, p. 259–75.

Ehrenfeucht, A., Haussler, D. (1988) "A new distance metric on strings computable in linear time," *Discrete Applied Mathematics*, Vol. 20, p. 191–203.

Faulk, R.D. (1964) "An inductive approach to language translation," *Communications of the ACM*, Vol. 7, No. 11, p. 647–53, November 1964.

Fischer, M.J., Paterson, M.S. (1974) "String-matching and other products," in Karp, R.M. (ed.) *Complexity of Computation*, SIAM-AMS Proceedings, Vol. 7, p. 113–25.

Fischetti, V.A., Landau, G.M., Schmidt, J.P., Sellers, P.H. (1992) "Identifying periodic occurrences of a template with applications to protein structure," in Apostolico, A., Crochemore, M., Galil, Z., Manber, U. (eds.) *Combinatorial Pattern Matching*, Lecture Notes in Computer Science, Vol. 644, p. 111–20, Springer-Verlag, Berlin.

Foster, M.J., Kung, H.T. (1979) *Design of Special-Purpose VLSI Chips: Example and Opinions*, Technical Report CMU-CS-79-147, Department of Computer Science, Carnegie-Mellon University, Pittsburgh, PA.

Foster, M.J., Kung, H.T. (1980) "The design of special-purpose VLSI chips," *Computer*, Vol. 13, No. 1, p. 26–40, January 1980.

Fredkin, E. (1959) *Trie memory*, Informal Memorandum, Bolt Beranek and Newman Inc., Cambridge, MA, 23 January 1959.

Fredkin, E. (1960) "Trie memory," *Communications of the ACM*, Vol. 3, No. 9, p. 490–9, September 1960.

Galil, Z. (1979) "On improving the worst case running time of the Boyer-Moore string searching algorithm," *Communications of the ACM*, Vol. 22, No. 9, p. 505–8.

Galil, Z., Seiferas, J. (1983) "Time-space optimal string matching," *Journal of Computer and System Sciences*, Vol. 26, p. 280–94.

Galil, Z., Giancarlo, R. (1986) "Improved string matching with k mismatches," *SIGACT News*, Vol. 17, p. 52–4.

Galil, Z., Giancarlo, R. (1988) "Data structures and algorithms for approximate string matching," *Journal of Complexity*, Vol. 4, p. 33–72.

Galil, Z., Park, K. (1989) "An improved algorithm for approximate string matching," in Ausiello, G., Dezani-Ciancaglini, M., Ronchi Della Rocca, S. (eds) *ICALP 89*, Proceedings of the 16th International Colloquium on Automata, Languages and Programming, Lecture Notes in Computer Science, Vol. 372, p. 394–404, Springer-Verlag, Berlin.

Galil, Z., Park, K. (1990) "An improved algorithm for approximate string matching," *SIAM Journal on Computing*, Vol. 19, No. 6, p. 989–99, December 1990.

Gallant, J.K., Maier, D., Storer, J.A. (1980) "On finding minimal length superstrings," *Journal of Computer and System Sciences*, Vol. 20, No. 1, p. 50–8, February 1980.

Gallant, J.K. (1982) *String Compression Algorithms*, Ph.D. Thesis, Department of Electrical Engineering and Computer Science, Princeton University, Princeton, NJ, June 1982.

Gokhale, M., Holmes, W., Kopser, A., Kunze, R., Lopresti, D., Lucas, S., Minnich, R., Olsen, P. (1990) *SPLASH: A Reconfigurable Linear Logic Array*, Technical Report SRC-TR-90-012, Supercomputer Research Center, Bowie, MD, 12 April 1990 (also in Kung, S.Y. (ed.) *Proceedings of the International Conference on Application-Specific Array Processors*, IEEE Computer Society Press, Los Alamitos, CA, 1990).

Gokhale, M., Holmes, W., Kopser, A., Lucas, S., Minnich, R., Sweely, D., Lopresti, D. (1991) "Building and using a highly parallel programmable logic array," *Computer*, Vol. 24, No. 1, p. 81–9, January 1991.

Gonnet, G.H. (1987) *The PAT Text Searching System*, Technical Report, Department of Computer Science, University of Waterloo, Waterloo, Ontario.

Gonnet, G.H., Baeza-Yates, R. (1991) *Handbook of Algorithms and Data Structures in Pascal and C*, Chapter 7: Text Algorithms, p. 251–88, 2nd edition, Addison-Wesley, Wokingham, UK.

Grossi, R., Luccio, F. (1989) "Simple and efficient string matching with k mismatches," *Information Processing Letters*, Vol. 33, No. 3, p. 113–20, 30 November 1989.

Guibas, L.J., Odlyzko, A.M. (1977) "A new proof of the linearity of the Boyer-Moore string searching algorithm," *Proceedings of the 18th Annual IEEE Symposium on Foundations of Computer Science*, p. 189–95 (also *SIAM Journal on Computing*, Vol. 9, No. 4, p. 672–82, 1980).

Hakata, K., Imai, H. (1992) "The longest common subsequence problem for small alphabet size between many strings," in Ibaraki, T., Inagaki, Y., Iwama, K., Nishizeki, T., Yamashita, M. (eds.) *Algorithms and Computation*, Lecture Notes in Computer Science, Vol. 650, p. 469–78, Springer-Verlag, Berlin.

Halaas, A. (1983) "A systolic VLSI matrix for a family of fundamental search problem," *Integration VLSI Journal*, Vol. 1, No. 4, p. 269–82, December 1983.

Hall, P.A.V., Dowling, G.R. (1980) "Approximate string matching," *Computing Surveys*, Vol. 12, No. 4, p. 381–402, December 1980.

Hamming, R. (1982) *Coding and Information Theory*, Prentice Hall, Englewood Cliffs, NJ.

Hardy, G.H. (1910) *Orders of infinity: the 'Infintarcalcul' of Paul Du Bois-Reymond*, Cambridge Tracts in Mathematics and Mathematical Physics, No. 12, Cambridge University Press, Cambridge, UK.

Hardy, G.H., Littlewood, J.E. (1914) "Some problems of Diophantine approximation," *Acta Mathematica*, Vol. 37, p. 155–238.

Harel, D., Tarjan, R.E. (1984) "Fast algorithms for finding nearest common ancestors," *SIAM Journal on Computing*, Vol. 13, No. 2, p. 338–55.

Harrison, M.C. (1971) "Implementation of the substring test by hashing," *Communications of the ACM*, Vol. 14, No. 12, p. 777–9, December 1971.

Haskin, R.L. (1980) "Hardware for searching very large text data-bases," *Proceedings of the 5th Workshop on Computer Architecture for Non-numeric Processing*, ACM, New York (published as a special issue of *SIGIR Forum*, Vol. 15, No. 2).

Haskin, R.L. (1981) "Special purpose processors for text retrieval," *Database Engineering*, Vol. 4, No. 1, p. 16–29, September 1981.

Haskin, R.L., Hollaar, L.A. (1983) "Operational characteristics of a hardware-based pattern matcher," *ACM Transactions on Database Systems*, Vol. 8, No. 1, p. 15–40, March 1983.

Haton, J.P. (1973) *Contribution à l'Analyse, Paramétrisation et la Reconnaissance Automatique de la Parole*, Thèse de doctorat d'état, Université de Nancy, France.

Hirata, M., Yamada, H., Nagai, H., Takahashi, K. (1987) "A versatile data string search VLSI," *CICC 87*, Proceedings of the IEEE Custom Integrated Circuits Conference, p. 563–6.

Hirata, M., Yamada, H., Nagai, H., Takahashi, K. (1988) "A versatile data string-search VLSI," *IEEE Journal of Solid-State Circuits*, Vol. 23, No. 2, p. 329–35, April 1988.

Hirschberg, D.S. (1975) "A linear space algorithm for computing maximal common subsequences," *Communications of the ACM*, Vol. 18, No. 6, p. 341–3, June 1975.

Hirschberg, D.S. (1977) "Algorithm for the longest common subsequence problem," *Journal of the ACM*, Vol. 24, No. 3, p. 664–75.

Hirschberg, D.S. (1978) "An information theoretic lower bound for the longest common subsequence problem," *Information Processing Letters*, Vol. 7, p. 40–1.

Hirschberg, D.S. (1983) "Recent results on the complexity of common subsequence problems," in Sankoff, D., Kruskall, J.B. (eds.) *Time Warps, String Edits, and Macromolecules: the Theory and Practice of Sequence Comparison*, Chapter 12, p. 325–30, Addison-Wesley, Reading, MA.

Hollaar, L.A., Roberts, D.C. (1978) "Current research into specialized processors for text information retrieval," *Proceedings of the 4th International Conference on Very Large Data Bases*, p. 270–9, ACM, New York (published as a special issue of *SIGMOD Record*, Vol. 9, No. 4).

Hollaar, L.A. (1979) "Text retrieval computers," *Computer*, Vol. 12, No. 3, p. 40–50, March 1979.

Horspool, R.N. (1980) "Practical fast searching in strings," *Software — Practice and Experience*, Vol. 10, No. 6, p. 501–6.

Hsu, W., Du, M. (1984) "Computing a longest common subsequence for a set of strings," *BIT*, Vol. 24, p. 45–59.

Huang, X. (1989) "A space-efficient parallel sequence comparison algorithm for a message-passing multiprocessor," *International Journal of Parallel Programming*, Vol. 18, No. 3, p. 223–39, June 1989.

Huang, X., Hardison, R.C., Miller, W. (1990) "A space-efficient algorithm for local similarities," *Computer Applications in the Biosciences* (CABIOS), Vol. 6, No. 4, p. 373–81.

Huang, X., Miller, W. (1991) "A time-efficient, linear-space local similarity algorithm," *Advances in Applied Mathematics*, Vol. 12, p. 337–57.

Huang, X. (1992) "A contig assembly program based on sensitive detection of fragment overlaps," *Genomics*, Vol. 14, p. 18–25.

Hume, A., Sunday, D. (1991) "Fast string searching," *Software — Practice and Experience*, Vol. 21, No. 11, p. 1221–48, November 1991.

Hunt, J.W., McIlroy, M.D. (1976) *An Algorithm for Differential File Comparison*, Computing Science Technical Report 41, AT&T Bell Laboratories, Murray Hill, NJ.

Hunt, J.W., Szymanski, T.G. (1977) "A fast algorithm for computing longest common subsequences," *Communications of the ACM*, Vol. 20, No. 5, p. 350–3, May 1977.

Irving, R.W., Fraser, C.B. (1992) "Two algorithms for the longest common subsequence of three (or more) strings," in Apostolico, A., Crochemore, M., Galil, Z., Manber, U. (eds.) *Combinatorial Pattern Matching*, Lecture Notes in Computer Science, Vol. 644, p. 214–29, Springer-Verlag, Berlin.

Itoga, S.Y. (1981) "The string merging problem," *BIT*, Vol. 21, p. 20-30.

Ivanov, A.G. (1984) "Distinguishing an approximate word's inclusion on Turing machine in real time," (Russian) *Izvestiia Akademii nauk SSSR, Seriia Matematicheskaia*, Vol. 48, p. 520–68 .

Jacobson, G., Vo, K.P. (1992) "Heaviest increasing/common subsequence problems," in Apostolico, A., Crochemore, M., Galil, Z., Manber, U. (eds.) *Combinatorial Pattern Matching*, Lecture Notes in Computer Science, Vol. 644, p. 52–66, Springer-Verlag, Berlin.

Jiang, T., Li, M. (1991) *Towards a DNA Sequencing Theory (Learning a String)*, Technical Report 91-08, Computer Science Department, McMaster University, Hamilton, Ontario.

Johnson, S.C. (1975) *YACC — yet another compiler-compiler*, Report CSTR-32, Bell Laboratories, NJ.

Jokinen, P., Tarhio, J., Ukkonen, E. (1991) *A Comparison of Approximate String Matching Algorithms*, Technical Report A-1991-7, Department of Computer Science, University of Helsinki, Finland, ISBN 951-45-5976-2.

Jokinen, P., Ukkonen, E. (1991) "Two algorithms for approximate string matching in static texts," in Tarlecki, A. (ed.) *Proceedings of the 16th International Symposium on Mathematical Foundations of Computer Science*, Lecture Notes in Computer Science, Vol. 520, p. 241–8, Springer-Verlag, Berlin.

Karlin, S., Morris, M., Ghandour, G., Leung, M.Y. (1988) "Efficient algorithms for molecular sequence analysis," *Proceedings of the National Academy of Sciences of the USA*, Vol. 85, p. 841–5.

Karp, R.M. (1972) "Reducibility among combinatorial problems," in Miller, R.E., Thatcher, J.W. (eds.) *Complexity of Computer Computations*, p. 85–103, The IBM Research Symposia Series, Plenum Press, New York.

Karp, R.M., Miller, R.E., Rosenberg, A.L. (1972) "Rapid identification of repeated patterns in strings, trees and arrays," *Proceedings of the 4th Annual ACM Symposium on Theory of Computing*, p. 125–36.

Karp, R.M., Rabin, M.O. (1987) "Efficient randomized pattern-matching algorithms," *IBM Journal of Research and Development*, Vol. 31, No. 2, p. 249–60, March 1987.

Kashyap, R.L., Oommen, B.J. (1983) "The noisy substring matching problem," *IEEE Transactions on Software Engineering*, Vol. SE-9, No. 3, p. 365–70, May 1983.

Kececioglu, J.D., Myers, E.W. (1993) *Combinatorial Algorithms for DNA Sequence Assembly*, Technical Report TR92-37, Department of Computer Science, University of Arizona, Tucson, AZ (revised 15 January 1993).

Kim, J.Y., Shawe-Taylor, J. (1992a) "Fast multiple keyword searching," in Apostolico, A., Crochemore, M., Galil, Z., Manber, U. (eds.) *Combinatorial Pattern Matching*, Lecture Notes in Computer Science, Vol. 644, p. 41–51, Springer-Verlag, Berlin.

Kim, J.Y., Shawe-Taylor, J. (1992b) "An approximate string-matching algorithm," *Theoretical Computer Science*, Vol. 92, p. 107–17.

Kimbrell, R.E. (1988) "Searching for text? Send an N-gram!," *BYTE*, Vol. 13, No. 5, p. 297–312, May 1988.

Knuth, D.E. (1973) *The Art of Computer Programming, Volume 3: Sorting and Searching*, 6.3: Digital Searching, Addison-Wesley, Reading, MA.

Knuth, D.E. (1976) "Big Omicron and Big Omega and Big Theta," *SIGACT News*, Vol. 8, No. 2, p. 18–24, April–June 1976.

Knuth, D.E., Morris, J.H., Pratt, V.R. (1977) "Fast pattern matching in strings," *SIAM Journal on Computing*, Vol. 6, No. 2, p. 323–50, June 1977.

Kohonen, T., Reuhkala, E. (1978) "A very fast associative method for the recognition and correction of misspelt words, based on redundant hash-addressing," *Proceedings of the 4th International Joint Conference on Pattern Recognition*, November 1978, Kyoto, Japan, p. 807–9, IEEE, 1979.

Kumar, S.K., Rangan, C.P. (1987) "A linear space algorithm for the LCS problem," *Acta Informatica*, Vol. 24, p. 353–62.

Landau, E. (1909) *Handbuch der Lehre von der Verteilung der Primzahlen*, Teubner, Leipzig.

Landau, G.M., Vishkin, U. (1985) "Efficient string matching in the presence of errors," *Proceedings of the 26th Annual IEEE Symposium on Foundations of Computer Science*, p. 126–36.

Landau, G.M., Vishkin, U. (1986a) "Efficient string matching with k mismatches," *Theoretical Computer Science*, Vol. 43, p. 239–49.

Landau, G.M., Vishkin, U. (1986b) "Introducing efficient parallelism into approximate string matching and a new serial algorithm," *Proceedings of the 18th ACM Symposium on Theory of Computing*, p. 220–30.

Landau, G.M., Vishkin, U. (1988) "Fast string matching with k differences," *Journal of Computer and System Sciences*, Vol. 37, No. 1, p. 63–78.

Landau, G.M., Vishkin, U. (1989) "Fast parallel and serial approximate string matching," *Journal of Algorithms*, Vol. 10, p. 157–69.

Lander, E., Mesirov, J.P., Taylor, W. (1988) "Protein sequence comparison on a data parallel computer," in Bailey, D.H. (ed.) *Proceedings of the 1988 International Conference on Parallel Processing*, Vol. 3 (Algorithms and Applications), p. 257–63, Pennsylvania State University Press, PA.

Lecroq, T. (1992) "A variation on the Boyer-Moore algorithm," *Theoretical Computer Science*, Vol. 92, No. 1, p. 119–44, January 1992.

Lee, D., Lochovsky, F. (1985) "Text retrieval machine," in Tsichritzis, D.C. (ed.) *Office Automation — Concepts and Tools*, section 14, Topics in Information Systems Series, Springer-Verlag, Berlin.

Lee, K.C., Frieder, O., Mak, V. (1988) "A parallel VLSI architecture for unformatted data processing," in Jajodia, S., Kim, W., Silberschatz, A. (eds.) *Proceedings of the International Symposium on Databases in Parallel and Distributed Systems*, p. 80–6, IEEE Computer Society Press, Washington, DC.

Lee, K.C., Mak, V.W. (1989) "Design and analysis of a parallel VLSI string search algorithm," in Boral, H., Faudemay, P. (eds.) *Database Machines*, Proceedings of the 6th International Workshop, Lecture Notes in Computer Science, Vol. 368, p. 215–29, Springer-Verlag, Berlin.

Levenshtein, V.I. (1965) "Binary codes capable of correcting deletions, insertions, and reversals," (Russian) *Doklady Akademii nauk SSSR*, Vol. 163, No. 4, p. 845–8 (also *Cybernetics and Control Theory*, Vol. 10, No. 8, p. 707–10, 1966).

Li, M. (1990) "Towards a DNA sequencing theory (learning a string)," *Proceedings of the 31st Annual IEEE Symposium on Foundations of Computer Science*, Vol. 1, p. 125–34.

Lipman, D.J., Pearson, W.R. (1985) "Rapid and sensitive protein similarity searches," *Science*, Vol. 227, No. 4693, p. 1435–41, 22 March 1985.

Lipton, R.J., Lopresti, D. (1985) "A systolic array for rapid string comparison," in Fuchs, H. (ed.) *Proceedings of the 1985 Chapel Hill Conference on Very Large Scale Integration*, p. 363–76, Computer Science Press, Rockville, MD.

Lipton, R.J., Lopresti, D. (1986) *Comparing Long Strings on a Short Systolic Array*, Technical Report CS-TR-026-86, Princeton University, Princeton, NJ (also in Moore, W., McCabe, A., Urquart, R. *Proceedings of the 1986 International Workshop on Systolic Arrays*, Hilger, Bristol, 1987).

Liu, H.H., Fu, K.S. (1984) "VLSI arrays for minimum-distance classifications," in Fu, K.S. (ed.) *VLSI for Pattern Recognition and Image Processing*, Springer-Verlag, Berlin.

Lopresti, D.P. (1987) "P-NAC: a systolic array for comparing nucleic acid sequences," *Computer*, Vol. 20, No. 7, p. 98–9, July 1987.

Lowrance, R., Wagner, R.A. (1975) "An extension of the string-to-string correction problem," *Journal of the ACM*, Vol. 22, No. 2, p. 177–83, April 1975.

Maier, D., Storer, J.A. (1977) *A Note on Complexity of the Superstring Problem,* Technical Report TR-233, Department of Electrical Engineering and Computer Science, Princeton University, Princeton, NJ, October 1977.

Maier, D. (1978) "The complexity of some problems on subsequences and super-sequences," *Journal of the ACM,* Vol. 25, No. 2, p. 322–36, April 1978.

Main, M.G., Lorentz, R.J. (1979) *An $O(n \log n)$ algorithm for recognizing repetition,* Technical Report CS-79-056, Computer Science Department, Washington State University, Pullman, WA.

Main, M.G., Lorentz, R.J. (1984) "An $O(n \log n)$ algorithm for finding all repetitions in a string," *Journal of Algorithms,* Vol. 5, p. 422–32.

Majster, M.E., Reiser, A. (1980) "Efficient on-line construction and correction of position trees," *SIAM Journal on Computing,* Vol. 9, No. 4, p. 785–807, November 1980.

Manber, U., Myers, E.W. (1990) "Suffix arrays: a new method for on-line string searches," *Proceedings of the 1st Annual ACM-SIAM Symposium on Discrete Algorithms,* p. 319–27, SIAM, Philadelphia, PA.

Manber, U., Baeza-Yates, R. (1991) "An algorithm for string matching with a sequence of don't cares," *Information Processing Letters,* Vol. 37, p. 133–6, 18 February 1991.

Manber, U., Wu, S. (1992) "Some assembly required: approximate pattern matching," *BYTE,* Vol. 17, No. 12, p. 281–92, November 1992.

Masek, W.J., Paterson, M.S. (1980) "A faster algorithm for computing string-edit distances," *Journal of Computer and Systems Sciences,* Vol. 20, No. 1, p. 18–31.

Masek, W.J., Paterson, M.S. (1983) "How to compute string-edit distances quickly," in Sankoff, D., Kruskall, J.B. (eds.) *Time Warps, String Edits, and Macromolecules: the Theory and Practice of Sequence Comparison,* Chapter 14, p. 337–49, Addison-Wesley, Reading, MA.

McCreight, E.M. (1976) "A space-economical suffix tree construction algorithm," *Journal of the ACM,* Vol. 23, No. 2, p. 262–72, April 1976.

Mead, C.A., Pashley, R.D., Britton, L.D., Daimon, Y.T., Sando, S.F. (1976) "128-bit multicomparator," *IEEE Journal of Solid-State Circuits,* Vol. SC-11, No. 5, p. 692–5.

Mehlhorn, K. (1984) *Data Structures and Algorithms 1: Sorting and Searching,* EATCS Monographs on Theoretical Computer Science, Springer-Verlag, Berlin.

Menico, C. (1989) "Faster string searches," *Dr. Dobb's Journal*, p. 74–5, July 1989.

Middendorf, M. (1993) "The shortest common nonsubsequence problem is NP-complete," *Theoretical Computer Science*, Vol. 108, p. 365–9.

Miller, W., Myers, E.W. (1985) "A file comparison program," *Software — Practice and Experience*, Vol. 15, No. 11, p. 1025–40.

Morrison, D.R. (1968) "PATRICIA — practical algorithm to retrieve information coded in alphanumeric," *Journal of the ACM*, Vol. 15, No. 4, p. 514–34.

Mukhopadhyay, A. (1978) "Hardware algorithms for non-numeric computation," *Proceedings of the 5th Annual Symposium on Computer Architecture*, p. 8–16, IEEE, New York (published as a special issue of *Computer Architecture News* (ACM SIGARCH), Vol. 6, No. 7, April 1978).

Mukhopadhyay, A. (1979) "Hardware algorithms for nonnumeric computation," *IEEE Transactions on Computers*, Vol. C-28, No. 6, p. 384–94, June 1979.

Mukhopadhyay, A. (1980) "Hardware algorithms for string processing," in Guy Rabbat, N.B. (ed.) *ICCC 80*, Proceedings of the IEEE International Conference on Circuits and Computers, p. 508–11.

Myers, E.W. (1986a) "An $O(ND)$ difference algorithm and its variations," *Algorithmica*, Vol. 1, p. 251–66.

Myers, E.W. (1986b) *Incremental Alignment Algorithms and their Applications*, Technical Report TR86-22, Department of Computer Science, University of Arizona, Tucson, AZ, 18 September 1986.

Myers, E.W., Miller, W. (1988) "Optimal alignments in linear space," *Computer Applications in the Biosciences* (CABIOS), Vol. 4, p. 11–7.

Myers, E.W. (1990) *A Sublinear Algorithm for Approximate Keyword Matching*, Technical Report TR90-25, Department of Computer Science, University of Arizona, Tucson, AZ (also to appear in *Algorithmica*).

Nakatsu, N., Kambayashi, Y., Yajima, S. (1982) "A longest common subsequence algorithm suitable for similar text strings," *Acta Informatica*, Vol. 18, p. 171–9.

Needleman, S.B., Wunsch, C.D. (1970) "A general method applicable to the search for similarities in the amino-acid sequence of two proteins," *Journal of Molecular Biology*, Vol. 48, p. 443–53.

Okuda, T., Tanaka, E., Kasai, T. (1976) "A method for the correction of garbled words based on the Levenshtein metric," *IEEE Transactions on Computers*, Vol. C-25, No. 2, p. 172–8, February 1976.

Oommen, B.J. (1987) "Recognition of noisy subsequences using constrained edit distances," *IEEE Transactions on Pattern Analysis and Machine Intelligence*, Vol. PAMI-9, No. 5, p. 676–85, September 1987.

Owolabi, O., McGregor, D.R. (1988) "Fast approximate string matching," *Software — Practice and Experience*, Vol. 18, No. 4, p. 387–93, April 1988.

Pearson, W.R., Lipman, D. (1988) "Improved tools for biological sequence comparison," *Proceedings of the National Academy of Sciences of the USA*, Vol. 85, p. 2444–8.

Pearson, W.R. (1990) "Rapid and sensitive sequence comparison with FASTP and FASTA," *Methods in Enzymology*, Vol. 183, p. 63–98.

Peterson, J.L. (1980) "Computer programs for detecting and correcting spelling errors," *Communications of the ACM*, Vol. 23, No. 12, p. 676–87, December 1980.

Pinter, R.Y. (1985) "Efficient string matching with don't care patterns," in Apostolico, A., Galil, Z. (eds.), *Combinatorial Algorithms on Words*, NATO ASI Series, Vol. F12, p. 11–29, Springer-Verlag, Berlin.

Pirklbauer, K. (1992) "A study of pattern-matching algorithms," *Structured Programming*, Vol. 13, p. 89–98.

Pratt, V.R. (1973) *Applications of the Weiner repetition finder*, Cambridge, MA, May 1973 (unpublished manuscript).

Quong, R.W. (1992) "Fast average-case pattern matching by multiplexing sparse tables," *Theoretical Computer Science*, Vol. 92, p. 165–79.

Rabin, M.O. (1985) "Discovering repetitions in strings," in Apostolico, A., Galil, Z. (eds.) *Combinatorial Algorithms on Words*, NATO ASI Series, Vol. F12, p. 279–88, Springer-Verlag, Berlin.

Räihä, K.J., Ukkonen, E. (1981) "The shortest common supersequence problem over binary alphabet is NP-complete," *Theoretical Computer Science*, Vol. 16, p. 187–98.

Raita, T. (1992) "Tuning the Boyer-Moore-Horspool string searching algorithm," *Software — Practice and Experience*, Vol. 22, No. 10, p. 879–84, October 1992.

Régnier, M. (1988) *Knuth-Morris-Pratt Algorithm: an Analysis*, INRIA, Rocquencourt, France (unpublished manuscript).

Reichert, T.A., Cohen, D.N., Wong, A.K.C. (1973) "An application of information theory to genetic mutations and the matching of polypeptide sequences," *Journal of Theoretical Biology*, Vol. 42, p. 245–61.

Riseman, E.M., Ehrich, R.W. (1971) "Contextual word recognition using binary digrams," *IEEE Transactions on Computers*, Vol. C-20, No. 4, p. 397–403, April 1971.

Riseman, E.M., Hanson, A.R. (1974) "A contextual postprocessing system for error correction using binary n-grams," *IEEE Transactions on Computers*, Vol. C-23, No. 5, p. 480–93, May 1974.

Rivest, R.L. (1977) "On the worst-case behaviour of string searching algorithms," *SIAM Journal on Computing*, Vol. 6, No. 4, p. 669–74.

Roberts, D.C. (1977) (ed.) *A Computer System for Text Retrieval: Design Concept Development*, Report RD-77-10011, Office of Research and Development, Central Intelligence Agency, Washington, DC.

Roberts, D.C. (1978) "A specialized computer architecture for text retrieval," *Proceedings of the 4th Workshop on Computer Architecture for Non-numeric Processing*, p. 51–9, ACM, New York.

Russell, R.C. (1918) "Index," US Patent Number 1261167 (filed on 25 October 1917).

Russell, R.C. (1922) "Index," US Patent Numbers 1435663 and 1435664 (filed on 28 November 1921).

Rytter, W. (1980) "A correct preprocessing algorithm for Boyer-Moore string-searching," *SIAM Journal on Computing*, Vol. 9, p. 509–12.

Sakoe, H., Chiba, S. (1970) "A similarity evaluation of speech patterns by dynamic programming," (Japanese) *Institute of Electronic Communications Engineering of Japan*, p. 136, July 1970.

Sakoe, H., Chiba, S. (1971) "A dynamic programming approach to continuous speech recognition," *1971 Proceedings of the International Congress of Acoustics*, Budapest, Hungary, Paper 20 C 13.

Sankoff, D. (1972) "Matching sequences under deletion-insertion constraints," *Proceedings of the National Academy of Sciences of the USA*, Vol. 69, p. 4–6.

Sankoff, D., Kruskall, J.B. (eds.) (1983) *Time Warps, String Edits, and Macromolecules: the Theory and Practice of Sequence Comparison*, Addison-Wesley, Reading, MA.

Schaback, R. (1988) "On the expected sublinearity of the Boyer-Moore algorithm," *SIAM Journal on Computing*, Vol. 17, No. 4, p. 648–58.

Schensted, C. (1961) "Largest increasing and decreasing subsequences," *Canadian Journal of Mathematics*, Vol. 13, p. 179–91.

Schieber, B., Vishkin, U. (1988) "On finding lowest common ancestors: simplification and parallelization," *SIAM Journal on Computing*, Vol. 17, No. 6, p. 1253–62.

Schönhage, A., Strassen, V. (1971) "Schnelle Multiplikation grosser Zahlen," *Computing (Arch. Elektron. Rechnen)*, Vol. 7, p. 281–92.

Sedgewick, R. (1983) *Algorithms*, Chapter 19: String Searching, p. 241–55, Addison-Wesley, Reading, MA.

Sedgewick, R., Vitter, J.S. (1986) "Shortest paths in Euclidean graphs," *Algorithmica*, Vol. 1, p. 31–48.

Sellers, P.H. (1980) "The theory and computation of evolutionary distances: pattern recognition," *Journal of Algorithms*, Vol. 1, p. 359–73.

Sibbald, P.R., White, M.J. (1987) "How probable are antibody cross-reactions?," *Journal of Theoretical Biology*, Vol. 127, p. 163–9.

Sleator, D.D., Tarjan, R.E. (1985) "Self-adjusting binary search trees," *Journal of the ACM*, Vol. 32, p. 652–86, July 1985.

Slisenko, A.O. (1983) "Detection of periodicities and string matching in real time," *Journal of Soviet Mathematics*, Vol. 22, No. 3, p. 1316–87 (translated from *Zapiski Nauchnykh Seminarov Leningradskogo Otdeleniya Matematicheskogo Instituta im. V.A. Steklova AN SSSR*, Vol. 105, p. 62–173, 1980).

Smit, G. de V. (1982) "A comparison of three string matching algorithms," *Software — Practice and Experience*, Vol. 12, p. 57–66.

Smith, P.D. (1991) "Experiments with a very fast substring search algorithm," *Software — Practice and Experience*, Vol. 21, No. 10, p. 1065–74, October 1991.

Smith, T.F., Waterman, M.S. (1981) "Identification of common molecular subsequences," *Journal of Molecular Biology*, Vol. 147, p. 195–7.

Staden, R. (1982) "Automation of the computer handling of gel reading data produced by the shotgun method of DNA sequencing," *Nucleic Acids Research*, Vol. 10, No. 15, p. 4731–51.

Stellhorn, W.H. (1974) "A processor for direct scanning of text," *Proceedings of the 1st Workshop on Computer Architecture for Non-numeric Processing*, ACM, New York.

Sunday, D.M. (1990) "A very fast substring search algorithm," *Communications of the ACM*, Vol. 33, No. 8, p. 132–42, August 1990.

Takahashi, K., Yamada, H., Nagai, H., Matsumi, K. (1986) "A new string search hardware architecture for VLSI," *Proceedings of the 13th Annual International Symposium on Computer Architecture*, p. 20–7, IEEE Computer Society Press, Washington, D.C. (published as a special issue of *Computer Architecture News* (ACM SIGARCH), Vol. 14, No. 2, June 1986).

Takahashi, K., Yamada, H., Hirata, M. (1987) "Intelligent string search processor to accelerate text information retrieval," *Proceedings of the 5th International Workshop on Database Machines*, p. 440–53, October 1987.

Tarhio, J., Ukkonen, E. (1986) "A greedy algorithm for constructing shortest common superstrings," in Gruska, J., Rovan, B., Wiedermann, J. (eds.) *Proceedings of the 12th International Symposium on Mathematical Foundations of Computer Science*, Lecture Notes in Computer Science, Vol. 233, p. 602–10, Springer-Verlag, Berlin.

Tarhio, J., Ukkonen, E. (1988) "A greedy approximation algorithm for constructing shortest common superstrings," *Theoretical Computer Science*, Vol. 57, p. 131–45.

Tarhio, J., Ukkonen, E. (1990a) *Approximate Boyer-Moore String Matching*, Technical Report A-1990-3, Department of Computer Science, University of Helsinki, Finland, ISBN 951-45-5361-6, March 1990.

Tarhio, J., Ukkonen, E. (1990b) "Boyer-Moore approach to approximate string matching," in Gilbert, J.R., Karlsson, R. (eds.) *SWAT 90*, Proceedings of the 2nd Scandinavian Workshop on Algorithm Theory, Lecture Notes in Computer Science, Vol. 447, p. 348–59, Springer-Verlag, Berlin.

Tarhio, J., Ukkonen, E. (1993) "Approximate Boyer-Moore String Matching," *SIAM Journal on Computing*, Vol. 22, No. 2, p. 243–60.

Thue, A. (1912) "Über die gegenseitige Lage gleicher Teile gewisser Zeichenreichen," *Norske Videnskabers Selskabs Skrifter Mat. Naturv. Klasse*, No. 1, p. 1–67.

Timkovskii, V.G. (1989) "Complexity of common subsequence and supersequence problems and related problems," *Kibernetika*, Vol. 25, p. 1–13 (Russian). (Translated in *Cybernetics*, Vol. 25, p. 565–80, 1990.)

Turner, J. (1986) *Approximation Algorithms for the Shortest Common Superstring Problem*, Technical Report WUCS-86-16, Department of Computer Science, Washington University, St. Louis, MO.

Turner, J. (1989) "Approximation algorithms for the shortest common superstring problem," *Information and Computation*, Vol. 83, p. 1–20.

Ukkonen, E. (1983) "On approximate string matching," in Karpinski, M. (ed.) *Foundations of Computation Theory*, Proceedings of the 1983 International FCT Conference, Lecture Notes in Computer Science, Vol. 158, p. 487–95, Springer-Verlag, Berlin.

Ukkonen, E. (1985a) "Algorithms for approximate string matching," *Information and Control*, Vol. 64, p. 100–18.

Ukkonen, E. (1985b) "Finding approximate patterns in strings," *Journal of Algorithms*, Vol. 6, No. 6, p. 132–7.

Ukkonen, E. (1990) "A linear-time algorithm for finding approximate shortest common superstrings," *Algorithmica*, Vol. 5, p. 313–23.

Ukkonen, E., Wood, D. (1990) *Approximate String Matching with Suffix Automata*, Technical Report A-1990-4, Department of Computer Science, University of Helsinki, Finland, ISBN 951-45-5390-X, April 1990.

Ukkonen, E. (1992a) "Approximate string-matching with q-grams and maximal matches," *Theoretical Computer Science*, Vol. 92, p. 191–211.

Ukkonen, E. (1992b) "Constructing suffix-trees on-line in linear time," in Leeuwen, J. van (ed.) *Algorithms, Software, Architecture: Information Processing 92*, Vol. 1, p. 484–92, Elsevier, Amsterdam.

Ukkonen, E. (1993) *On-line construction of suffix-trees*, Report A-1993-1, Department of Computer Science, University of Helsinki, Finland, February 1993, ISBN 951-45-6384-0.

Ukkonen, E., Wood, D. (1993) "Approximate string matching with suffix automata," *Algorithmica* (in press).

Ullmann, J.R. (1977) "A binary n-gram technique for automatic correction of substitution, deletion, insertion and reversal errors in words," *The Computer Journal*, Vol. 20, No. 2, p. 141–7.

Velichko, V.M., Zagoruyko, N.G. (1970) "Automatic recognition of 200 words," *International Journal of Man-Machine Studies*, Vol. 2, p. 223–34.

Vintsyuk, T.K. (1968) "Speech discrimination by dynamic programming," *Cybernetics*, Vol. 4, No. 1, p. 52–7 (also (Russian) *Kibernetika*, Vol. 4, No. 1, p. 81–8).

Vo, K.P. (1986) *More* `<curses>`: *the* `<screen>` *library*, Technical Report, AT&T Bell Laboratories.

Wagner, R.A., Fischer, M.J. (1974) "The string-to-string correction problem," *Journal of the ACM*, Vol. 21, No. 1, p. 168–73, January 1974.

Wagner, R.A. (1975) "On the complexity of the extended string-to-string correction problem," *Proceedings of the 7th Annual ACM Symposium on Theory of Computing*, p. 218–23 (also in Sankoff, D., Kruskall, J.B. (eds.) *Time Warps, String Edits, and Macromolecules: the Theory and Practice of Sequence Comparison*, Addison-Wesley, Reading, MA, 1983).

Waterman, M.S., Eggert, M. (1987) "A new algorithm for best subsequence alignments with application to tRNA-rRNA comparisons," *Journal of Molecular Biology*, Vol. 197, p. 723–8.

Watson, B.W., Zwaan, G. (1992) *A Taxonomy of Keyword Pattern Matching Algorithms*, Computing Science Note 92/27, Department of Mathematics and Computing Science, Eindhoven University of Technology, The Netherlands.

Weiner, P. (1973) "Linear pattern matching algorithm," *Proceedings of the 14th IEEE Symposium on Switching and Automata Theory*, p. 1–11.

Wong, C.K., Chandra, A.K. (1976) "Bounds for the string editing problem," *Journal of the ACM*, Vol. 23, No. 1, p. 13–6, January 1976.

Woude, J. van der (1989) "Playing with patterns, searching for strings," *Science of Computer Programming*, Vol. 12, No. 3, p. 177–90.

Wu, S., Manber, U., Myers, E.W., Miller, W. (1990) "An $O(NP)$ sequence comparison algorithm," *Information Processing Letters*, Vol. 35, p. 317–23, September 1990.

Wu, S., Manber, U. (1991) *Fast Text Searching with Errors*, Technical Report TR-91-11, Department of Computer Science, University of Arizona, Tucson, AZ, June 1991.

Wu, S., Manber, U. (1992a) "`agrep` — a fast approximate pattern matching tool," *Proceedings of the Winter 1992 USENIX Conference*, p. 153–62, USENIX Association, Berkeley, CA.

Wu, S., Manber, U. (1992b) "Fast text searching allowing errors," *Communications of the ACM*, Vol. 35, No. 10, p. 83–91, October 1992.

Yamada, H., Hirata, M., Nagai, H., Takahashi, K. (1987a) "A character string search processor," *ISSCC Digest of Technical Papers*, IEEE 34th International Solid-State Circuits Conference, p. 272–3.

Yamada, H., Hirata, M., Nagai, H., Takahashi, K. (1987b) "A high-speed string-search engine," *IEEE Journal of Solid-State Circuits*, Vol. SC-22, No. 5, p. 829–34, October 1987.

Index

ϵ (empty string), 2, 205, 207
$\lhd$ (subsequence relation), 48, 205
$\rhd$ (supersequence relation), 50, 205
$\prec$, 203
$\succ$, 203
$\sim$, 203
Θ-notation, 204
O-notation, 203
o-notation, 204
Ω-notation, 204
C (alphabet), 205
C_x (alphabet), 112, 116, 154, 205
C_{xy} (alphabet), 117, 168

Abrahamson, K., 124
agrep, 113, 119, 149, 184
Aho, A.V., 11, 21, 37, 46, 74, 86, 87, 124, 192
Aho-Corasick automaton, 11, 12, 51, 88, 99, 117, 123
Alberga, C.N., 41
Alignment
  global, 48
    Myers-Miller algorithm, 48
  local, 47, 126
    k best, non-intersecting, 47, 48
    Huang-Hardison-Miller algorithm, 48, 126
    Huang-Miller algorithm, 48
    Waterman-Eggert algorithm, 47
    Smith-Waterman algorithm, 47, 126
  multiple-string, 126
Allison, L., 45

Alphabet, 2, 207
Altschul, S.F., 48
Amino-acid sequences, 125, 126
Angell, R.C., 41, 128
Aoe, J., 12
Apostolico, A., 7, 22, 45, 46, 47, 67, 88, 93, 110, 192, 194, 200, 201
Arlazarov, V.L., 44, 68
Arnold, J.M., 130, 133
Arratia, R., 125
Associative memory, 130, 131, 132
Asymptotic notation, 203
Atallah, M.J., 114
Automaton
  Aho-Corasick, 11, 12, 51, 88, 99, 117, 123
  suffix, 117, 120, 121
  Crochemore's algorithm, 117, 120
Bachman, P., 203
Baeza-Yates, R.A., 8, 9, 10, 12, 17, 18, 29, 36, 37, 49, 113, 115, 119, 123, 124, 141, 149, 156, 157, 184, 189
Baker, B.S., 193, 199
Baskin, H., 41
Bellman, R., 42
Best-match searching, 114, 119
Bickel, M.A., 42
Big Oh, 203
Big Omega, 204
Big Theta, 204
Bird, R.M., 130
Blair, C.R., 127
Blum, A., 51